GONE PRO NORTH CAROLINA

Tar Heel Stars Who Became Pros

Tim W. Jackson

CLERISY PRESS

Gone Pro North Carolina: Tar Heel Stars Who Became Pros

For further information, contact the publisher at:

Clerisy Press
306 Greenup Street
Covington, KY 41011
clerisypress.com

a division of Keen Communications, Birmingham, Alabama

Library of Congress Cataloging-in-Publication Data:
Jackson, Tim W.
Gone pro : North Carolina : Tar Heels stars who became pros / Tim W. Jackson.
pages cm
Includes bibliographical references and index.
ISBN 978-1-57860-545-3 (paperback) -- ISBN 1-57860-545-8 ()
eISBN 978-1-57860-546-0
1. University of North Carolina at Chapel Hill--Sports--History.
2. University of North Carolina at Chapel Hill--Students--Biography.
3. College athletes--United States--Biography. I. Title.
GV691.U57J33 2014
796.04'309756--dc23
2014005128

Distributed by Publishers Group West
Printed in the United States of America
First edition, first printing
Editor: Andy Sloan
Cover design: Scott McGrew
Index: Rich Carlson
Interior design: Annie Long and Donna Collingwood
Interior photos courtesy of University of North Carolina Chapel Hill Sports Information Department

TABLE of CONTENTS

Acknowledgments

Thanks, first, to Bob Sehlinger, Molly Merkle, and Steve Millburg, who first got me involved in this project. From there, thanks must be extended to the entire gang at Keen Communications for their patience while I toiled away on this book, pushing back the deadline month after month. I know it is truly a team effort to publish a book, and I appreciate all who were involved in this project—editors, designers, the marketing team, and everyone else.

Thanks to the University of North Carolina at Chapel Hill for assistance with information and photos.

And then there's my wife, Taryn Chase Jackson, who was an immense help in researching and editing. I'm glad we made it through the process together! Thank you so much, Taryn.

About Gone Pro

Welcome to Gone Pro, a series of books that celebrates college athletes who have continued their sporting exploits in the professional ranks or the Olympics. Each book focuses on a single college or university. The one you're holding salutes the storied sports legacy of the Tar Heels of the University of North Carolina.

In it, we applaud, with a biographical sketch or at least a listing of basic information, the North Carolina athletes, male and female, who have performed in a top-level professional league or the Olympic Games. Some stars, of course, get more notice than others. You can catch up with old (or not-so-old) favorites, relive (or learn about) the glory days gone by, and maybe even learn something you didn't know. You might be a new fan of the Tar Heels, or you may have followed UNC athletics for decades, but either way you will surely enjoy reading about so many Tar Heels who left Chapel Hill to play with the best athletes in their fields.

While Carolina has long been recognized for its prowess on the hardwood, you will learn that UNC is in no way "just a basketball school." One of the impressive things about Carolina athletics is that it is all-encompassing. The Tar Heels have had major stars in just about every sport. Think Mia Hamm in soccer, Lawrence Taylor in football, B. J. Surhoff in baseball, Marion Jones (despite her fall from grace) in track & field, Davis Love III in golf, and Vic Seixas in tennis. And even in basketball, it's easy to consider Michael Jordan, James Worthy, and Vince Carter, but think about the greats from the women's teams, such as Charlotte Smith, Ivory Latta, and Sylvia Crawley.

And one of the amazing things about Carolina athletics is that behind all of these great players who have gone pro have been some excellent coaches with remarkably long careers. No other university can boast of coaches with tenures such as those of Anson Dorrance in soccer, Sylvia Hatchell in women's basketball, Dean Smith in men's basketball, and Donna Pappa in softball, just to name a few.

WEBSITE

Your Gone Pro experience doesn't have to end when you've finished the book. You can extend it indefinitely by hanging out at the Gone Pro website, **goneprobooks.com.** Click on over for regular updates about Tar Heels in the pro ranks, advance excerpts from new books in the series, and plenty of fun stuff for the Gone Pro community.

TELL US MORE

We hope this book stirs warm memories and tells you some things you didn't know about North Carolina's athletic heroes. But there's always more to learn and more to tell. If we missed something about one of your favorites, we'd like to know about it. Please contact us at:

Gone Pro
PO Box 43673
Birmingham, AL 35243

You can also reach us through the website, **goneprobooks.com,** or follow us on Twitter: **@GoneProBks.**

Introduction

The University of North Carolina at Chapel Hill offers a long history of academic and athletic excellence. The school claims 39 team national championships in six different sports, eighth all-time, and 51 individual national championships. Currently 13 men's and 15 women's sports are sanctioned by the National Collegiate Athletic Association (NCAA).

UNIVERSITY OF NORTH CAROLINA HISTORY AND MISSION

The University of North Carolina at Chapel Hill is the nation's oldest state university, measured by when instruction actually began, which was 1795. For 136 years, it was simply known as the University of North Carolina, but as the UNC system began to grow and the UNC name appeared in cities such as Greensboro, Charlotte, Asheville, and Wilmington, "at Chapel Hill" was needed to distinguish the original from the rest. For the purposes of this book, however, when we refer to the University of North Carolina or UNC, the reference is always to the University of North Carolina at Chapel Hill.

Today the whole UNC system has as its mission the following:

> *The University of North Carolina is a public, multi-campus university dedicated to the service of North Carolina and its people. It encompasses the 16 diverse constituent institutions and other educational, research, and public service organizations. Each shares in the overall mission of the University. That mission is to discover, create, transmit, and apply knowledge to address the needs of individuals and society. This mission is accomplished through instruction, which communicates the knowledge and values and imparts the*

THE UNIVERSITY
of NORTH CAROLINA
at CHAPEL HILL

skills necessary for individuals to lead responsible, productive, and personally satisfying lives; through research, scholarship, and creative activities, which advance knowledge and enhance the educational process; and through public service, which contributes to the solution of societal problems and enriches the quality of life in the State. In the fulfillment of this mission, the University shall seek an efficient use of available resources to ensure the highest quality in its service to the citizens of the State.

Teaching and learning constitute the primary service that the University renders to society. Teaching, or instruction, is the primary responsibility of each of the constituent institutions. The relative importance of research and public service, which enhance teaching and learning, varies among the constituent institutions, depending on their overall missions.

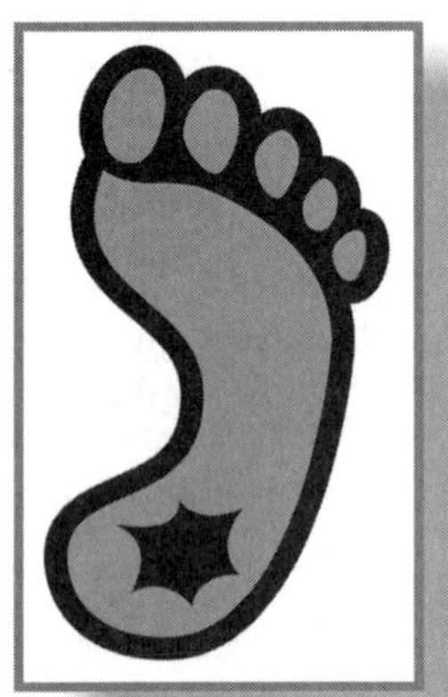

WHAT IS A TAR HEEL?

Now that we know a bit about the origins of the school and its mission, here comes the obvious question: What is a Tar Heel?

The nickname of the school and its athletic teams also applies to North Carolina citizens. Unfortunately no one really knows its origins. The following are listed as the two possibilities.

1. During the Revolutionary War, after fording a river in eastern North Carolina, British troops discovered that their feet were covered with tar, a product of the state's many pine trees. Legend suggests that the North Carolinians dumped it in the river to slow down the invading army. The British observation was that if you waded in North Carolina rivers, you'd get tar on your heels.

2. The second story is also rooted in a time of conflict, the Civil War. North Carolina soldiers supposedly rebuked their comrades for fleeing the battlefield when the going got tough. North Carolina soldiers proposed to stick tar on the heels of retreating soldiers to keep them in the battle. General Robert E. Lee is said to have commented, "God bless the Tar Heel boys!"

SCHOOL COLORS

Throughout the nineteenth century, students were required to be members of either the Dialectic or the Philanthropic Literary Societies. The Dis' color was light blue; the Phis' was white. At official functions, those in charge, such as a chief marshal or manager, wore both colors to represent the entire student body. When UNC first fielded intercollegiate athletic teams in 1888, the school colors were a natural choice. Light blue and white had come to symbolize unity at the university. Light blue and white have been considered the official colors ever since. Perhaps you're familiar with the popular saying, which became a bumper sticker, that God must be a Tar Heel because he made the sky Carolina Blue. I suppose the white clouds only back up that claim.

FOR WHOM THE BELL TOLLS

While not an athletic icon, one of the most recognized features on the UNC campus is the Morehead-Patterson Bell Tower. Completed in 1931, it was a gift to UNC from John Motley Morehead and Rufus Lenoir Patterson II. The 172-foot tower is located behind the Wilson Library.

UNIVERSITY OF NORTH CAROLINA CLUB SPORTS

Club sports are University-recognized student organizations that are student-run and student-funded. They are not recognized by the NCAA. They are typically year-round clubs that compete in intercollegiate competitions on a local, regional, and/or national scale. UNC has about 50 club sports, ranging from aikido to wrestling, with an array of activities in between, such as ballroom dance, crew, ice hockey, judo, sailing, water polo, and many more.

FACILITIES

Dean E. Smith Center

OPENED: 1986 **SEATING CAPACITY:** 21,750

Basketball fans everywhere know of the "Dean Dome," the name affectionately given to the Dean E. Smith Center, a multiuse facility named for legendary Tar Heels Coach Dean E. Smith. When the term "home-court advantage"

UNC/Smith Center

is bandied about, this facility typically comes to mind. In fact, fantastic UNC wins have been the hallmark of this building from the start. The first game featured No. 1 Carolina defeating No. 3 Duke, 95–92, in a battle of unbeatens on January 18, 1986. The Tar Heels have been undefeated at home during four seasons since moving into the Smith Center.

Numerous renovations have taken place here over the years, the most recent being the men's basketball offices and the team's varsity hallway prior to the 2010–11 season. As for other uses, Kenny Rogers staged the first concert in the arena on April 12, 1986. Other acts who have performed include such big names as the Grateful Dead, Bon Jovi, Bruce Springsteen, Guns n' Roses, and Elton John. In 1987, U.S. Olympic Festival basketball brought in a Smith Center–record attendance of 23,713 for the gold medal game. In 1994, the Smith Center hosted the NCAA Division I Wrestling Championships.

Kenan Stadium

OPENED: 1927 **SEATING CAPACITY:** 63,000

Known as one of the more beautiful settings for a football game, Kenan Stadium is set amid the Carolina pines on the campus of UNC. Originally seating 24,000, the capacity increased to 48,000 in 1963, 50,000 in 1979, 52,000 in

Kenan Stadium

1988, 57,500 in 1997, and 60,000 in 1998. The stadium is named for William R. and Mary Hargrave Kenan. William Rand Kenan Jr. was born in Wilmington in 1872 and graduated from UNC in 1894. He quickly became an active chemical and mechanical engineering advisor and went on to become a successful businessman in numerous ventures.

Boshamer Stadium

OPENED: 1972 **SEATING CAPACITY:** 5,000

While Boshamer Stadium has been the home of UNC baseball since 1972, the current facility is completely new, built in 2009 within the same footprint as the old Boshamer Stadium. It's recognized as a top facility in collegiate baseball.

The original stadium opened in 1972 and hosted five ACC Tournaments along with NCAA regionals in 1983, 2006, and 2007. The Tar Heels have already hosted three regionals in the new Boshamer, plus two super regionals. The original stadium resulted from a gift by 1917 UNC graduate Cary C. Boshamer. The playing surface at the new facility—Bryson Field—honors former player Vaughn Bryson and his wife, Nancy.

Boshamer Stadium

Carmichael Arena

OPENED: 1965 **SEATING CAPACITY:** 6,822

Carmichael offers a lot of history, as it was originally home to the UNC men's basketball and wrestling teams. While the wresting team remains a tenant, the men's basketball team moved to the Dean E. Smith Center midway through the 1985–86 season. The men's basketball team earned a 169–20 record at Carmichael Arena. Not too shabby.

Carmichael Arena is named for the late William D. Carmichael Jr., who served as the university's comptroller, then as its vice president. He also served for many years as the Consolidated University's acting president. The venerable area underwent a complete renovation in 2010 at a cost of $30 million. The new hallways are decorated in graphics depicting UNC's most outstanding athletes in the school's many intercollegiate sports. It adjoins Woollen Gymnasium, the current home of physical education and intramural activities.

Cone-Kenfield Tennis Center

OPENED: 1992 **SEATING CAPACITY:** 2,000

This indoor-outdoor tennis facility was named for Caesar Cone and John Kenfield. Cone was a 1928 alumnus and former tennis player. He was a successful businessman and regular benefactor to UNC. Kenfield is the legendary UNC tennis coach who compiled a record of 434-30-2 in dual match play from 1928 to 1955. His teams were conference champions 17 times (15 Southern Conference, two ACC) while he was at UNC. Kenfield actually coached Cone in Cone's senior season.

The $2 million facility includes six indoor and 12 outdoor hard-surface tennis courts, outdoor seating for 2,000, dressing facilities, weight-training rooms, offices, and public restrooms. The UNC men's teams have hosted NCAA regional tournaments at the Cone-Kenfield Tennis Center several times since 2004.

Fetzer Field/Belk Track

OPENED: 1935 **SEATING CAPACITY:** 5,700

Rarely has one facility seen so much greatness year in and year out in multiple sports. Fetzer Field has been home to UNC track and field since it was constructed in 1935 as a Works Project Administration project during the Great Depression. Later came men's soccer in 1947, men's lacrosse in 1949, women's soccer in 1979, and finally women's lacrosse in 1996. All the programs have achieved remarkable success with Fetzer Field as their home.

Named for UNC athletic director and track coach Bob Fetzer, the facility has undergone numerous renovations over the years, the most recent being the 2011 addition of locker rooms under the field's stands. Over the years, the facility has been home to women's and men's soccer NCAA and ACC Championship events, ACC Outdoor Track and Field Championships, North Carolina High School Athletic Association Track and Field Championships, National Junior Olympics, men's and women's lacrosse and soccer ACC Tournaments, and NCAA tournament play.

Finley Golf Course

OPENED: 1949

The course was redesigned in 1999 into a par 72 course. A recently renovated clubhouse doubles the space of the old one. It's also home to the A. E. Finley Memorabilia Room. The course's namesake was instrumental in the construction of the original golf course. Finley Golf Course is recognized as one of the best daily-fee courses in North Carolina. In fact, a few years ago, Finley Golf Course was recognized by the Golf Channel as the nation's No. 7 college course in America.

Koury Natatorium

OPENED: 1986 **SEATING CAPACITY:** 2,000

The Maurice J. Koury Natatorium has hosted multiple ACC Men's and Women's Swimming and Diving Championships and an array of other significant competitions, in addition to being home to the UNC swimming and diving teams. The pool measures 50 meters in length by 25 yards in width. The pool is seven feet in depth at its shallowest point and 18 feet at its deepest point. It offers continuous-flow gutters and has a state-of-the-art lighting system. The gallery area provides seating for roughly 2,000 spectators.

McCaskill Soccer Center

OPENED: 1999

With such amazing success by UNC soccer teams, the programs needed updated facilities. While games are still played at Fetzer Field, McCaskill Soccer Center is a two-story structure that houses locker rooms for the men's and women's soccer teams, as well as a team meeting room on the first floor. The second floor houses offices for both sports, as well as a large conference room that can be used by all of the UNC Olympic sports teams. The $1.8

McCaskill Soccer Center

million building was named in honor of the McCaskill family, specifically Mildred McCaskill, and facilitated through her brother Norman and his wife, Carol McCaskill.

Francis E. Henry Stadium

OPENED: 1999 **CAPACITY:** 1,086

This 12,000-square-foot facility houses locker rooms, a film and meeting room, a sports medicine treatment room, equipment storage areas, concession stands, restrooms, and a sizable trophy case in the entranceway. Renovations in 2008 brought a new surface with a top-notch watering system that recycles the field water. The stadium is named for UNC alumnus Francis E. Henry, who lettered in soccer for the Tar Heels from 1964 to 1966 and now resides in Wilmington, North Carolina.

Anderson Softball Stadium

OPENED: 2002 **SEATING CAPACITY:** 500

This lighted facility offers a field that measures 200 feet from home plate to the outfield wall in all fields. The team building includes a locker room, on-site training room, coaches' offices, an equipment room, and a team room.

Chapman Golf Center

OPENED: 2001

The Chapman Golf Center houses offices for the men's and women's golf coaches, men's and women's locker rooms, a team meeting room, and a reception area. The 4,500-square-foot facility underwent renovations in 2010. The golf center also includes a teaching area with two hitting bays, plus the Williamson Golf Team Practice Facility, which offers a practice range, putting and chipping greens, and bunkers.

Eddie Smith Field House/Dick Taylor Indoor Track

OPENED: 2001

This is the home for UNC track and field during the indoor season. The Dick Taylor Track offers a six-lane, 200-meter track that has regularly been the spot of ACC Indoor Championships. The facility also houses the John Pope Practice Field, which is used by the football team. Locker rooms, coaching offices, and a scoreboard finish out the field house.

UNC Boathouse at University Lake

The UNC crew calls this facility its home. A three-bay boathouse stores the UNC fleet of hulls. An 80-foot wooden dock is included and utilized by the teams. The lake, managed by the Orange Water and Sewer Authority, is a public watershed that offers a 2,700-meter stretch of navigable water.

RIVALRIES

Four teams in the ACC are from the state of North Carolina. In addition to UNC, these include Duke, North Carolina State, and Wake Forest. With Duke and NC State in such close geographic proximity to UNC, those two schools are the primary rivals of the Tar Heels. The rivalry between UNC and Duke is particularly strong in basketball because of how competitive both programs have been over the past several decades—and the fact that the campuses are only about 10 miles apart. In basketball, UNC ranks as the program with the second-most wins. Duke is fourth. The two teams met for the first time in 1920, although Duke was still known as Trinity College back then. Over the decades, the two have combined to win about 80% of ACC regular-season titles and 60% of ACC tournament titles. Overall, UNC holds a 132-104 record vs. Duke.

UNC and Duke were once equally as bitter in their football rivalry, but UNC dominance in the last three decades has cooled the heat just a bit. The two schools, though, do have fierce rivalries in just about every sport in which the two compete. Women's basketball, men's or women's soccer, men's or women's lacrosse—you name it, the two schools desperately want to beat each other.

In football, UNC dominated the rivalry with NC State early on (with the first game being played between the two in 1894), but the series became more fierce starting in the mid-1950s when the Wolfpack began a winning streak over the Tar Heels that continued for the next 25 years. Since then, the series has been marked by a handful of winning streaks. NC State had five-game winning streaks from 1988 to 1992 and 2007–11. UNC had seven-game winning streaks from 1969 to 1975 and 1983–89. Overall, the Tar Heels hold a 64-32-6 advantage. Like UNC and Duke, UNC and NC State are major rivals in pretty much every sport in which the two face each other. The fact that the campuses are a mere 25 miles apart adds to the intensity.

CONFERENCE AFFILIATIONS

In 1894, the University of North Carolina became a founding member of the Southern Intercollegiate Athletic Association, one of the first college conferences. The other original members were Alabama, Auburn (then known as Alabama Polytechnic Institute), Georgia, Georgia Tech (then known as the Georgia School of Technology), Sewanee (officially called University of the South), and Vanderbilt. Invited to join as charter members the following year, 1895, were Clemson, Cumberland, Kentucky, LSU, Mercer, Mississippi, Mississippi State (then known as Mississippi A&M), Rhodes (then known as Southwest Presbyterian University), Tennessee, Texas, Tulane, and the University of Nashville (then known as Peabody Normal School, which ceased operations in 1909).

Most of the conference's larger schools defected in 1921 because of a dispute over whether freshmen should be eligible to play. The larger schools opposed freshman eligibility; the smaller schools favored it. The SIAA continued as a small-school conference until it disbanded in 1942.

In February 1921, the Southern Conference was formed, which included Alabama, Auburn, Clemson, Georgia, Georgia Tech, Kentucky, Maryland, Mississippi State, North Carolina, North Carolina State (then known as North Carolina College of Agriculture and Mechanic Arts), Tennessee, Virginia, Virginia Tech (then officially known as Virginia Agricultural and Mechanical College and Polytechnic Institute), and Washington & Lee.

In 1922, more SIAA refugees joined: Florida, LSU, Mississippi, South Carolina, Tulane, and Vanderbilt. Sewanee came aboard in 1923, followed by Virginia Military Institute in 1924, and Duke in 1929.

From the beginning, it was a sprawling aggregation. Geographically, it was especially unwieldy in the days before routine air travel and interstate highways. The Southern Conference soon spawned two of today's most prominent sports leagues, the Atlantic Coast Conference and the Southeastern Conference.

The last original member—Virginia Tech—left in 1965. But the Southern Conference didn't die. It's still an NCAA Division I league. In football, its members compete in the Football Championship Subdivision, formerly called Division IAA. Current conference members are Appalachian State, Tennessee-Chattanooga, The Citadel, College of Charleston, Davidson, Elon, Furman, Georgia Southern, Samford, North Carolina-Greensboro, Western Carolina, and Wofford. Associate members Campbell, Gardner-Webb, Southern Illinois-Edwardsville, and Virginia Military Institute participate in wrestling only.

The Atlantic Coast Conference was founded in 1953 with seven charter members: Clemson, Duke, Maryland, North Carolina, North Carolina State, South Carolina, and Wake Forest. A few of the conference names that weren't adopted included Colonial, Dixie, East Coast, Mid Atlantic, Mid South, Piedmont, Seaboard, Shoreline, and the Southern Seven.

The ACC operated with seven members until 1978 when Georgia Tech was admitted.

Over the years, the conference has continued to expand with Florida State in 1991, Miami and Virginia Tech in 2004, Boston College in 2005, and Syracuse and Pittsburgh in 2013. The ACC also announced in 2012 that Notre Dame would become part of the conference in all sports except football and hockey. The ACC finally lost a member in 2012 when Maryland left for the Big Ten Conference. However, the ACC quickly invited Louisville to replace Maryland.

ATHLETICS DIRECTORS

Lawrence R. (Bubba) Cunningham is the director of athletics at the University of North Carolina. He began his duties in Chapel Hill on November 14, 2011, succeeding Dick Baddour. Cunningham is only the seventh director of athletics in UNC history, following Robert A. Fetzer (1923–52), Chuck Erickson (1953–67), Homer Rice (1969–75), Bill Cobey (1976–80), John Swofford (1980–97), and Baddour.

Lawrence R. (Bubba) Cunningham is just the seventh director of athletics in UNC history.

ALL-AMERICA, ALL-CONFERENCE, ALL-WHAT?

You won't see a whole lot of mention in this book of All-America, All-Conference, or other All-Whatever lists. Nor do we cite many Player of the Year, Coach of the Year, or similar awards. We don't mean to slight anyone. But All-America and other such designations have proliferated to such an extent that what was once an honor has become almost an entitlement. If you have a halfway-decent season, somebody somewhere will put you on an All-America team—even if it's the second team. Or the third. Or the . . . you get the point.

In football, the NCAA recognizes All-America teams selected by the Associated Press, American Football Coaches Association, Football Writers Association of America, *Sporting News*, and Walter Camp Football

Foundation. Of those, the AFCA, FWAA, and *Sporting News* pick only a first team. The Walter Camp Foundation, which traces its roots back to the first All-America selections in 1889, picks a first team and a second team. The AP picks first, second, and third teams.

If all five selectors list you on the first team, you're a "unanimous" All-America selection. If three of the five do so, you're a "consensus" pick.

Those five are not the only organizations that publish an All-America football team. Others who get in on the fun include (at the moment, anyway) *Sports Illustrated, Pro Football Weekly,* ESPN, CBS Sports, *College Football News,* **scout.com,** and Yahoo! Sports, not to mention lots of individual newspapers and lesser-known websites.

And that's just the Division I Football Bowl Subdivision (formerly Division IA). It doesn't include the Division I Football Championship Subdivision (formerly Division IAA) or Division II or III, or the National Association of Intercollegiate Athletics, or the Academic All-America recognition bestowed by the College Sports Information Directors of America.

So when we see someone described as an All-American, we're not sure what that means. According to whom? First team, second, or third? Consensus? Unanimous? We're similarly uncertain about such designations as Player of the Year and Coach of the Year.

Therefore, we try to steer clear of this thicket as much as we can. We think you'll enjoy reading about the players in this book, regardless of whether they made somebody's All-Something list.

TITLE IX

More than 40 years after the federal law commonly known as Title IX was enacted, it still stirs passions—for and against.

The 1972 law reads, in part: "No person in the United States shall, on the basis of sex, be excluded from participation in, be denied the benefits of, or be subjected to discrimination under any education program or activity receiving Federal financial assistance."

Virtually every U.S. college and university receives federal funds. In effect, Title IX has forced most schools to provide intercollegiate athletic opportunities for women in proportion to their representation in the student body. Basically, if a college with a 50-50 gender split among students fields men's teams that total 100 athletes, then it more or less has to field women's teams that total 100 athletes as well.

No one disputes that Title IX has greatly increased the opportunities for—and numbers of—female collegiate athletes. Critics say it has also reduced opportunities for—and numbers of—male collegiate athletes. If our hypothetical school with the 50-50 gender split among the general student body has slots for 100 male athletes but for only 50 female athletes, it can either add women's sports or cut men's sports, or both.

Often, it's easier and cheaper to cut men's sports, especially if they're "nonrevenue" sports—in other words, if the costs to field the team exceed the income generated from ticket sales and other revenue sources. Except for football and basketball, most sports at most universities are nonrevenue.

Without Title IX, would North Carolina have both men's *and* women's varsity soccer teams—and, therefore, one of the NCAA's most successful programs in UNC women's soccer? Without Title IX, would the Tar Heels have a women's field hockey, gymnastics, or volleyball team? It's hard to know for sure, but UNC stands as a beacon for both men's and women's athletics; to have it any other way would be a shame.

MASCOT

In 1924, Vic Huggins, UNC's head cheerleader, decided that Carolina needed a mascot—some sort of animal perhaps. Jack Merrit, known as the "Battering Ram," was a popular member of the Tar Heel football team. Huggins came up with the idea of a ram as the University of North Carolina's mascot. As legend has it, Huggins asked UNC business manager Charles T. Woollen for $25 to buy a ram. The first mascot was then ordered from Texas.

FIGHT SONGS

That's right, we said songs. Plural. While most universities have a single fight song officially affiliated with the school, the University of North Carolina has several. Those include "Carolina Victory," "Hark the Sound," "Here Comes Carolina," "North Carolina," and "I'm a Tar Heel Born." The most popular is "I'm a Tar Heel Born," which has its origins as a tag, or an add-on, to the UNC alma mater. Its lyrics are as follows:

I'm a Tar Heel born, I'm a Tar Heel bred.
And when I die, I'm a Tar Heel dead.
So it's rah-rah, Car'lina-'lina!
Rah-rah, Car'lina-'lina!

Rah-rah, Car'lina-'lina!
Rah, rah, rah!

That last *rah, rah, rah* part was typically replaced with "Go to hell, State," from the 1970s through the early '90s. In recent decades, it's most often replaced with "Go to hell, Duke." Of course, it can also depend on who the opponent is at the time.

The other popular fight song is "Here Comes Carolina," which is most often heard as a sports team enters the field of play.

SPORTS AND SEASONS

Baseball (men)

February through May and then playoffs through June

Basketball (men and women)

November through March

Cross Country (men and women)

Late August through mid-November

Fencing (men and women)

October through March

Field Hockey (women)

Late August through mid-November

Football (men)

September through early December, plus the possibility of a bowl game as late as early January

Golf (men and women)

September–October; February–April; and then conference and NCAA tournaments through May

Gymnastics (women)

January through mid-March; conference and NCAA tournaments through April

Lacrosse (men and women)

February through April; conference and NCAA tournaments through May

Rowing (women)

October through November; March through May

Soccer (men and women)

August through early November; conference and NCAA tournaments into December

Softball (women)

February through early May; conference and NCAA tournaments into June

Swimming and Diving (men and women)

October through January; conference and NCAA tournaments through March

Tennis (men and women)

September through November; January through April; conference tournaments though May

Track and Field (men and women)

January through April; conference and NCAA tournaments through early June

Wrestling (men)

October through February; conference and NCAA tournaments through March

BASKETBALL

MEN

The names are legendary. Not just in the annals of Tar Heel history, but also in the history of basketball: Bob McAdoo, Walter Davis, Bobby Jones, Mitch Kupchak, Vince Carter, James Worthy, and the incomparable Michael Jordan. These are just a few of the University of North Carolina players to have gone pro in the sport about which most Tar Heel fans are most passionate.

Basketball at UNC had quite humble beginnings. The first intercollegiate varsity team, back in 1910–11, finished with 7 wins and 4 losses. In those days there was no Dean Smith Center. Games were played at Bynum Gymnasium, a facility gifted to UNC by Judge William Preston Bynum in memory of his grandson, William Preston Bynum Jr., an early Tar Heel football player who died of typhoid fever in the spring of 1893. You may know the venerable building today as Bynum Hall—the graduate admissions office.

It didn't take long, though, for UNC teams to excel at basketball. In the 1920s, UNC basketball began racking up Southern Conference championships: 1922, '24, '25, and '26. The 1924 team was undefeated, 26-0, and was voted National Champion by the Helms Athletic Foundation. (Yeah, we know Duke fans say that championship doesn't count. Suck it up, Dookies.) Speaking of that team, its coach was Norman Shepard. It was his first season as a coach and his only season coaching UNC. You gotta love it: 26-0, National Champs, Shepard out! (It also was the first season that UNC played in the Indoor Athletic Center, more commonly known as the Tin Can.)

Winning teams became a habit in Chapel Hill. Memorable games were routine. UNC didn't win all of those memorable games, though. The 1946 NCAA championship game in New York's Madison Square Garden is one example.

DEAN SMITH. Legendary coach Dean Smith won 859 games, including two NCAA Championships, during his 36-year career with the Tar Heels.

The Tar Heels battled with Oklahoma A&M but came up short, 43–40. Still, that game and the entire 1946 team, with its 30-5 record, are legendary.

Speaking of going pro, UNC's first truly great coach ended up leaving Chapel Hill to go pro. Back in 1952, Frank McGuire left his coaching job at St. John's to head south to Chapel Hill. He brought with him a gritty brand of New York City basketball that was immediately a success for the team in Carolina blue and white. McGuire won 164 games in nine seasons before leaving for the NBA. His most outstanding team was the 1957 squad, which finished as national champions with a 32-0 record. Losing McGuire was considered a big blow. Too bad the young whippersnapper that followed him wasn't that good. Dean Smith had an 8-9 record in his first year. A 15-6 record followed, which gave fans some hope that perhaps this guy had some coaching chops. Smith followed that with a 12-12 record, though. By the end of 1964, some wondered if Smith was a poor choice to follow McGuire. Three decades and one Dean Dome later, most Carolina fans are happy the administration stuck with Smith.

Despite the rocky start, Smith finished his esteemed coaching career having won 78% of his games. He took his team to the NCAA Tournament 27 times in his 36 seasons at UNC. His tourney success included 11 Final Fours and two National Championships. Yeah, you could say Smith worked out okay.

Now under the tutelage of Roy Williams, who came to Chapel Hill after 15 successful seasons at the University of Kansas, Carolina basketball is enjoying continued success. Originally from Western North Carolina, the home-state boy has done good (as we'd say around Marion and Spruce Pine—Williams's old stompin' grounds). In a decade on the bench of the Dean Dome, Williams has won two National Championships and continues to churn out players who go pro.

Head Coaching Records

(In chronological order, including record and winning percentage; a tie counts as half a win, half a loss, per NCAA practice)

YEARS	COACH	RECORD	WINNING PCT.
1911–14	Nat Cartmell	25-24	.510
1915–16	Charles Doak	18-16	.529
1917–19	Howell Peacock	14-7	.622
1920–21	Fred Boye	19-17	.671
1922–23	No Coach	30-7	.811
1924	Norman Shepard	26-0	1.000
1925	Monk McDonald	20-5	.800
1926	Harlan Sanborn	20-5	.800
1927–31	James Ashmore	80-37	.684
1932–35	George Shepard	69-16	.812
1936–39	Walter Skidmore	65-25	.722
1940–44	Bill Lange	85-41	.675
1945–46	Ben Carnevale	52-11	.825
1947–52	Tom Scott	100-65	.606
1953–61	Frank McGuire	164-58	.739
1962–97	Dean Smith	879-254	.776
1997–2000	Bill Guthridge	80-28	.741
2001–03	Matt Doherty	53-43	.552
2003–14	Roy Williams	282-79	.781

(Ranked by victories)

RECORD	COACH	YEARS	WINNING PCT.
879-254	Dean Smith	1962–97	.776
282-79	Roy Williams	2003–14	.781
164-58	Frank McGuire	1953–61	.739

RECORD	COACH	YEARS	WINNING PCT.
100-65	Tom Scott	1947–52	.606
85-41	Bill Lange	1940–44	.675
80-28	Bill Guthridge	1997–2000	.741
80-37	James Ashmore	1927–31	.684
69-16	George Shepard	1932–35	.812
65-25	Walter Skidmore	1936–39	.722
53-43	Matt Doherty	2001–03	.552
52-11	Ben Carnevale	1945–46	.825
30-7	No Coach	1922–23	.811
26-0	Norman Shepard	1924	1.000
25-24	Nat Cartmell	1911–14	.510
20-5	Monk McDonald	1925	.800
20-5	Harlan Sanborn	1926	.800
19-17	Fred Boye	1920–21	.671
18-16	Charles Doak	1915–16	.529
14-7	Howell Peacock	1917–19	.622

(Ranked by winning percentage; a tie counts as half a win, half a loss, per NCAA practice)

WINNING PCT.	COACH	YEARS	RECORD
1.000	Norman Shepard	1924	26-0
.825	Ben Carnevale	1945–46	52-11
.812	George Shepard	1932–35	69-16
.811	No Coach	1922–23	30-7
.800	Monk McDonald	1925	20-5
.800	Harlan Sanborn	1926	20-5
.781	Roy Williams	2003–14	282-79
.776	Dean Smith	1962–97	879-254
.741	Bill Guthridge	1997–2000	80-28
.739	Frank McGuire	1953–61	164-58
.722	Walter Skidmore	1936–39	65-25
.684	James Ashmore	1927–31	80-37
.675	Bill Lange	1940–44	85-41

WINNING PCT.	COACH	YEARS	RECORD
.671	Fred Boye	1920–21	49-24
.622	Howell Peacock	1917–19	23-14
.606	Tom Scott	1947–52	100-65
.552	Matt Doherty	2001–03	53-43
.529	Charles Doak	1915–16	18-16
.510	Nat Cartmell	1911–14	25-24

Top 25 All-Time Division I College Teams

(Ranked by wins through the 2012–13 season; includes winning percentage and number of seasons played)

RECORD	TEAM	WINNING PCT.	SEASONS
2,111-661	Kentucky	.761	110
2,101-812	Kansas	.721	115
2,090-745	**North Carolina**	**.737**	**103**
2,001-840	Duke	.704	108
1,874-832	Syracuse	.693	112
1,814-992	Temple	.646	117
1,754-931	St. John's (NY)	.653	106
1,753-779	UCLA	.692	94
1,748-949	Notre Dame	.648	108
1,719-966	Indiana	.640	113
1,706-1,020	Pennsylvania	.626	113
1,697-869	Louisville	.661	99
1,690-910	Illinois	.650	108
1,690-1,026	Brigham Young	.622	111
1,685-936	Utah	.643	105
1,683-1,095	Washington	.606	111
1,675-844	Western Kentucky	.665	94
1,675-994	Texas	.628	107
1,658-972	Purdue	.630	115
1,654-1,251	Oregon State	.569	112
1,646-963	Cincinnati	.631	112

RECORD	TEAM	WINNING PCT.	SEASONS
1,645-900	Arizona	.646	108
1,636-1,025	Princeton	.615	113
1,634-1,024	West Virginia	.615	104
1,617-980	North Carolina State	.623	101
1,589-888	Connecticut	.642	110
1,584-903	Villanova	.637	93
1,575-892	Missouri State	.638	101
1,569-962	Georgetown	.620	105
1,568-950	Alabama	.623	100
1,558-1,009	Ohio State	.607	112
1,558-1,080	Oklahoma State	.591	104
1,556-880	Arkansas	.639	90
1,553-1,054	Missouri	.596	107

(Ranked by winning percentage through 2012–13 season)

WINNING PCT.	TEAM	RECORD
.761	Kentucky	2,111-661
.737	**North Carolina**	**2,090-745**
.721	Kansas	2,101-812
.713	Nevada-Las Vegas	1,158-466
.704	Duke	2,001-840
.693	Syracuse	1,874-832
.692	UCLA	1,753-779
.665	Western Kentucky	1,675-844
.661	Louisville	1,697-869
.653	St. John's (NY)	1,754-931
.650	Illinois	1,690-910
.648	Notre Dame	1,748-949
.646	Temple	1,814-992
.646	Arizona	1,645-900
.643	Utah	1,685-936
.643	Virginia Commonwealth	818-455

WINNING PCT.	TEAM	RECORD
.643	Murray State	1,501-835
.642	Connecticut	1,589-888
.640	Indiana	1,719-966
.639	Arkansas	1,556-880
.639	Weber State	945-535
.638	Missouri State	1,575-892
.637	Villanova	1,584-903
.632	Memphis	1,441-838
.631	Cincinnati	1,646-963
.630	Purdue	1,658-972
.628	Texas	1,675-994
.626	Pennsylvania	1,706-1,020
.624	Alabama-Birmingham	695-418
.623	Alabama	1,568-950
.623	North Carolina State	1,617-980
.622	Marquette	1,520-922
.622	Brigham Young	1,690-1,026
.620	Georgetown	1,569-962
.615	Princeton	1,636-1,025

Atlantic Coast Conference Teams

(Ranked by wins through 2012–13 season; includes winning percentage and number of seasons played)

RECORD	TEAM	WINNING PCT.	SEASONS
2,090-745	**North Carolina**	**.737**	**103**
2,001-840	Duke	.704	108
1,617-980	North Carolina State	.623	101
1,455-1,127	Wake Forest	.564	107
1,454-1,132	Virginia	.562	108
1,428-1,002	Maryland	.588	94
1,355-1,129	Virginia Tech	.545	105
1,280-1,140	Georgia Tech	.529	98

RECORD	TEAM	WINNING PCT.	SEASONS
1,211-1,220	Clemson	.498	102
1,128-880	Boston College	.562	80
1,060-781	Florida State	.576	66
897-688	Miami	.566	61

(Ranked by winning percentage through 2012–13 season)

WINNING PCT.	TEAM	RECORD
.737	**North Carolina**	**2,090-745**
.704	Duke	2,001-840
.623	North Carolina State	1,617-980
.588	Maryland	1,428-1,002
.576	Florida State	1,060-781
.566	Miami	897-688
.564	Wake Forest	1,455-1,127
.562	Boston College	1,128-880
.562	Virginia	1,454-1,132
.545	Virginia Tech	1,355-1,129
.529	Georgia Tech	1,280-1,140
.498	Clemson	1,211-1,220

Atlantic Coast Conference Championships

(Regular season, through 2013)

29 North Carolina
19 Duke
7 North Carolina State
5 Virginia
5 Maryland
4 Wake Forest
2 Georgia Tech
1 Clemson
1 Miami
1 South Carolina

(Tournament, through 2013)

19 Duke
17 North Carolina
10 North Carolina State
4 Wake Forest
3 Georgia Tech
3 Maryland
1 Florida State
1 Virginia
1 South Carolina

Top 20 Division I Home Attendance Leaders

(2012–13, with per-game average and season total)

TEAM	AVERAGE PER-GAME ATTENDANCE	TOTAL SEASON ATTENDANCE
Kentucky	23,099	415,775
Syracuse	22,439	426,347
Louisville	21,571	345,129
North Carolina	**19,350**	**309,603**
Indiana	17,412	330,832
Creighton	17,155	291,643
Wisconsin	16,843	303,172
Tennessee	16,635	282,794
Ohio State	16,524	297,428
Kansas	16,438	295,889
Memphis	16,336	294,044
North Carolina State	16,299	277,087
Brigham Young	15,986	287,750
Nevada-Las Vegas	15,196	334,320
Marquette	15,033	240,530
New Mexico	15,022	240,351
Illinois	15,013	255,213
Michigan State	14,341	258,138
Arizona	14,157	226,505
Arkansas	13,750	261,242

Atlantic Coast Conference Home Attendance

(2012–13, with per-game average and season total)

TEAM	AVERAGE PER-GAME ATTENDANCE	TOTAL SEASON ATTENDANCE
North Carolina	**19,350**	**309,603**
North Carolina State	16,299	277,087
Maryland	12,489	262,264
Wake Forest	9,614	153,831

TEAM	AVERAGE PER-GAME ATTENDANCE	TOTAL SEASON ATTENDANCE
Virginia	9,403	206,876
Duke	9,314	149,024
Clemson	7,743	116,151
Florida State	7,537	135,673
Georgia Tech	7,365	125,200
Virginia Tech	6,202	105,442
Miami	5,814	87,212

North Carolina in the NCAA Tournament

(Through 2013; includes furthest round achieved)

Year	Round	Year	Round	Year	Round
1941	Elite Eight	**1982**	**NCAA Champion**	**1997**	National Semifinals
1946	National Championship	**1983**	Elite Eight	**1998**	National Semifinals
1957	**NCAA Champion**	**1984**	Sweet Sixteen	**1999**	First Round
1959	First Round	**1985**	Elite Eight	**2000**	National Semifinals
1967	National Semifinals	**1986**	Sweet Sixteen	**2001**	Second Round
1968	National Championship	**1987**	Elite Eight	**2004**	Second Round
1969	National Semifinals	**1988**	Elite Eight	**2005**	**NCAA Champion**
1972	National Semifinals	**1989**	Sweet Sixteen	**2006**	Second Round
1975	Sweet Sixteen	**1990**	Sweet Sixteen	**2007**	Elite Eight
1976	First Round	**1991**	National Semifinals	**2008**	National Semifinals
1977	National Championship	**1992**	Sweet Sixteen	**2009**	**NCAA Champion**
1978	First Round	**1993**	**NCAA Champion**	**2011**	Elite Eight
1979	Second Round	**1994**	Second Round	**2012**	Elite Eight
1980	Second Round	**1995**	National Semifinals	**2013**	Third Round
1981	National Championship	**1996**	Second Round		

North Carolina in the NIT

(Postseason NIT only; through 2013; includes furthest round achieved)

Year	Round	Year	Round	Year	Round
1970	First Round	**1973**	Fourth Round	**2003**	Third Round
1971	**Champion**	**1974**	First Round	**2010**	Championship Game

NCAA Championships

(Through 2013, teams with more than one championship)

11, UCLA	**3,** Connecticut	**2,** Michigan State
8, Kentucky	**3,** Kansas	**2,** North Carolina State
5, Indiana	**3,** Louisville	**2,** Oklahoma State
5, North Carolina	**2,** Cincinnati	**2,** San Francisco
4, Duke	**2,** Florida	

NIT Championships

(Postseason NIT only; through 2013)

* **6,** St. John's (New York)	**1,** Baylor	**1,** Penn State
4, Bradley	**1,** California	**1,** Princeton
3, Dayton	**1,** CCNY	**1,** Purdue
** **3,** Michigan	**1,** Colorado	**1,** Seton Hall
2, Brigham Young	**1,** Connecticut	**1,** Southern Illinois
2, Kentucky	**1,** DePaul	**1,** Southern Mississippi
2, Long Island	**1,** Duquesne	**1,** San Francisco
*** **2,** Minnesota	**1,** Fresno State	**1,** St. Bonaventure
2, Ohio State	**1,** Holy Cross	**1,** St. Louis
2, Providence	**1,** Indiana	**1,** Texas
2, South Carolina	**1,** LaSalle	**1,** UCLA
2, Stanford	**1,** Louisville	**1,** Utah
2, Temple	**1,** Marquette	**1,** Vanderbilt
2, Tulsa	**1,** Maryland	**1,** Villanova
2, Virginia	**1,** Memphis	**1,** Wake Forest
2, Virginia Tech	**1,** Nebraska	**1,** Wichita State
2, West Virginia	**1, North Carolina**	**1,** Xavier

* *Includes the 2003 title, which the NCAA vacated because of an ineligible player*

** *Includes the 1997 title, which the NCAA vacated because of ineligible players*

*** *Includes the 1998 title, which the NCAA vacated because of academic fraud*

Player Bios

HARRISON BARNES ■ 6' 8" 210 ■ *Forward*

COLLEGE: 2010–12 **NBA:** 2012–13

Still so young, Harrison Bryce Jordan Barnes has plenty of potential for a long pro career. And he's no late bloomer. It seems Barnes has always been a great basketball player. Playing for Ames High School in Iowa, Barnes led his team to back-to-back state championships, each team going undefeated. He averaged 26.1 points, 10 rebounds, 3.1 steals, and 3 assists during his senior year. As the season ended, he was selected to the McDonald's All-American Team and the *USA Today* All-USA First Team. He also won the Morgan Wootten Player of the Year Award, which goes to the nation's top high school player. With a few recruiting services ranking Barnes as the nation's top prospect, he had his choice of schools. Iowa State, Kansas, and Oklahoma were all closer to home. Duke and UNC were strongly considered in the East, as was UCLA in the West. In the end, he chose Chapel Hill. Perhaps because one of his names is Jordan? At any rate, Barnes wasted no time making an impact as a Tar Heel.

Before the start of his freshman season, he was named an All-American by the Associated Press. Now *there's* some pressure. Barnes didn't blink, though. He just got better as the 2011–12 season progressed. He began with a 14-point outing against Lipscomb and had a 40-point performance against Clemson in the ACC Tournament. He started all but one game his freshman year, finishing with a 15.7 points-per-game scoring average. He was the ACC Freshman of the Year. Tar Heel fans held their breath as the season ended, thinking Barnes could be one and done. The opportunity was certainly there, as most experts thought Barnes would be a lottery pick in the NBA for the 2011 draft. Fans were able to finally breathe a sigh of relief when Barnes decided to return for his sophomore season.

Barnes avoided a sophomore slump, increasing his average points per game to 17.3. He also increased his field goal and three-point shot percentages. Ending with a First Team All-ACC selection, Barnes' sophomore season would be his last in Chapel Hill. He entered the 2012 NBA Draft, where he was the seventh overall pick. In his rookie season for the Golden State Warriors, Barnes had a solid season, averaging nearly 10 points a game and helping the Warriors make the playoffs.

LARRY BROWN ■ 5' 9" 160 ■ *Guard*

COLLEGE: 1959–63 **ABA:** 1967–72 **OLYMPICS:** 1964, assistant coach 2000, head coach 2004

Younger readers probably know Lawrence Harvey Brown as a basketball coach rather than a player—and with good reason. Brown is a longtime coach who has been on the sidelines in the NBA, ABA, and for college teams. Currently the coach of the Southern

Methodist University Mustangs, Brown previously coached nine NBA teams and is one of the few men to surpass 1,000 career victories in basketball's top echelon. He was inducted to the Basketball Hall of Fame in 2002. We'll get back to Brown as a coach, but we want to inform those who don't know that Larry was a pretty good ballplayer.

Larry Brown was a stellar point guard in Chapel Hill, but at 5-foot-9 he was considered too small for a career in the NBA. He played for five seasons in the ABA, and perhaps it was there that he developed a penchant of moving on rather quickly. In those five seasons, he played for the New Orleans Buccaneers, the Oakland Oaks (who became the Washington Capitols and then the Virginia Squires), and the Denver Rockets, winning an ABA championship in his year with Oakland. (One of his teammates at Oakland was fellow UNC alumnus Doug Moe, who went on to become a pretty good coach too.) As a point guard, Brown averaged 11.2 points per game and 6.7 assists in his ABA career. He gave up playing to become the head coach of Davidson College back in North Carolina. Before he could coach a game, though, the ABA lured him back as coach of the Carolina Cougars, where he led the team to a first-place finish in the league's East Division.

Brown coached Carolina one more year before leaving for Denver, which was transitioning from its former name, the Rockets, to its new name, the Nuggets. Brown and the new Nuggets finished first in the West in the last two years of the ABA's existence, making it to the ABA finals for the 1975–76 season. Brown then led the Nuggets as one of the ABA teams to merge with the NBA, but alas, Denver has never returned to a finals series. One of Brown's stars on those last-two ABA and first-two NBA teams was Bobby Jones, fresh out of the University of North Carolina.

BILLY CUNNINGHAM ■ 6' 6" 210 ■ *Forward / Center*

COLLEGE: 1961–65 **ABA:** 1972–74 **NBA:** 1965–72, 1974–76

William John Cunningham, known during his playing days as "The Kangaroo Kid," is another guy younger readers may remember in a role other than player. For several years beginning in the late 1980s, Billy Cunningham was a color commentator for CBS's NBA coverage. Prior to that he was the very successful head coach of the Philadelphia 76ers for eight seasons. Billy Cunningham came to fame, though, as a scrappy forward for the North Carolina Tar Heels.

Cunningham arrived in Chapel Hill as a much-heralded player from Brooklyn, New York, finishing high school as a *Parade* All-American in 1961. Cunningham was a star on the team as a young Dean Smith tried to find his coaching stride. Cunningham had to sit out his freshman season by rule, as the Tar Heels finished with a disappointing 8-9 record. In his sophomore year, the 1962–63 season, UNC improved to 15-6. The team finished third in the ACC, and Cunningham received All-ACC honors. In his junior year, the team suffered a setback, finishing 12-12, but Cunningham continued to impress. He had an amazing 27 rebounds in one game

VINCE CARTER ■ 6' 6" 215 ■ *Guard / Forward*

COLLEGE: 1995–98 **NBA:** 1998–13 **OLYMPICS:** 2000

VINCE CARTER. With a long NBA career plus an Olympic gold medal, Vince Carter's basketball career has been legendary.

Upon Michael Jordan's retirement from the NBA, many looked at fellow Tar Heel Vince Carter as potentially being "the next Michael Jordan." While that never came to fruition, Carter still had an extraordinary career and is considered to be among the top five Tar Heels to ever go pro in basketball. It was clear early on in Daytona Beach, Florida, that Carter would be a star. In his senior season at Mainland High School, Carter led his team to a state championship while earning Florida Mr. Basketball honors and McDonald's All-American status for himself (in addition to winning the McDonald's All-American Slam Dunk Contest). Carter then went to UNC to play for Coach Dean Smith. In his freshman and sophomore years under Smith, the Tar Heels reached the NCAA Tournament, making it to the Final Four his sophomore season. Two months before the start of Carter's junior season, Smith announced his retirement, and longtime assistant Bill Guthridge was named head coach. In that season, UNC registered a school record–tying 34 wins and an appearance in the Final Four, where it lost to Utah. During his sophomore and junior seasons, Carter helped lead North Carolina to consecutive ACC Tournament titles and Final Four appearances. He averaged 15.6 points per game and was named second-team All-American his junior year. He then decided to forego his senior year and go pro.

Carter was selected as the fifth pick in the 1998 NBA draft by the Golden State Warriors but was immediately traded to the Toronto Raptors for Tar Heel teammate Antawn Jamison, who had been chosen as the fourth pick. Carter made an immediate splash. Not only did he win the Rookie of the Year Award in 1999, but he was also named to the All-Rookie First Team. His star continued to rise early in his career. A highlight was leading the U.S. Olympics basketball team in scoring on the way to a gold medal in the 2000 Olympic Games in Sydney, Australia. Back in the NBA, Carter caught the attention of even casual fans

continued on next page

with his performance in the 2000 NBA Slam Dunk Contest, which he won. His best scoring season came in 2000–01 when he averaged a career-high 27.6 points per game. With this sort of high-flying success and the Tar Heel connection, you can see why Carter was being tagged as "the next Michael Jordan." But injuries became more common for Carter.

Interestingly enough, Carter gave up his roster spot in the 2003 All-Star Game to Michael Jordan. Carter had an injury and couldn't play, while Jordan was retiring (again) and got the chance to play a final All-Star game, this one as a Washington Wizard. Injuries and discontent with the Toronto Raptors' management led to a trade to New Jersey, where Carter had some great years with the Nets. He has since played for the Orlando Magic, the Phoenix Suns, and, since 2011, the Dallas Mavericks. Over the course of his career, Carter has been an eight-time All-Star selection and has averaged more than 20 points per game. With more than 22,000 career points, Carter is among the top 30 scorers of all time in the NBA. He scored 51 points in a game on two occasions.

Carter established the Embassy of Hope nonprofit foundation in 1998 "to help address the needs of children and their parents." The Embassy of Hope is a Florida-based 501(c)(3) charitable organization. Through the Foundation's annual fundraisers, the Embassy of Hope has helped kids in Florida, New Jersey, Toronto, and elsewhere.

In 2010, he and his mother, Michelle Carter-Scott, opened Vince Carter's, a restaurant in Daytona Beach.

BILLY CUNNINGHAM *continued from page 30*

that season (against Clemson). Cunningham then finished with a flourish in his senior year, setting a UNC single-game scoring record against Tulane while finishing with numerous conference (including ACC Player of the Year) and All-America honors. He ended his collegiate career with 1,709 points (24.8 per game) and 1,062 rebounds (15.4 per game).

In the 1965 NBA draft, Cunningham was chosen fifth overall, going to the Philadelphia 76ers. After seven seasons with the 76ers, Cunningham spent two seasons with the Carolina Cougars of the ABA before going back to Philadelphia for two more seasons prior to his retirement. For his pro career, Cunningham averaged 21.2 points and 10.4 rebounds per game. He proved to be a solid passer as well, finishing with 4.3 assists per game, which isn't bad for a forward. He always proved to be a reliable and solid player. He had good fundamentals and skills in all aspects of the game.

He also avoided injuries for the better part of his career, though an injury early in the 1975–76 season forced him into retirement. Cunningham later said of the injury, "In a way, the injury made things easy for me. I never had to agonize over that decision all athletes face."

His accolades as a pro player include:

- **Four-time NBA All-Star**
- **Three-time All-NBA First Team**
- **All-NBA Second Team**
- **NBA All-Rookie First Team**
- **All-ABA First Team**
- **ABA Most Valuable Player**
- **NBA Champion**

After his retirement from playing, Cunningham also picked up honors such as ABA All-Time Team, NBA 50th Anniversary All-Time Team, and having his jersey number (32) retired by the 76ers. Just a year after his retirement as a player, Cunningham took the reins of the 76ers as head coach. The 76ers reached the playoffs in each of his eight seasons. His teams lost in the NBA finals in 1980 and 1982 before winning the championship in 1983. His teams won at least 50 regular season games in seven of his eight years as coach, and he reached the milestones of 200, 300, and 400 wins faster than any other coach in NBA history. Known as a fierce competitor and intense player on the court, Cunningham grew weary of the NBA lifestyle, surprising everyone with his retirement after such quick and sustained success.

Former Philadelphia 76ers executive Pat Williams talked to *New Miami* magazine about Billy Cunningham in 1992. "When you think about Billy's life, it is amazing," Williams said. "He was a high school superstar. Then he went to North Carolina and was an All-American. He was a No. 1 draft choice. Then an All-Star. Then he goes into coaching and, percentage-wise, becomes one of the best ever. He rises to the highest level of broadcasting. . . . I don't know anything he has done that hasn't worked. It's a remarkable life."

ED DAVIS ■ 6' 10" 245 ■ *Forward*

COLLEGE: 2008–10 **NBA:** 2010–13

As the son of NBA player Terry Davis, who played in the league for 10 seasons, it seemed Edward Adam Davis was meant to follow in his father's footsteps. With Terry standing 6-foot-10, weighing 225 pounds, it looked like young Ed would come close to that same size. Playing for Richmond's Benedictine High School, he led the team to two state championships. In his senior year, he was ranked as a top-five player, accumulating accolades such as McDonald's and *Parade* All-American and Virginia's Mr. Basketball.

He then moved on to Chapel Hill to play for Coach Roy Williams. His freshman season, Davis got a lot of playing time but only started two games on a team rife with

BRAD DAUGHERTY ■ 7' 0" 245 ■ *Center*

COLLEGE: 1982–86 **NBA:** 1986–94

You may know Brad Daugherty as just another 7-foot, African American NASCAR commentator. Wait, what? The guy who loves fishing, hunting, and golf? Oh, yeah, that guy.

Before all that, Daugherty was known as a basketball player. A native of Black Mountain, North Carolina, near Asheville, he led Charles D. Owen High School to the state finals his senior year. He then moved to Chapel Hill to begin his basketball tutelage under Coach Dean Smith, just after the team won its 1981–82 National Championship. By the end of his four years at UNC, Daugherty was considered one of the best big men to ever play in Carolina blue and white.

BRAD DAUGHERTY. Now known as a NASCAR commentator, Brad Daugherty had a sterling career for the Cleveland Cavaliers before injuries led to an early retirement.

UNC had great success during Daugherty's four years on campus in Chapel Hill, as the team won 28 games in three of his seasons and 27 in the other. The team never had quite the success it expected in the NCAA Tournament, though. Nonetheless, two Sweet Sixteen and two Elite Eight finishes are not too shabby. Individually, Daugherty got better each year. As a young freshman (he had just turned 17 when the season began), Daugherty averaged a modest 8.2 points and 5.2

talent. He finished the year averaging 6.7 points and 6.6 rebounds per game, but more important was how the team finished. The 2008–09 Tar Heels won the ACC and went on to beat Michigan State in the NCAA Tournament for the National Championship. In that game, Davis scored 11 points and got a team-high 8 rebounds, thus propelling conversation that he would leave Chapel Hill after the season and enter the NBA Draft. Davis decided to come back for his sophomore season. In February 2010, he suffered a broken wrist in a loss to Duke, putting a damper on what was shaping up to be a great sophomore season in which Davis averaged 13.2 points and 9.6 rebounds per game.

Davis did decide to go pro after his sophomore year at UNC and was the 13th overall pick in the 2010 NBA Draft, chosen by the Toronto Raptors. After two and a half solid seasons with Toronto, he was part of a three-team trade in January 2013 that saw him land with the Memphis Grizzlies and subsequently make it to the

rebounds per game. Those numbers increased to 10.5 and 5.6 as a sophomore, 17.3 and 9.7 as a junior, and 20.2 and 9.0 as a senior. He was a two-time All-ACC selection and First-Team All-American his senior year. His tremendous success at UNC led him to be the No. 1 overall pick in the 1986 NBA draft. Chosen by the Cleveland Cavaliers, he played all eight of his NBA seasons for the Cavs.

Daugherty was named to the NBA All-Rookie Team in 1987, a year in which he averaged 15.7 points and 8.1 rebounds per game. These were solid numbers, yet they were the lowest averages of his career. At his peak, in 1990–91, Daugherty averaged 21.6 points and 10.9 rebounds in 76 games for Cleveland. Recurring back problems limited him in the 1993–94 season, allowing for only 50 games played. At age 28, it turned out to be his final NBA season. After two inactive seasons, he officially retired in 1996. While not the longest NBA career, it was certainly productive. A five-time NBA All-Star, he finished his career as Cleveland's top scorer and rebounder, though both those marks have since been passed. His jersey number, 43, was retired by the Cavs.

Oh yeah, about that number. Back in 1977, Daugherty met Richard Petty, the King of NASCAR, who drove the No. 43 car. Meeting Petty stirred in Daugherty a fascination with racing that continues to this day. As a young NBA player, Daugherty cofounded a late-model stock race team with driver Robert Pressley. Daugherty later was influential as an owner in the NASCAR Nationwide Series and Craftsman Truck Series. In 2008, he became part owner of JTG-Daugherty Motorsports, which races cars in both the NASCAR Sprint Cup and the NASCAR Nationwide Series. He joined ESPN as a NASCAR analyst in 2007. He began his broadcast career as a game analyst for the Cavaliers from 1996 to 1998, also working some as an analyst for the San Antonio Spurs. He then served as a college basketball sideline reporter and analyst for ESPN and ABC (1999–01).

playoffs for the first time. Though he's averaged just over 7 points and just under 7 rebounds per game in his early NBA career, if Davis can avoid injuries, he could have a lot of playing days left.

WALTER DAVIS ■ 6' 6" 193 ■ *Guard / Forward*

COLLEGE: 1973–77 **NBA:** 1977–92 **OLYMPICS:** 1976

Best known for his years with the Phoenix Suns, Walter Davis was a six-time NBA All-Star, Olympian, and 1978 NBA Rookie of the Year. Born in Pineville, North Carolina, the youngest of 14 children, he graduated from Charlotte's South Mecklenberg High School. He earned the nickname "Sweet D" in Chapel Hill due to his smooth, graceful style of play. Davis averaged at least 14 points per game in each of his four years

HUBERT DAVIS. A fantastic shooting guard for the Tar Heels, Hubert Davis played in the NBA, served as a college basketball analyst, and is now on the UNC coaching staff.

HUBERT DAVIS ■ 6' 5" 183 ■ *Guard*

COLLEGE: 1988–92 **NBA:** 1992–04

Hubert Ira Davis, Jr., seemed destined to be a UNC basketball legend. He's the nephew of former UNC basketball star Walter Davis (as it should happen, the next guy on this list). He was born in North Carolina at Winston-Salem. During Davis's years as a Tar Heel (1988–92), UNC had a record of 102-37, won the ACC Tournaments in 1989 and 1991, and played in the 1991 Final Four. As a 6-foot-5 shooting guard, Davis averaged 21.4 points, 1.6 assists, and 2.3 rebounds per game his senior year while earning second-team All-ACC honors. He scored a career-high 35 points at Duke in March of 1992. As a junior, Davis had a three-point percentage of .489—second best in UNC history. He shares the UNC single-game record for three-pointers, making eight at Florida State his senior year.

Scoring more than 1,600 career points for a storied basketball program typically gets you drafted by the NBA in the first round. That was the case with Davis, who was chosen 20th overall by the New York Knicks in 1992. He played four seasons

WALTER DAVIS *continued from page 35*

with the Tar Heels. He was on the 1976 Olympics basketball team coached by Dean Smith that went undefeated in the Games and finished with a gold medal. In 1977, he was the fifth overall pick of the NBA draft.

Davis needed no transition time to adjust to the professional level. In fact, the highest scoring average of his NBA career came in his rookie season when he averaged 24.2 points per game. He played 11 years with the Phoenix Suns, battling injuries and drug problems along the way. He played two and a half seasons with the Denver Nuggets before being traded to the Portland Trail Blazers for half a season. He returned to Denver for the 1991–92 season, which would be his last. Over his career, Davis averaged 18.9 points per game, 3.8 assists, and 3 rebounds. Always a great free-throw shooter, he finished with a career average of 85 percent. He also hit 51 percent of his shots from the field, which is particularly impressive for an outside shooter.

After his retirement he worked as an announcer for the Nuggets and as a scout for the Washington Wizards. His number, 6, was retired by the Phoenix Suns in 1994, and in 2004 he entered the team's Ring of Honor. In 2012, Davis sold his Olympic gold medal at auction for $108,000. He is the uncle of the aforementioned Hubert Davis.

in New York before playing for a year with the Toronto Raptors and then moving on to the Dallas Mavericks. While he kept his reputation as a fine three-point shooter, Davis was never a prolific scorer on a consistent basis. Playing for Dallas in the 1999–2000 season, he led the NBA in three-point percentages at .491, but he averaged only 7.4 points per game. (Davis did average double-digit points per game during four of his NBA seasons, three of those early on with the Knicks.) He went on to play for the Washington Wizards, Detroit Pistons, and New Jersey Nets before hanging up his sneakers after the 2003–04 season. He finished his career averaging 8.2 points per game and an impressive .441 three-point percentage.

In 2008, Davis began working for ESPN as a college basketball analyst, enjoying considerable success and notoriety. He left broadcasting in 2012 to head back to UNC, this time as a coach. "For the last four or five years, Hubert has always been on my mind in case a spot did come open," said UNC Head Coach Roy Williams about the idea of hiring Hubert Davis as an assistant in Chapel Hill. "I didn't know if I could get him to come back, but I knew I wanted him to be the first option. Coaching is about teaching, relationships, and passion, and I feel Hubert is the perfect choice. Our student-athletes will benefit greatly from what he adds to our staff." In Davis's first season as an assistant coach at UNC, the team finished the season 25-11, 12-6 in ACC play to finish in third place. After defeating Villanova, the Tar Heels lost to Kansas in the NCAA Tournament.

WAYNE ELLINGTON ■ 6' 4" 200 ■ *Guard*

COLLEGE: 2006–09 **NBA:** 2009–13

Wayne Ellington made an immediate impact for the Tar Heels, playing in all 38 games his freshman year and averaging 11.7 points per game. He averaged 16.6 points per game as a sophomore. That season included a career-high 26 points in a game at Clemson that saw Ellington nail a game-winning three-point shot. He initially declared for the 2008 NBA Draft but decided to instead come back for his junior year in Chapel Hill. That decision made Tar Heel fans happy, as Ellington led the team to a National Championship; he was named NCAA Tournament Most Outstanding Player in the process. Ellington did indeed forego his senior year and was drafted by the Minnesota Timberwolves 28th overall in the NBA Draft.

Thus far, Ellington has not made a major impact in the NBA. After three seasons with Minnesota, in which he managed just 13 starts and fewer than 7 points per game, he was traded to the Memphis Grizzlies in 2012. After 40 games, he was traded again, this time to the Cleveland Cavaliers, where he started the most games of his career (17) and averaged 10.4 points per game.

PHIL FORD ■ 6' 2" 175 ■ *Guard*

COLLEGE: 1974–78 **NBA:** 1978–85
OLYMPICS: 1976

The pride of Rocky Mount, Phil Jackson Ford Jr. made his home state proud by signing with the Tar Heels after a spectacular high school career. He was the first freshman during Dean Smith's tenure to start in the first game of his Carolina career. Ford went on to become UNC's all-time leading scorer with 2,290 points—a record he held for more than 30 years. In his senior season he averaged 20.8 points per game and was voted the ACC Player of the Year. In 1977 and 1978, he was awarded the Anthony J. McKevlin Award as the ACC Athlete of the Year. And we can't forget his contributions to the 1976

PHIL FORD. His pro career didn't match the success of his collegiate days at UNC, but Phil Ford remains a Tar Heel legend.

RAYMOND FELTON ■ 6' 1" 198 ■ *Guard*

COLLEGE: 2002–05 **NBA:** 2005–13

After being named the Naismith Award winner by the Atlanta Tipoff Club as the 2002 National High School Player of the Year, Raymond Felton headed to Chapel Hill with high expectations. In his first season at UNC, Felton was named the team's MVP, the first time a freshman won the award. He set the freshman single-game assist record with 10 against Penn State. He averaged 12.9 points and 6.7 assists per game that year. He put up similar numbers the next two years, helped lead the team to a National Championship in 2005, and won the Bob Cousy Award as the nation's best collegiate point guard.

Felton was selected fifth overall by the Charlotte Bobcats in the 2005 NBA Draft and played five solid seasons. In 2010, he signed as a free agent with the New York Knicks and then was dealt mid-season to the Denver Nuggets. At the end of the season, he was traded to the Portland Trail Blazers. At the end of the 2012 season, he was traded back to the Knicks. Whew! Got all that? Throughout it all, he has averaged 13.5 points per game and 6.6 assists through the 2012–13 season.

RICK FOX ■ 6' 7" 230 ■ *Forward*

COLLEGE: 1987–91 **NBA:** 1991–04

Canadian-born and raised in the Bahamas, Ulrich Alexander Fox, known to you and me simply as Rick, finished high school in basketball-crazy Indiana and then went

Olympics basketball team, which won a gold medal. All that led to his selection by the Kansas City Kings as the second overall pick in the 1978 NBA Draft.

His pro career started off well enough. His rookie campaign ended with Ford averaging 15.9 points per game, along with 8.6 assists, 2.2 steals, and 2.3 rebounds. His scoring average increased each of the next two years, and it appeared that Ford would be an NBA superstar. In his fourth year in the league, though, his productivity dropped across the board, and he only averaged 9.9 points per game. At the end of that season, he was traded to the New Jersey Nets, who traded him early in the season to the Milwaukee Bucks. After a lackluster season, Ford signed with the Houston Rockets, playing two seasons. For his career he averaged 11.6 points and 6.4 assists per game.

Ford returned to Chapel Hill in 1988 to be an assistant for the Tar Heels. He held the job until 2000. He was inducted into the North Carolina Sports Hall of Fame in 1991. After a couple of stints in the NBA as an assistant coach, he is now back at UNC, working for the Educational Foundation, the fundraising arm of the North Carolina athletic department.

on to star for the Tar Heels. In his senior year he averaged 16.9 points, 6.6 rebounds, and 3.7 assists per game—good enough to be chosen 24th overall in the 1991 NBA Draft by the Boston Celtics.

Fox had a solid career with the Celtics, averaging double-digit scoring seasons in three of his six years there. In 1997, he signed with the Los Angeles Lakers. In his first season with the Lakers, Fox averaged 12 points, 4.4 rebounds, and 3.4 assists per game. His NBA career had pretty much peaked in terms of individual production, but it was just getting started in terms of team success. Fox was a valuable contributor as the Lakers won three consecutive NBA Championships 2000–02. He played two more seasons after the championship run and retired in 2004 after a 13-year career with the NBA's two most decorated teams.

Formerly married to singer Vanessa Williams, Fox has appeared on a number of TV shows and in a few films. He competed on ABC's *Dancing with the Stars* in 2010. He continues to act and stays busy behind the camera developing film and television projects for his production company, 1744 Entertainment. He is the father of two and lives in Los Angeles.

DANNY GREEN ■ 6' 6" 210 ■ *Forward*

COLLEGE: 2005–09 **NBA:** 2009–13

Tons of college superstars turn out to be duds in the pros. The jury is still out, but nearly the opposite could prove to be true with Danny Green. To be fair, he wasn't exactly a dud in college. He was a solid contributor at UNC and was a starter on the 1999 National Championship team. And in four years, he's also the only Tar Heel ever to reach 1,000 points (1,368), 500 rebounds (590), 200 assists (256), 100 blocks (155), and 100 steals (160). That ain't bad! But for his career in Chapel Hill, he only averaged 9.4 points per game and was not considered nearly as much of a superstar as some of his UNC teammates. Nonetheless, he was taken in the second round of the NBA Draft by the Cleveland Cavaliers.

To say Green got off to a slow start would be an understatement. In his rookie year, he scored 40 points—total. Just before the start of his second NBA season he was waived by the Cavs. As the 2010 season began, he was picked up by the San Antonio Spurs. The Spurs waived him a week later. He played in Slovenia and bounced around in developmental leagues. Finally, in March 2011, he was again signed by the Spurs. UNC Coach Roy Williams and Spurs Coach Gregg Popovich had a little heart-to-heart with Green. "Roy and I teamed up and gave him a big dose of honesty," Popovich told reporters during the 2013 playoffs. "We both got on him pretty good, just being honest, to let him know where he stood. It was all about his head—about his approach, his aggressiveness and confidence." Apparently the conversation paid off.

In the 2011–12 season, Green played in 66 games for the Spurs, starting 38. He averaged 9.1 points and 10.5 rebounds. For 2012–13, Green started in all 80 games he played and became a bona fide star in the playoffs. In the 2013 NBA Finals, Green set a record for most three-pointers in a finals series, though the Spurs went on to lose in seven games to the Miami Heat. If Green can build on that momentum, he may finally claim a new level of basketball success.

TYLER HANSBROUGH ■ 6' 9" 250 ■ *Forward*

COLLEGE: 2005–09 **NBA:** 2009–13

In sports, it's a compliment if your opponents and rivals hate you. Tyler Hansbrough is a Carolina legend but is despised by many for reasons not exactly known. In 2013, the sports and entertainment website *grantland* had a tournament of most hated college basketball players of the past 30 years. Hansbrough made it to the finals vs. Duke's Christian Laettner. Just as it should be: UNC vs. Duke for the championship. In this case, perhaps it's best that the Duke guy won?

The star of Missouri's Poplar Bluff High School made an immediate impact in Chapel Hill, scoring 18.9 points and grabbing 7.8 rebounds per game and garnering ACC Freshman of the Year honors. That was just the beginning. His collegiate accomplishments could take up the next couple pages, so we'll just go with a few highlights: ACC Player of the Year (2008), AP National Player of the Year (2008), Naismith College Player of the Year (2008), Adolph Rupp Trophy (2008), Oscar Robertson Trophy (2008), and NCAA champion (2009). That's definitely enough to make rivals hate you.

Hansbrough was selected by the Indiana Pacers in the first round of the 2009 NBA Draft. Through the 2012–13 season, he had not established himself as an elite NBA player. His second season was his best, averaging 11 points and 5.2 rebounds per game in 70 games, starting 29 of those. In the 2012–13 season, Hansbrough played in 81 games but started just eight. He averaged 7 points and 4.6 rebounds per game.

BRENDAN HAYWOOD ■ 7' 0" 268 ■ *Center*

COLLEGE: 1997–01 **NBA:** 2001–13

Playing for Greensboro's James B. Dudley High School, Brendan Haywood was the Gatorade North Carolina Player of the Year and a McDonald's All-American. He made Carolina fans very happy when he decided to attend the state's flagship school. He was a solid contributor off the bench his freshman season and became a starter as a sophomore. He finished his career as the Tar Heels' all-time leader in blocked shots and was the first Carolina player to ever record a triple-double, a feat he accomplished vs. Miami in 2008: 18 points, 14 rebounds, 10 blocks.

In the 2001 NBA Draft, Haywood was selected in the first round by the Cleveland Cavaliers, who then traded him to the Orlando Magic, who then traded him to the Washington Wizards. One day, three teams: Welcome to the NBA! He played eight full seasons with the perennially woeful Wizards before being dealt to the Dallas Mavericks during the 2009–10 season. He then played two full seasons with the Mavs—winning an NBA Championship in 2011—before signing with the Charlotte Bobcats for the 2012–13 season. While only averaging double digits in scoring for one season (10.6 points per game in 2007–08), Haywood is a big body who can plug the middle, grab some rebounds, and be a disruptive force with his shot-blocking.

JOHN HENSON ■ 6' 11" 220 ■ *Forward*

COLLEGE: 2009–12 **NBA:** 2012–13

Like the aforementioned Brendan Haywood, John Henson was born in Greensboro and was a McDonald's All-American in high school (though he went to high school in Texas and then graduated in Florida). At Carolina he was the ACC's Defensive Player of the Year his sophomore and junior seasons. He was a solid scorer but excelled in rebounding and shot-blocking. He left Carolina after his junior year and was chosen in the first round by the Milwaukee Bucks. In his first season with the Bucks, Henson averaged 6 points, 4.7 rebounds, and 0.7 blocks per game. He played in 63 games, starting six. In the regular-season finale, he flashed a glimpse of his NBA potential as he led Milwaukee to a 95–89 victory over Oklahoma City. Henson had a career-high 28 points and 16 rebounds in the win.

ANTAWN JAMISON ■ 6' 8" 223 ■ *Forward*

COLLEGE: 1995–98 **NBA:** 1998–2013

Known as the guy who had his name misspelled on his birth certificate, Antawn (instead of Antwan) Cortez Jamison went to Chapel Hill from Providence High School in Charlotte. He quickly became one of the best-liked Tar Heels to wear the Carolina blue. In his three seasons he averaged 19 points and 9.9 rebounds per game. His junior year, he averaged a double-double: 22.2 points and 10.5 rebounds per game. For that 1997–98 season he was awarded the Naismith and Wooden awards and was named AP Player of the Year. He came to Carolina at the same time as Vince Carter, and the two were always linked as star players. Carter had the most flash, but Jamison was the solid, dependable player. Jamison's UNC number, 33, was retired in 2000. Jamison and Carter found themselves linked yet again as they both entered the NBA Draft, each bypassing his senior year. Jamison was drafted as the fourth pick overall by the Toronto Raptors. Carter was drafted as the fifth pick overall by the Golden State Warriors. Then they were traded for each other.

ANTAWN JAMISON. The high-flying Antawn Jamison has thrilled NBA audiences since 1998, playing for six teams in a distinguished pro career.

GEORGE KARL ■ 6' 2" 185 ■ *Guard*

COLLEGE: 1969–73 **ABA:** 1973–76 **NBA:** 1976–78

Younger basketball fans may not realize that longtime NBA coach George Karl is a Tar Heel. We'll get to his extensive accomplishments as a coach, but we want to explore his days as a player first. Karl, a 1973 graduate of the University of North Carolina, played as a guard under Coach Dean Smith. Karl led the team to the 1971 National Invitation Tournament title and a 1972 Final Four appearance in the NCAA Tournament. In his senior year, Karl averaged 17 points and 5.8 assists per game. He was then chosen in the fourth round by the New York Knicks in the 1973 NBA draft but chose to begin his career instead with the ABA's San Antonio Spurs, where he had three solid seasons. His best year was his second, when he averaged 8.1 points and 4.1 assists per game. By Karl's fourth pro season, the Spurs had merged into the NBA, and his career stats quickly diminished. Rarely seeing playing time, Karl retired in April 1978 and then

The two have gone on to long, distinguished NBA careers. Jamison played his first five years with Golden State and was on his way to a great career, averaging at least 19 points per game in four of those five seasons. He was then traded to the Dallas Mavericks, where he finally was on a winning team but had to settle for a sixth-man role. After starting every game the previous three seasons for Golden State, he only started two games in 2003–04 for Dallas and saw his points per game drop to 14.8. After one season in Dallas, he was traded to the Washington Wizards. He played five full seasons with the Wizards and saw his production rise back up to Golden State levels. He was having yet another solid season with the Wizards when he was dealt to the Cleveland Cavaliers for the 2009–10 season.

An aging player, Jamison saw signs of slowing down with Cleveland—playing fewer games per year, for example—but his productivity on the court was still high. During the 2011–12 season, his 14th in the league, he averaged 17.2 points per game for the Cavs while grabbing 6.3 rebounds. After 14 seasons, Jamison had never come close to a championship, though. As a free agent, he yearned to latch on to a team with a chance to go all the way. Dwight Howard was teaming up with Kobe Bryant and Pau Gasol, so Jamison signed on with the Los Angeles Lakers to accept a spot as a role player in hopes to make a run at the title. Unfortunately, the Lakers chemistry and coaching never materialized as he hoped, and Jamison averaged the fewest points per game of his career. Nevertheless, Jamison made it to a couple of All-Star Games (both with the Wizards) and had a sterling career while playing on some teams that struggled to find wins.

became an assistant coach with the Spurs. His first head coaching gig came with the Continental Basketball Association's Montana Golden Nuggets, where he won CBA coach of the year in 1981 and 1983. His status as an up-and-coming coach was solidified, and he became head coach of the NBA's Cleveland Cavaliers in 1984.

He has since been head coach for the Golden State Warriors, Seattle SuperSonics, Milwaukee Bucks, and Denver Nuggets. His most successful stint was his seven years with Seattle, in which his teams won at least 64% of their games each year and made the playoffs annually. His 1996 Sonics team faced Michael Jordan and the Bulls in the NBA Finals. Chicago won the series four games to two. Two more seasons followed, in which Seattle won its division but was defeated in the conference semifinals each year. Karl was fired but was snatched up quickly by the Milwaukee Bucks, with whom he spent five seasons, four of which included playoff appearances. Still, the Bucks could never get over the hump of being consistently around .500.

Following a one-year hiatus from coaching, Karl was hired to lead the Denver Nuggets in 2004. In nine seasons, he has led the team into the playoffs each year

BOBBY JONES ■ 6' 9" 210 ■ *Forward*

COLLEGE: 1970–74 **ABA:** 1974–76
NBA: 1976–86 **OLYMPICS:** 1972

BOBBY JONES. A member of the 1972 Olympic basketball team, Bobby Jones saw pro success in the ABA and the NBA.

As a star for South Mecklenberg High School in Charlotte, Robert Clyde Jones was taught the right way to play basketball: hustle, selflessness, tough on defense, smart on offense, and always a gentleman. He took that game to Chapel Hill and became a star there as well, earning second-team All-American honors his senior year of 1974. But before he left UNC, Jones had the opportunity to play on the 1972 U.S. Olympics basketball team, which is best known for its controversial loss to the Soviet Union in the gold medal game.

During the height of the Cold War and with the game in Munich, Germany, the United States battled the Soviets for gold. With officials inexplicably stopping the game and putting more time on the clock as it wound down, Bobby Jones and the U.S. team lost a heartbreaker 51–50 to settle for the silver medal. It was the first loss for a U.S. team since basketball was accepted as an Olympics sport in 1936. The team refused to accept its silver medals.

That on-court disappointment in the Olympics was an aberration in the career of Bobby Jones. After his sterling career at UNC, he was selected by the Houston Rockets as the fifth choice in the 1974 NBA draft. Jones instead decided to sign with the Denver Nuggets of the American Basketball Association. While the ABA would merge with the NBA after Jones played just a couple of seasons with Denver, he left an indelible mark on the ABA: All-Rookie First Team in 1975, All-ABA Second Team and an ABA All-Star in 1976, and ABA All-Defensive First Team in 1975–76. After the merger, the accolades kept coming for Jones in his next two seasons with Denver and another eight with the Philadelphia 76ers. He was an eight-time NBA All-Defensive First Team choice (1976–84) and then made the second team in 1985. He was also a four-time NBA All-Star, including in 1983 when he didn't even start for the 76ers but did win the league's first Sixth Man of the Year award. The 1983–84 season was also a championship season for the 76ers, a team filled with talented players, including Moses Malone, Julius Erving, Maurice Cheeks, and Andrew Toney.

Over his career, Jones racked up some impressive numbers. Never known as a prolific scorer, Jones still managed 12.1 points per game in his pro career and ranks as the ABA's all-time leader in field-goal percentage at 59%. Hitting 55% of his field goals in the NBA, Jones ranks 14th all-time in that league. Throughout his career in both leagues, Jones averaged 6.1 rebounds, 2.7 assists, 1.5 steals, and 1.4 blocks per game.

Always known for his Christian values, Jones was a leader in getting chapel services established for NBA teams. It shouldn't be a surprise that, today, Jones coaches basketball and tennis at Carmel Christian School in Charlotte and operates summer basketball camps at the school.

GEORGE KARL *continued from page 43*

but has struggled to get the Nuggets past the first round. Nevertheless, Karl's career numbers as a coach rank him near the top of his profession. In 2010, he became just the seventh NBA coach to record 1,000 wins. He led Denver to a franchise-best 57 wins and was named NBA Coach of the Year for 2012–13. Less than a month later, he was fired by the Nuggets.

Karl is a survivor of prostate cancer and neck and throat cancer. His son, Coby, who played college ball at Boise State and had a couple years in the NBA, is a survivor of thyroid cancer. The elder Karl, a winner of the Jimmy V Perseverance Award, is actively involved with several cancer-related organizations.

MITCH KUPCHAK ■ 6' 9" 230 ■ *Forward / Center*

COLLEGE: 1972–76 **NBA:** 1976–86 **OLYMPICS:** 1976

Mitch Kupchak is remembered as being a Carolina great under Coach Dean Smith in the 1970s and playing for Smith in the 1976 Olympics, winning gold for the USA. He averaged double-doubles for UNC in his junior and senior seasons: 18.5 points and 10.8 rebounds per game as a junior; 17.6 points and 11.3 rebounds per game as a senior. He was then a first-round draft choice by the Washington Bullets in 1976.

Arguably his best NBA season was his second. He helped lead the Bullets to an NBA Championship by averaging 15.9 points and 6.9 rebounds per game. After five solid seasons, he signed with the Los Angeles Lakers as a free agent for the 1981–82 season. Individually he was off to a great start—averaging 14.3 points and a career-high 8.1 rebounds per game—but he injured his knee in just the 26th game of the season, and the Lakers missed the playoffs. He missed the entire 1982–83 season due to the injury before coming back for three more years with the Lakers. His productivity was never the same, though he did win a title with the 1984–85 Lakers.

While with the Lakers, Kupchak began preparing for his career off the court by learning the front office from Laker Legend Jerry West. He received an MBA from UCLA in 1987 and became the team's general manager in 2000. There he has won four NBA Championships as part of Lakers management.

MICHAEL JORDAN ■ 6' 6" 195 ■ *Guard / Forward*

COLLEGE: 1981–84 **NBA:** 1984–98, 2001–03
OLYMPICS: 1984, 1992

MICHAEL JORDAN. What can you say about Michael Jordan? He's simply the greatest of all time.

Michael Jordan may just be the state of North Carolina's biggest export. We all know the basics of his story, right? He didn't make the varsity team in 10th grade at Emsley A. Laney High School in Wilmington. Crushed, he was determined to get better. He did get better in an outstanding year on the junior varsity team, and he grew about four inches that year too. He easily made the varsity team and became a star in his final two years at Laney High, where he made the McDonald's All-American team after a senior season that saw him averaging a triple-double: 29.2 points, 11.6 rebounds, and 10.1 assists.

MJ was just beginning his climb to the top of the basketball world, though. His career under Coach Dean Smith at UNC set the stage for a phenomenal pro career. In his first year at Chapel Hill, Jordan was named ACC Freshman of the Year as he averaged 13.4 points per game. Then came his sophomore year when Jordan cemented his name and legacy in the annals of basketball history. A consensus First Team All-American season ended with Jordan making the game-winning shot against Georgetown in the NCAA Tournament's national championship game.

During his junior season, it looked like Jordan would lead UNC to another title. Ranked No. 1 for most of the season, the team jumped out to a 21-0 record before losing a one-point game to Arkansas. The team finished its regular season at 26-1, 14-0 in the ACC. After beating Duke twice in the regular season, the nemesis Blue Devils finally got the upper hand in the ACC tournament, winning by two points in the semifinal game. Still a favorite to win the NCAA tournament, UNC's season ended abruptly in a Sweet 16 loss to Indiana. Nonetheless, Jordan's fantastic season, which included winning the Naismith and Wooden player of the year awards, gave him an easy decision to skip his senior year and go pro.

Drafted third by the Chicago Bulls, Jordan began a steady climb to the top of the basketball world. Before we get into the phenomenal accomplishments of Jordan on the court, we would be remiss if we didn't mention his cachet as a marketing icon. Major endorsement deals early on with Gatorade and Nike helped make Jordan a household name in the United States and gave him notoriety across the globe. Gatorade's "Be Like Mike" campaign was ubiquitous and highly successful. Nike created the Air Jordan shoe, eventually expanding the shoe to the Jordan Brand division of the company. Its commercials staring MJ and Spike Lee as the Mars Blackmon character were constants on TV. A Nike commercial showed Looney Tunes character Bugs Bunny playing basketball with MJ against a host of Martian characters. The commercial inspired the 1996 movie *Space Jam*. Over the years, Jordan has been a spokesman for other major brands, including Ball Park Franks, Chevrolet, Coca-Cola, Hanes, McDonald's, MCI, Rayovac, and Wheaties.

But let's get back to basketball. We could write an entire book on Jordan's accomplishments on the hardwood, and many people have. Before tackling his feats with the Chicago Bulls, we should mention Jordan's two Olympics gold medals. Along with UNC teammate Sam Perkins, and back when the U.S. Olympics Team was made up of all amateur players, Jordan led the 1984 team to gold in the Summer Olympics in Los Angeles. The 1992 U.S. Olympics basketball team was the first to feature active NBA players. Dubbed "The Dream Team," it featured MJ alongside the likes of Magic Johnson, Larry Bird, Charles Barkley, David Robinson, John Stockton, and Bulls teammate Scottie Pippen. They dominated their Olympics opponents, winning each contest by an average of 44 points on the way to gold.

Playing for the Bulls, Jordan quickly became a superstar. His popularity increased the profile of the NBA in general and made the Chicago Bulls the league's No. 1 team. Even today, most high school and college players wearing the jersey number 23 are doing so in honor of MJ. Known for his high-flying dunks (he was a two-time NBA Slam Dunk Contest winner) and prolific scoring, sometimes people forget just how good of a defender Jordan was. He led the league in steals three times, and his 2,514 career steals rank him third on the NBA's all-time list.

Let's take a look at some of Jordan's other NBA highlights at a glance:

- **Six-time champion**
- **Six-time Finals MVP**
- **Five-time MVP**
- **14-time All-Star**
- **Three-time All-Star Game MVP**
- **Naismith Memorial Basketball Hall of Fame (Class of 2009)**
- **10 scoring titles**
- **Nine-time All-Defensive First Team**
- **Rookie of the Year (1984–85)**
- **Defensive Player of the Year (1987–88)**

YORK LARESE ■ 6' 4" 183 ■ *Guard*

COLLEGE: 1957–61 **NBA:** 1961–62

The NBA career of York Bruno Larese was short, but we wanted to make sure we got in a Chicago Packers reference. Yes, Larese was drafted in the second round of the 1961 NBA Draft by the Chicago Packers. (The Chicago Packers franchise evolved into what is today the Washington Wizards.) He played a whopping eight games for the Packers before being waived and picked up by the Philadelphia Warriors. He averaged 5.1 points per game in that, his only NBA season. Larese's biggest claim to fame that year was that he played in Wilt Chamberlain's 100-point game for the Warriors, who were coached by none other than former UNC coach Frank McGuire, who had been Larese's coach at Carolina.

Larese played in the Continental Basketball Association until 1969 when he became head coach of the ABA's New York Nets for the 1969–70 season, for which he had a record of 39-45. Prior to his pro career, Larese was a three-time All-ACC guard for the Tar Heels and averaged 17.9 points per game. He scored 36 points against Duke in 1959 as part of the Dixie Classic.

Larese worked in the footwear business for Puma and Converse, dabbled in brokering, and was a scout for a while with the NBA. He's known as a regular at Carolina's basketball camp.

TY LAWSON ■ 5' 11" 195 ■ *Guard*

COLLEGE: 2006–09 **NBA:** 2009–13

Tywon Ronell Lawson arrived in Chapel Hill by way of Oak Hill Academy in Virginia, where he was an all-everything point guard. He played three seasons as a Tar Heel, going out on a winning note. Lawson averaged 16.6 points, 6.6 assists, and 3 rebounds during 2009 as the Tar Heels won the National Championship. He was named the ACC's Player of the Year. It was the first time a point guard had received the honor since Carolina's own Phil Ford in 1978.

Lawson was selected in the first round of the 2009 NBA Draft by the Minnesota Timberwolves, who then traded him to the Denver Nuggets. In four seasons with the Nuggets, Lawson's stats have steadily improved. In 2012–13, he averaged 16.7 points and 6.9 assists per game. His most memorable game came in 2011 when he became the first player in NBA history to make his first 10 three-point attempts to start a game. Lawson finally missed on his last three-point attempt but finished the game with a career-high 37 points, 7 rebounds, and 6 assists.

JEFF LEBO ■ 6' 2" 180 ■ *Guard*

COLLEGE: 1985–89 **NBA:** 1989–90

Jeff Lebo's pro career as a player was negligible, but he has been a longtime coach in the college ranks. Before all that, he was an incredibly consistent player in his four years at UNC. Points per game: 9.2, 13.5, 12.2, 12.2. Rebounds per game: 2.5, 2.1, 2.6, 2.6. His workmanlike career for a legendary coach and program earned Lebo a free agency contract with the San Antonio Spurs in 1989. He managed just six points in four games before getting waived.

He decided instead that his professional career would be as a coach. He was an assistant at East Tennessee State, Vanderbilt, and South Carolina before landing his first head-coaching gig at Tennessee Tech. He went on to lead Chattanooga and Auburn and is now the head coach at East Carolina, where he finished with a record of 23-12 in the 2012–13 season.

GEORGE LYNCH ■ 6' 8" 218 ■ *Forward*

COLLEGE: 1989–93 **NBA:** 1993–05

Coming from Virginia with a name like George DeWitt Lynch III, he may sound more like one of our nation's founding fathers. In fact, George Lynch was a hotshot high school basketball player who landed a scholarship to play for the Tar Heels. His Carolina career culminated in the 1993 National Championship, a season in which he averaged 14.7 points and 9.6 rebounds per game. He was then chosen by the Los Angeles Lakers in the first round of the 1993 NBA Draft.

Lynch's pro career began well enough. He started 46 of the 71 games he played in as a rookie for the Lakers, averaging 9.6 points and 5.8 rebounds per game. His production actually went down the next two seasons, though; in 1996, he was dealt to the Vancouver Grizzlies. In his second season with the Grizzlies, he played all 82 games but started none. So he signed as a free agent with the Philadelphia 76ers in 1998 and had three solid seasons. His second season in Philly was his best; he averaged 9.6 points and 7.8 rebounds per game. He even hit 42% of his three-point attempts that year.

Then Lynch was traded to Charlotte, where he played one season. He followed it up with two seasons with the New Orleans Hornets. Lynch was never a star in the NBA. He was only a full-time starter for a few of his dozen seasons in the league, primarily his three seasons with the Philadelphia 76ers. He's still involved in basketball, though. He was the founder and director (2006–10) of Flight Nine Basketball, a nonprofit youth basketball program in Dallas. He then served for two years on the UC Irvine basketball staff before joining the Southern Methodist University Mustangs. He currently serves as the strength and conditioning coach.

KENDALL MARSHALL ■ 6' 4" 195 ■ *Guard*

COLLEGE: 2010–12 **NBA:** 2012–13

More and more players are leaving college early for the pros, leaving them little time to build up an extraordinary body of work before they join the NBA. Kendall Marshall arrived in Chapel Hill from Bishop O'Connell High School in Arlington, Virginia, where he had All-Metro and McDonald's All-American Honors. He took over the starting point guard role midway through his freshman season, finishing the year by averaging 6.2 points and 6.2 assists per game. His sophomore year at Carolina saw him set the all-time UNC record for assists in a season (351). For the year, he averaged 8.1 points and 9.8 assists, winning the Bob Cousy Award as the nation's top collegiate point guard.

After his sophomore year, Marshall decided to go pro. He was selected by the Phoenix Suns in the first round of the 2012 NBA Draft. Although Marshall was known as a phenomenal passer, his inadequacies in shooting got him sent to the Suns' developmental league team. After a while, he was called back up and played in 48 games for the Suns as a rookie. To extend his career in the NBA, it's apparent that Marshall will need to continue working on his shooting. If that improves, he could become a longtime NBA point guard.

SEAN MAY ■ 6' 9" 266 ■ *Forward*

COLLEGE: 2002–05 **NBA:** 2005–10

The fact that Sean May chose to play basketball for UNC is still a bit amazing. The highly recruited player from Bloomington, Indiana, is the son of Scott May, a star on the Indiana University 1975–76 National Championship team. Sean's brother, Scott Jr., was a player on the Indiana team that made it to the 2002 National Championship game before losing to Maryland. Sean May, though, was determined to establish his own identity and win big for another program. His junior year, he averaged 17.5 points and 10.7 rebounds per game to lead Carolina to a National Championship. He was named the Most Outstanding Player of the NCAA Tournament in the process. May thought it was time to go pro.

Some players never seem to fulfill their potential due to injuries. Thus far, it seems that Sean May is one of those. He was a first-round draft choice in 2005 for the Charlotte Bobcats. An injury just 23 games into his rookie season ended his year. In fact, injuries prevented May from playing more than 82 games from 2005 to 2009. He inked a one-year deal with the Sacramento Kings for the 2009–10 season but didn't have a lot of production. He signed a one-year contract with the New Jersey Nets for 2010–11 but suffered a stress fracture in his foot before the season began and was released. Since then, he has been playing basketball in Europe.

RASHAD McCANTS ■ 6' 4" 207 ■ *Guard*

COLLEGE: 2002–05 **NBA:** 2005–09

Rashad McCants is what we might call "a character." A Carolina native born in Asheville, he was a star at Erwin High School before transferring to New Hampton School in New Hampshire, where he led his team to the 2002 New England Prep School Class A championship, being named MVP of the title game. He then headed back to Carolina as part of a stellar recruiting class. He led the team in scoring as a freshman, led the entire ACC in scoring as a sophomore, and as a junior helped lead the team to an NCAA title with a 75–70 win over Illinois in the NCAA Championship Game.

This was also a guy who once described his time in Chapel Hill as a prison and who tattooed "Born To Be Hated" on one arm and "Dying To Be Loved" on the other. Concerns about his attitude were persistent, but the Minnesota Timberwolves took a chance and chose him as the overall 14th pick of the 2005 NBA Draft. He played three full seasons with the Timberwolves, having his best year in that third year. In his fourth year with the team, his minutes and overall productivity dropped a bit and he was dealt to the Sacramento Kings for the rest of the season. After that season, McCants never made it to another NBA roster. He has played in the NBA's development league, attempted to catch on with teams in the Philippines, France, and China, and been a part-time actor. After all, he always did have a flair for the dramatic.

JEFF McINNIS ■ 6' 4" 190 ■ *Guard*

COLLEGE: 1993–96 **NBA:** 1996–08 (with the 1996–97 season in Greece and the 1997–98 season in the CBA)

Jeff McInnis turned an exceptional career at UNC into a solid pro career as a basketball journeyman. After attending high school in Virginia, McInnis arrived in Chapel Hill as yet another high school standout. He had a solid year in a part-time role as a freshman before blooming into a top player in his sophomore and junior seasons. As a junior, he averaged 16.5 points and 5.5 assists per game. He then decided to turn pro and was a second-round pick of the Denver Nuggets in the 1996 NBA Draft.

McInnis began his first year with the Nuggets but was waived from the team in December. He latched onto a team in Greece that season and played a year in the CBA before returning to the NBA with the Washington Wizards for 35 games in 1998–99. He then played with the Los Angeles Clippers, Portland Trail Blazers, Cleveland Cavaliers, and New Jersey Nets before finishing his career in the city of his birth, Charlotte. His best pro season was with the Clippers in 2001–02, when he averaged 14.6 points and 6.2 assists per game. He averaged double-digit points per game in four of his NBA seasons. He's recently been involved as a coach in Charlotte on the youth basketball circuit.

BONES McKINNEY ■ 6' 6" 185 ■ *Forward / Center*

COLLEGE: 1945–46 (at UNC after two years at NC State and time served in WWII) **NBA:** 1946–52

It's a tough job to choose which players to profile substantially in a book like this, but, even if we didn't know his many basketball accomplishments, we'd have to feature a guy named Bones. (Seriously, Bones!) Horace Albert McKinney was born in North Carolina and starred for Durham High School teams that won 69 straight games

BOB McADOO ■ 6' 9" 210 ■ *Center / Forward*

COLLEGE: 1971–72 (transfer) **NBA:** 1972–86

The basketball career of Bob McAdoo was filled with ups and downs. A star athlete (and saxophone player) at Smith High School in Greensboro, his grades weren't good enough for him to get into UNC after high school, so he spent two years at Vincennes Junior College in Indiana, where he won the junior college national championship in 1970. He then played one season at Carolina, leading the team to a Final Four appearance. He averaged 19.5 points and 10.1 rebounds per game as a Tar Heel. He was then chosen as the second overall pick in the 1972 NBA Draft by the Buffalo Braves.

BOB MCADOO. Bob McAdoo went on to a long and successful NBA career and has been a long-time assistant coach for the Miami Heat.

Averaging an impressive 18 points and 9.1 rebounds per game, McAdoo was named NBA Rookie of the Year. During his next three seasons in Buffalo, McAdoo averaged 30 points per game and became one of the league's stars. He was the NBA's MVP in 1974–75, a season in which he led the league in points, field goals, rebounds, free-throw attempts, and minutes played. During the 1975–76 season, *Sports Illustrated* described McAdoo as "the quickest tall man, finest shooter, and most astounding outside scoring machine ever to play basketball." As his contract was coming to an end, the Braves decided to trade McAdoo during the 1976–77 season across the state to the New York Knicks. He finished the year with the Knicks and played one full season with them before being traded again during

and three consecutive state titles. He graduated in 1940 and attended (gulp) North Carolina State. Unfortunately for McKinney but fortunately for Carolina fans, he was drafted into the Army during World War II. He returned to college when the war ended, but this time he attended UNC, where he led the Tar Heels to the NCAA Championship Game in 1946, where Carolina lost to Oklahoma A&M (now Oklahoma State).

He then entered the NBA in 1946 as a 28-year-old rookie for the Washington Capitols. He averaged double-digits in points per game his first three years. His scoring productivity slipped a bit his fourth year. He then became player-coach for 1950–51, but the team folded midway through the season and McKinney

the season, this time to the Boston Celtics, where he finished out the 1978–79 season. And thus began the pattern. Brief stints followed with the Detroit Pistons and the New Jersey Nets. Having still been a prolific scorer through the 1979–80 season, when he averaged 21.1 points per game with the Pistons, McAdoo evolved into a role player. He had injuries and squabbles with management for the Pistons and Nets before being acquired by the Los Angles Lakers in 1981.

While his productivity had diminished, he had some solid seasons with the Lakers, who needed a backup big man after former UNC star Mitch Kupchak went down with injuries. While he was no longer a star and was instead backing up a star—Kareem Abdul-Jabbar—he did achieve basketball heights he had never experienced as a pro: championships. The Lakers won the NBA title in 1982 and 1985, the last year of McAdoo's contract with the Lakers. Despite his solid play and two championships in his four years in Los Angeles, McAdoo was not re-signed and it looked like his career might be over. Finally, the Philadelphia 76ers signed him as a free agent in January 1976, and McAdoo played 29 games for Philly. McAdoo was again productive as a role player, but the 76ers were not willing to sign him to a new contract after the season. McAdoo refused to retire, though.

Now in his mid-30s, he instead chose to play in Italy. In his first year in Europe, he led Milan to the Italian and European Championship, averaging 26.1 points and 10.2 rebounds per game. In all, he played seven years for three teams, finishing with career Italian League averages of 26.6 points and 8.7 rebounds per game. He finally retired in 1992 at age 41.

McAdoo was inducted into the Naismith Hall of Fame in 2000, and he's still winning championships. As a longtime assistant coach with the Miami Heat, McAdoo has been part of three NBA titles since the start of the 2005 season. McAdoo and his wife, Patrizia (whom he met in Italy), live in Boca Raton, Florida, with their children, Rasheeda and Ryan. McAdoo's eldest son Robert III and daughter Rita live in New York, while their other sons, Ross and Russell, live in Miami.

ended up as a Boston Celtic. He played one more full season for the Celtics before retiring at 33.

McKinney then became an assistant coach for Wake Forest and took over as head coach in 1957. He had winning seasons in five of his eight years at Wake Forest, making it to the Final Four in 1962. He later coached the Carolina Cougars of the ABA (1969–71) and provided color commentary for college basketball games thereafter. He died in 1997, at age 78, not long after a stroke. His obituary in the *Raleigh News & Observer* said this: "He made people laugh, not with biting or snippy cracks, but simply with stories: about himself, about his teams, about life. He was a blithe spirit, a raconteur, a basketball coach, a speechmaker and an ordained Baptist minister rolled into one 6-foot-6 frame."

LARRY MILLER ■ 6' 4" 190 ■ *Guard / Forward*

COLLEGE: 1964–68 **ABA:** 1968–75

A name that might not be familiar to younger fans, Lawrence James Miller was a high school star from Pennsylvania who made his way south to become a Carolina legend. He was named ACC MVP and ACC Tournament MVP in 1967 and 1968. He led the Tar Heels to consecutive Final Fours, making the 1968 All-Final Four Team. He averaged 21.8 points and 9.2 rebounds per game as a Tar Heel. He was then drafted by the Los Angeles Stars of the ABA in 1968.

He ended up bouncing around quite a bit in the ABA, playing for the Los Angeles Stars, Carolina Cougars, San Diego Conquistadors, Virginia Squires, and Utah Stars (yes, these Stars were the ones formerly in Los Angeles). His pro career was solid but not nearly as spectacular as his collegiate performance. Miller averaged 13.6 points, 5 rebounds, and 2.4 assists in his ABA career, but he also holds a record that will never be broken. As a 6-foot-4 guard with the Carolina Cougars, Miller scored 67 points versus the Memphis Pros on March 18, 1972. That scoring total was a record for most points in an ABA game. It was also the most points a pro basketball guard had ever scored. That record, of course, has since been broken by a handful of NBA players, but because the ABA disbanded decades ago Miller's ABA record will always stand.

ERIC MONTROSS ■ 7' 0" 270 ■ *Center*

COLLEGE: 1990–94 **NBA:** 1994–02

Eric Montross was a great athlete for Lawrence North High School in Indianapolis. He was at one point drafted as a pitcher for the Chicago Cubs. But Montross loved basketball and had a slew of accolades when he rolled into Chapel Hill. He played four seasons for the Tar Heels and was a key to the team winning the 1993 National Championship over Michigan. He was a first-round draft choice of the Boston Celtics in 1994.

He averaged 10 points and 7.3 rebounds in his first year with Boston and was seemingly on his way to a successful NBA career. As it turns out, his rookie year was his best as a pro. He ended up jumping around from team to team—Dallas, New Jersey, Philadelphia, Detroit, Toronto—never averaging more than 4 points per game after his third year in the league. He retired in 2002. He joined UNC's Rams Club staff in August 2009 and provides color commentary for the UNC Basketball radio broadcast, working alongside Jones Angell. He is married with two children and lives in Chapel Hill.

MIKE O'KOREN ■ 6' 7" 207 ■ *Forward / Guard*

COLLEGE: 1976–80 **NBA:** 1980–88

A solid player who seemed to always rise to the occasion in big games, Mike O'Koren averaged double digits in points per game in all four of his seasons as a Tar Heel. His best year as a scorer was his sophomore year, when he averaged 17.3 points per game

DOUG MOE ■ 6' 5" 215 ■ *Forward / Guard*

COLLEGE: 1958–61 **ABA:** 1967–72

DOUG MOE. Doug Moe averaged 20.4 points and 14 rebounds per game as a senior at UNC. He went on to play in the ABA and then won 628 games as an NBA coach.

Brooklyn-born Douglas Edwin Moe was a phenomenal basketball player on the playgrounds and in the church leagues of Brooklyn. He eventually found his way down to Chapel Hill where he was an all-everything performer for the Tar Heels. In his senior year, he scored 20.4 points and grabbed 14 rebounds per game. Moe was drafted in 1961 by the NBA's Chicago Packers, but he never made it to the league. As part of a widespread point-shaving scandal, Moe was called to testify in 1961. According to Moe, he listened to a price-fixing pitch in New Jersey but wanted no part of it. He was given $75 to cover his expenses back to Chapel Hill, though.

"After that, I was blackballed by the NBA," Moe said in a *Sports Illustrated* article in 1988. "It was kind of a numbing experience. All my life I wanted to play ball, and suddenly I was being told I wouldn't be allowed to. I didn't realize at the time how many people actually thought I did something. It hurt at first, but I was immature enough that life was still fun and games to me. There was nothing I could do. I was banned and that was it."

So Moe went into the Army for six months, was an assistant at Elon College for a while, and finally went to Italy for a couple successful years of pro ball there. Finally, the ABA began, and Moe returned to the States to play for the New Orleans Buccaneers. He averaged 24.2 points and 10.2 rebounds per game as a 29-year-old rookie. That was his best season as a pro. In the always volatile ABA, he played his second year for the Oakland Oaks, the next for the Carolina Cougars, and the next two for the Virginia Squires before ending his pro career. He later coached for 15 years in the NBA (four with the San Antonio Spurs, 10 with the Denver Nuggets, one with the Philadelphia 76ers), finishing with a 628-529 record. His teams won at least 50 games in a season three times.

and had a remarkable .643 field goal percentage. As of 2013, O'Koren is the only player in North Carolina history to have at least 1,500 points (1,765), 800 rebounds (815), and 300 assists (348). He was selected in the first round of the 1980 NBA draft by the New Jersey Nets as the sixth overall pick.

SAM PERKINS ■ 6' 9" 235 ■ *Forward / Center*

COLLEGE: 1980–84 **NBA:** 1984–01 **OLYMPICS:** 1984

SAM PERKINS. With an NCAA championship and an Olympic gold medal, Sam Perkins narrowly missed adding an NBA championship to his résumé, as his teams made the NBA finals three times.

A member of the much-heralded 1982 Tar Heel team that won the NCAA Tournament championship, Sam Perkins had a great run as a basketball player on several levels. "Big Smooth" was just a sophomore on that 1982 team (which also starred the likes of Michael Jordan and James Worthy). He continued to rack up accolades in his junior and senior seasons when he was an All-ACC and consensus All-American.

Perkins was the fourth player taken in the 1984 NBA draft, just behind Tar Heel teammate Michael Jordan. In his 17-year career, Perkins played for four teams and had considerable success, yet surprisingly he never made an NBA All-Star team. Nonetheless, he started his career off with a bang for the Dallas Mavericks, being named to the All-Rookie team while averaging 11 points and 7.4 rebounds per game. In a game against the Houston Rockets in 1986, the 6-foot-9 power forward-center recorded the first 30-20 game in Mavericks history: 31 points and a career-high 20 rebounds. He scored a career-high 45 points while still with the Mavericks in 1990.

From Dallas, Perkins went on to play for the Los Angeles Lakers, Seattle SuperSonics, and Indiana Pacers. He averaged 11.9 points and 6 rebounds over the course of his career. For a big man, Perkins was known for his silky smooth outside shot. In fact, he tied an NBA record by hitting eight three-pointers without a miss with the Seattle SuperSonics in 1997.

Perkins also reached great basketball heights as a co-captain for the United States basketball team in the 1984 Olympic Games in Los Angeles. The U.S. breezed through the Olympics tournament, crushing Spain 96–65 in the gold medal game.

J. R. REID ■ 6' 9" 247 ■ *Forward*

COLLEGE: 1986–89 **NBA:** 1989–2001 (with the exception of 1996–97 when he played in France) **OLYMPICS:** 1988

If you ask Carolina fans about the Virginian named Herman Reid Jr., you might get a blank stare. Ask them about J. R. Reid, as the man is better known, and you'll get plenty of tales of his hardwood feats as a Tar Heel. Reid arrived in Chapel Hill from Kempsville High in Virginia Beach with heavy expectations. He was named the 1986 Gatorade and *USA Today* high school player of the year, ranked as the top recruit in the country by most, and was as highly recruited as any player of his era. He immediately lived up to the hype by averaging 14.7 points and 7.4 rebounds per game as a freshman. He was named ACC Rookie of the Year in 1987, won an Olympics bronze medal with Team USA in 1988, and was the ACC Tournament MVP in 1989. He led the Tar Heels to an 88-15 record in his three seasons in Chapel Hill and was a three-time All-ACC player. He decided to forego his senior year and was drafted as the fifth overall pick by the Charlotte Hornets in 1989.

J. R. REID. J. R. Reid followed up an outstanding career in Chapel Hill as a journeyman player in the NBA.

Reid's pro career began well enough. He played—and started—in all 82 games his rookie season and averaged 11.1 points and 8.4 rebounds per game, making the NBA All-Rookie Team in the process. Unfortunately, Reid could never progress beyond that and ended up being just another NBA journeyman. He had stops with the San Antonio Spurs and New York Knicks, played a season in France, and came back to Charlotte again. Then he went to the Los Angeles Lakers, Milwaukee Bucks, and Cleveland Cavaliers. After he was waived by Cleveland and it was apparent his NBA career was over, Reid went on to play another year in France and one final pro season in Spain. He has recently been an assistant coach for Patrick Henry Community College in Martinsville, Virginia.

MIKE O'KOREN *continued from page 55*

O'Koren scored 11 points per game as a rookie. He became a part-time starter in his second year and bumped his average up to 11.4 points per game, but he would never match that offensive production for the rest of his career.

He played six seasons with New Jersey before being traded to the Washington Bullets for a season. He made it back to the Nets during the 1987–88 season to play four games before ending his pro playing career. He followed up his playing days as an assistant coach in the NBA for several years with the New Jersey Nets, Washington Wizards, and Philadelphia 76ers.

CHARLIE SCOTT ■ 6' 5" 175 ■ *Guard / Forward*

COLLEGE: 1966–70 **ABA:** 1970–72 **NBA:** 1972–80 **OLYMPICS:** 1968

In statistical terms, Charlie Scott was one of the greatest players in Carolina history—maybe *the* greatest. He was also the first black scholarship athlete at UNC. He played in an era when freshmen didn't play with the varsity. With his 1966–67 UNC freshman squad, though, he averaged 24.2 points and 14.3 rebounds per game. Could he match those numbers with the varsity? Not quite for rebounding, but for scoring, yes. His scoring figures with the varsity were pretty amazing: 17.6, 22.3, and 27.1 points per game. His rebounding figures increased each year too: 6, 7.1, and 8.6. He helped Carolina to three conference titles, one NCAA Final Four, and one NCAA Final, in which the Tar Heels lost the championship to the decade's dominant team, the UCLA Bruins. And just for good measure, Scott won Olympics gold for Team USA in 1968.

Scott was drafted by the Boston Celtics in 1970 but instead chose to play in the ABA for the Virginia Squires, where he was named ABA Rookie of the Year. His second year in the ABA, he led the league in field goal attempts, field goals made, and points per game (34.6, the ABA record for highest scoring average in a season). He played in the 1971 and 1972 ABA All-Star Games. Scott then decided to try his hand in the NBA. In his first three years with the Phoenix Suns, he averaged 25 points per game and made three NBA All-Star Games. He then played two and a half seasons with the Celtics, the team that originally drafted him. He had two solid years and won a title with the Celtics in 1976. His numbers began to fade, and he was traded to the Lakers midway through the 1977–78 season. After that season, he was traded to the Denver Nuggets, where he finished his career two years later.

Scott's career since his playing days has included stints with sports apparel companies (Champion, Russell Athletics), a telemarketing firm, and the administration of the Washington Wizards. His eldest son Shannon plays for Ohio State. His son Shaun is a student at UNC. In addition to the two boys, Scott and his wife, Trudy, have a daughter, Simone.

KENNY SMITH ■ 6' 3" 170 ■ *Guard*

COLLEGE: 1983–87 **NBA:** 1987–97

Younger basketball enthusiasts may only know Kenny Smith for going pro as a television analyst. Smith typically sits next to Charles Barkley on Turner Sports basketball sets to offer insights into the game he once played—and played well. In his days as a Tar Heel, he was known for his quickness and speed, which made him a force on offense and defense and earned him the nickname "The Jet." He finished his UNC career as the school's all-time leader in steals. His 195 career steals still ranks fourth overall.

KENNY SMITH. Kenny "The Jet" Smith won NBA titles with the Houston Rockets in 1994 and '95. He's now an NBA analyst for TBS.

Smith came out of the gates in Chapel Hill as a star. He was one of only 10 players to start in his first game as a freshman for Coach Dean Smith. His statistics and contributions to the team continued to improve each year. In his senior season, he was a consensus All-America, first-team All-ACC choice, and was named by the *Basketball Times* as its Player of the Year after averaging 16.9 points per game and leading the team with 209 assists.

At 6-foot-3, Smith was expected to be the first point guard taken in the 1987 NBA draft, and he was, going as the sixth selection in the first round to the Sacramento Kings, where he was an NBA All-Rookie First Team choice. In his 10-year NBA career, Smith bounced around quite a bit, playing for six different clubs. His greatest successes came as a member of the Houston Rockets, where his team won NBA championships in 1994 and 1995. In addition to the Kings and Rockets, Smith also suited up for the Atlanta Hawks, Detroit Pistons, Orlando Magic, and Denver Nuggets. Smith finished his career averaging 12.8 points and 5.5 assists per game.

Some forget that Smith was also a gold medalist in 1986 as a participant for the United States basketball team in the FIBA Basketball World Cup. His 23 points led all scorers in a two-point victory over the Soviet Union in the gold medal game. And while his playing days are long over, Smith still teaches the game to a new generation of players at the Kenny Smith Carolina Basketball Camp, which takes place annually in Chapel Hill, with a mission to "help youth learn the productive mechanisms of team sports, teamwork, discipline, cooperation, setting goals, strong work ethics, and establishing moral values."

JERRY STACKHOUSE ■ 6' 6" 218 ■ *Guard / Forward*

COLLEGE: 1993–95 **NBA:** 1995–2013

Carolina fans would have loved to have Jerry Stackhouse in Chapel Hill a little longer. He had two fantastic seasons for UNC, especially his sophomore year, when he led the team in scoring with 19.2 points per game while averaging 8.2 rebounds per game. While leading UNC to a Final Four appearance he was named National Player of the Year by *Sports Illustrated*. He was then the third pick overall in the 1995 NBA Draft, chosen by the Philadelphia 76ers in what was the beginning of a long pro career.

In his first year with Philadelphia he was named to the NBA All-Rookie Team while averaging 19.2 points per game. He upped his average slightly in his second year but was traded to the Detroit Pistons during his third year. His best years in the NBA came in Detroit. In 2000–01, he averaged 29.8 points, 5.1 assists, and 3.9 rebounds per game while leading the league in field goal attempts, free throws, and total points. Of course, he led the league in turnovers that year too. He made the NBA All-Star Game in 2000 and 2001. He was traded by Detroit in 2004 to the Washington Wizards, where he played two seasons, the first of which was the last time he averaged more than 20 points per game in a season.

He then spent five solid seasons with Dallas before bouncing to Milwaukee, Miami, Atlanta, and finally Brooklyn, where he played the 2012–13 season. His older brother, Tony Dawson, spent a bit of time in the NBA (but mostly in the CBA and in Europe), and Stackhouse is the uncle to former Wake Forest player Craig Dawson.

MARVIN WILLIAMS ■ 6' 9" 230 ■ *Forward*

COLLEGE: 2004–05 **NBA:** 2005–13

Marvin Gaye Williams was a highly decorated basketball star at Bremerton High School in Washington state. Following an intense recruiting battle, he went east to Chapel Hill. His time at UNC was short but fruitful. In one season as Carolina's sixth man, he contributed heavily to an NCAA Championship. He averaged 11.3 points and 6.6 rebounds coming off the bench. He then declared for the NBA Draft, where he was selected in the first round (second overall) by the Atlanta Hawks.

Williams was a consistent player with the Hawks. His highest scoring average was 15.4 points per game and his lowest was 12. Similarly, his highest rebounding average was 7.1 boards per game and his lowest was 5.6. After seven seasons in Atlanta, Williams was traded to Utah for the 2012–13 season. Still in his mid-twenties, Williams should have plenty of pro years ahead of him.

SCOTT WILLIAMS ■ 6' 10" 230 ■ *Forward / Center*

COLLEGE: 1986–90 **NBA:** 1990–2005

Scott Williams was a star for Glen A. Wilson High School in Hacienda Heights, California, leading the 1986 team to a state title. He then went across the country to play

RASHEED WALLACE ■ 6' 10" 225 ■ *Forward / Center*

COLLEGE: 1993–95 **NBA:** 1995–10, 2012–13

RASHEED WALLACE. As part of his long NBA career, Rasheed Wallace holds NBA records for the most technical fouls in a season and a career.

The basketball career of Rasheed Wallace closely resembles that of UNC teammate Jerry Stackhouse. Both came to Chapel Hill in 1993, led Carolina to the Final Four in 1995, and left for the NBA after their sophomore years. And they both had very long careers in the pros. Wallace was a first-round draft choice by the Washington Bullets in 1995, the fourth overall pick. After just one year in Washington, Wallace was traded to Portland, one of two teams for which he is most known. In all, he spent eight seasons with the Trail Blazers. He offered a lot of productivity but was also known as one of the league's most volatile players.

He made two All-Star teams while with Portland and scored 19 points per game twice. In 2003–04, Wallace began the season with Portland, was traded to Atlanta, where he played a single game, and then was traded again to Detroit, where he finished the season. In five full seasons and one partial season with the Pistons, Wallace was a solid and consistent player, making two more All-Star Games and winning an NBA Championship. He then played a year with the Boston Celtics before retiring after the season in 2010. After being out of the game for two years, Wallace came out of retirement to play briefly with the New York Knicks. He retired a second time after being waived by the Knicks. Regarding that volatility: Wallace holds NBA records for most technical fouls in a season and in a career. The antics that led to his technical fouls and ejections could fill a chapter. Wallace was an intense competitor, which no doubt led him to much success on the court.

for Dean Smith and the Tar Heels. In his four years at Chapel Hill, Carolina made it to the NCAA's Sweet Sixteen twice and its Elite Eight twice. But despite averaging 10.9 points and 6.2 rebounds per game for UNC, Williams wasn't drafted.

Instead of being the top draft pick who never realized his potential, Williams became the undrafted player who went on to a lengthy NBA career. He had the good fortune to sign as a free agent with the Chicago Bulls in 1990, where he was a role player who won NBA titles in 1991, '92, and '93. He signed as a free agent with the Philadelphia 76ers in 1994 and played four full seasons. He then bounced about

SCOTT WILLIAMS *continued from page 61*

to Milwaukee, Denver, Phoenix, Dallas, and Cleveland. He never averaged even 8 points per game in a season. The most starts he had in a season was 52, which was in 1996–97 with the 76ers. But still, to be a part of 15 NBA seasons, including three titles, as an undrafted free agent is quite a success.

Following his playing days, Williams has stayed close to the game. He has been a color commentator for the Cleveland Cavaliers, Milwaukee Bucks, and Phoenix Suns and most recently was an assistant coach for the Idaho Stampede in the NBA's development league.

SHAMMOND WILLIAMS ■ 6' 1" 201 ■ *Guard*

COLLEGE: 1994–98 **NBA:** 1998–2004, 2006–07 (plus two seasons playing abroad)

Shammond Omar Williams has been known as a shooter. A member of two Final Four teams at Carolina, he finished his collegiate career with school records for career, season, and single-game three-pointers made, in addition to having the highest career and season free-throw percentages. He scored an impressive 16.8 points per game as a senior, to go with 4.2 assists and 3.2 rebounds. He was a second-round draft choice by the Chicago Bulls in 1998 but was then dealt immediately to the Atlanta Hawks.

He struggled to make a major impact but eked out a pro career with impressive longevity. He only played in two games for the Hawks. After being waived, he was picked up before the next season by the Seattle SuperSonics. His three seasons with Seattle were the most he spent with any team. He also played for Boston, Denver, Orlando, New Orleans, and the Los Angeles Lakers while also playing in Turkey, Russia, and Spain intermittently. Then after his final stint in the NBA with the Lakers, he played for teams in Spain, Cyprus, and Italy before finally calling it quits in 2011. He was briefly an assistant coach for Furman University.

JOE WOLF ■ 6' 11" 230 ■ *Forward / Center*

COLLEGE: 1983–87 **NBA:** 1987–99

Back in 2005, a vote was conducted by the *Milwaukee Journal Sentinel* to name the best high school player ever in Wisconsin. The winner: Joe Wolf. Following high school, Wolf took his skills to Chapel Hill, where he played four seasons for Dean Smith and helped lead the Tar Heels to two Sweet Sixteen and two Elite Eight appearances in the NCAA Tournament. He averaged 15.2 points and 7.1 rebounds as a senior and was then chosen in the first round of the 1987 NBA Draft by the Los Angeles Clippers.

Wolf scored more than 7 points per game as a rookie, a barrier he only crossed once more—in 1990–91 for Denver. Yet another journeyman story, Wolf went on to play for Boston, Portland, Baloncesto León (in a Spanish league), Charlotte, Orlando, Milwaukee, Denver, and again with Charlotte. He then left his playing days behind and began coaching. He was an assistant at William & Mary for a year, and then coached in the CBA and the NBA's development league. From 2008 to 2013, he was an assistant coach for the Milwaukee Bucks.

AL WOOD ■ 6' 6" 193 ■ *Guard / Forward*

COLLEGE: 1977–81 **NBA:** 1981–87 **OLYMPICS:** 1980

Martin Alphonzo Wood arrived in Chapel Hill by way of Gray, Georgia, and had a remarkable four years for the Tar Heels. He started a bit slow as a freshman, scoring fewer than 10 points per game, but then he averaged 17.8, 19, and 18.1 points per game in his final three years. Wood was also named to the 1980 Olympics basketball team, but the U.S. boycotted the Games held in Moscow. The team did play in a series versus a handful of all-star teams, though.

Wood was a first-round draft choice by the Atlanta Hawks. He started his rookie campaign with the Hawks but was traded to the San Diego Clippers. Wood didn't stick with any team, nor with the league, for long. He made it with the Seattle SuperSonics for three years and then went to Dallas for a year before being waived and ending his career. He averaged 11.8 points per game in six NBA seasons. Wood is now the director of the South Carolina chapter of Team Focus, a nonprofit with a mission of helping boys who lack a father.

BRANDAN WRIGHT ■ 6' 9" 205 ■ *Forward*

COLLEGE: 2006–07 **NBA:** 2007–13 (except for 2009–10 when he had a shoulder injury)

High school phenom Brandan Wright led his Brentwood Academy (Tennessee) team to four straight state championships while he was being named Mr. Basketball for his division an unprecedented three consecutive times. At UNC, Wright was one and one. His freshman season, he averaged 14.7 points on an ACC-best 64.6% field goal shooting. He led his team in blocks and was second in scoring and rebounding. He was named ACC Tournament MVP and ACC Rookie of the Year.

He was chosen in the first round of the 2007 NBA Draft by the Charlotte Bobcats, who then traded him immediately to the Golden State Warriors. The jury is still out on Wright's NBA career. He hasn't lived up to expectations, but he's still young. He's played for the Warriors, New Jersey Nets, and most recently the Dallas Mavericks. It's promising that in 2012–13 he had his best NBA season, averaging 8.5 points and 4.1 rebounds per game.

TYLER ZELLER ■ 7' 0" 250 ■ *Center*

COLLEGE: 2008–12 **NBA:** 2012–13

Basketball is in the blood of the Zeller family. Tyler Zeller's brothers, Cody and Luke, are both NBA players. His uncle, Al Eberhard, was an NBA player. Tyler, though, was

JAMES WORTHY ■ 6' 9" 225 ■ *Forward*

COLLEGE: 1979–82 **NBA:** 1982–94

JAMES WORTHY. With seven All-Star appearances and three NBA titles, James Worthy is one of the top Tar Heels to play pro basketball.

Born and raised in Gastonia, North Carolina, James Worthy is a home-state basketball legend. As a high school senior at Ashbrook High, his 21.5 points, 12.5 rebounds, and 5.5 assists per game led the team to the state championship game and got Worthy named as a McDonald's All-American. Even if his basketball days ended there, Worthy would still be discussed in conversations about North Carolina hoops. But by playing for Dean Smith as a University of North Carolina Tar Heel, Worthy continued building his legend.

Worthy started well as a freshman but broke his ankle 14 games into the season. He came back as a sophomore determined to prove himself after missing more than half of his freshman year. Worthy became an All-ACC forward as a sophomore. He averaged 14.2 points and 8.4 rebounds per game. His junior year at UNC, however, was one of the most magical years in Tar Heel basketball history. Also featuring the likes of Sam Perkins and Michael Jordan, the Tar Heels won the NCAA Tournament in a remarkable championship game against Georgetown, as Worthy stole a Fred Brown pass to seal UNC's win. He also scored 28 points on 13-for-17 shooting and was named Most Outstanding Player at the Final Four. For the season, Worthy was named a consensus First-Team All-American, averaging 15.6 points, 6.3 rebounds, and 2.4 assists while shooting .573 from the floor. He shared national Player of the Year honors with Virginia's Ralph Sampson. After a season filled with such superlatives, he decided to forego his senior season and go pro.

Worthy was chosen as the No. 1 overall pick in the 1982 NBA draft. As luck would have it, the team that chose him was the Pat Riley–coached Los Angeles Lakers, who had just won an NBA Championship over the Philadelphia 76ers and were on the verge of having a remarkable run of success. Showtime in Los Angeles had begun, and Worthy was right in the thick of it. Joining a team already loaded with talent (Kareem Abdul-Jabbar, Magic Johnson, Jamaal Wilkes, Michael Cooper, Norm Nixon, and even former Tar Heel Bob McAdoo), young James Worthy only started one game but saw considerable playing time. He averaged 13.4 points and 5.2 rebounds per game and was unanimously selected to the All-Rookie Team. The Lakers made it to the finals in Worthy's rookie season, but a late-season injury kept him out of the playoffs. Playing without his solid contributions, the Lakers were swept in the Finals by the 76ers.

In his second season, Worthy started 53 games. His 17.3 points-per-game average was third on the team, just a fraction behind Magic Johnson's 17.6. The Lakers once again fell in the championship, though, this time to the Boston Celtics. Worthy's career was starting to blossom, however, and he would win championships in 1985, '87, and '88, and be named MVP of the championship series in 1988. He and the Lakers also got to the finals in 1989 and '91 but lost to the Detroit Pistons and Chicago Bulls respectively. The 1991 championship was the first for fellow Tar Heel Michael Jordan. During his 12-year career, Worthy averaged 17.6 points, 5.1 rebounds, and 3 assists per game. He averaged more than 20 points per game in four of his NBA seasons. Worthy was also a seven-time NBA All-Star and was inducted into the Naismith Memorial Basketball Hall of Fame in 2003.

"I don't think there has been or will be a better small forward than James, and I don't think people appreciated that," said Pat Riley to the *Los Angeles Daily News* upon Worthy's retirement. "He was always such a quiet guy. But when he was in his prime, I can guarantee you, there wasn't anybody who could touch him."

Since his retirement, Worthy has been a basketball analyst and operates the James Worthy Foundation, which has as its mission to "help at-risk youth, military veterans, and their communities build an 'Earned Pathway to Success' in Gaston County, North Carolina." He's even had a couple of acting gigs, including a cameo spot in the sitcom *Everybody Loves Raymond* and the role of Klingon Koral in an episode of *Star Trek: The Next Generation.*

TYLER ZELLER *continued from page 63*

the biggest of the bunch at 7 feet. An injury early in his freshman year sidelined him until mid-February 2009. He only played in 15 games, averaging just 3.1 points per game, but still enjoyed contributing on UNC's National Championship team.

Zeller's numbers increased steadily throughout his four years in Chapel Hill, culminating with a senior season averaging 16.3 points and 9.6 rebounds per game. He was named ACC Player of the Year for that effort. He was chosen in the first round of the 2012 NBA Draft by the Dallas Mavericks but was traded the next day to the Cleveland Cavaliers. In his first season with the Cavs, Zeller started 55 of the 77 games in which he played, averaging 7.9 points and 5.7 rebounds per game. His NBA potential remains strong.

Other Pro Players

NAME	POSITION	COLLEGE	NBA	STATS
Dudley Bradley	Guard-Forward	1975–79	1979–89	5.2/1.8/1.9
Played For: Indiana Pacers, Phoenix Suns, Chicago Bulls, Washington Bullets, Milwaukee Bucks, New Jersey Nets, Atlanta Hawks				
Pete Brennan	Forward	1954–58	1959	2.5/1.9/0.4
Played For: New York Knicks				
Steve Bucknall	Guard	1985–89	1990	1.3/0.4/0.6
Played For: Los Angeles Lakers				
Bill Bunting	Forward-Center	1966–69	1969–72 (ABA)	4.3/2.9/0.7
Played For: Carolina Cougars, New York Nets, Virginia Squires (ABA)				
Bill Chamberlin	Forward	1970–72	1973–74 (NBA); 1972–73 (ABA)	5.3/2.5/1.4
Played For: Phoenix Suns (NBA); Memphis Tams and Kentucky Colonels (ABA)				
Pete Chilcutt	Forward-Center	1987–91	1991–2000	4.3/3.3/0.8
Played For: Sacramento Kings, Detroit Pistons, Houston Rockets, Vancouver Grizzlies, Utah Jazz, Cleveland Cavaliers, Los Angeles Clippers				

PETE CHILCUTT was an NBA journeyman, playing for seven teams over nine seasons. He earned a championship ring playing for the Houston Rockets.

NAME	POSITION	COLLEGE	NBA	STATS
Geoff Crompton	Center	1973–78	1978–84	1.2/1.7/0.3
Played For: Denver Nuggets, Portland Trail Blazers, Milwaukee Bucks, San Antonio Spurs, Cleveland Cavaliers				
Darrell Elston	Guard	1972–74	1976–77 (NBA); 1974–75 (ABA)	7.8/2.2/2.6
Played For: Indiana Pacers (NBA); Virginia Squires (ABA)				
Joseph Forte	Guard	1999–01	2001–03	1.2/0.7/0.7
Played For: Boston Celtics, Seattle SuperSonics				
George Glamack	Center-Forward	1937–41	1948–49	9.3/-/1.7
Played For: Indianapolis Jets				
Dick Grubar	Guard	1967–69	1969–70	2.0/0.0/0.5
Played For: Indiana Pacers				
Tommy Kearns	Guard	1956–58	1958–59	2.0/0.0/0.0
Played For: Syracuse Nationals				
John Kuester	Guard	1973–77	1977–80	3.3/1.0/2.3
Played For: Kansas City Kings, Denver Nuggets, Indiana Pacers				
Tom LaGarde	Center-Forward	1973–77	1977–82; 1984–85 (Olympics 1976)	7.6/5.1/1.5
Played For: Denver Nuggets, Seattle SuperSonics, Dallas Mavericks, New Jersey Nets				
Bobby Lewis	Guard	1964–68	1967–71	5.8/2.1/2.2
Played For: San Francisco Warriors, Cleveland Cavaliers				
Bill Miller	Forward	1947–48	1948–49	1.9/-/0.7
Played For: Chicago Stags, St. Louis Bombers				
Makhtar N'Diaye	Forward	1996–98 (transfer)	1998–99	1.3/1.3/0.3
Played For: Vancouver Grizzlies				
David Noel	Forward	2002–06	2006–07	2.7/1.8/1.0
Played For: Milwaukee Bucks				
Derrick Phelps	Guard	1990–94	1994–95	0.0/0.0/0.3
Played For: Sacramento Kings				
Dave Popson	Forward-Center	1983–87	1988–92	1.9/1.1/0.3
Played For: Los Angeles Clippers, Miami Heat, Boston Celtics, Milwaukee Brewers				
Stephen Previs	Guard	1970–72	1972–73 (ABA)	1.8/0.5/0.8
Played For: Carolina Cougars (ABA)				
Lennie Rosenbluth	Forward	1955–57	1957–59	4.2/1.8/0.4
Played For: Philadelphia Warriors				

NAME	POSITION	COLLEGE	NBA	STATS
Kevin Salvadori	Center	1990–94	1996–98	1.1/1.2/0.3
Played For: Sacramento Kings				
Lee Shaffer	Forward	1957–60	1961–64	16.8/6.3/1.2
Played For: Syracuse Nationals, Philadelphia 76ers				
Donald Washington	Forward	1973	1974–76 (ABA)	3.9/1.8/0.6
Played For: Denver Nuggets, Utah Stars (ABA)				
Matt Wenstrom	Center	1989–93	1993–94	1.6/1.1/0.0
Played For: Boston Celtics				
Jawad Williams	Forward	2001–05	2008–11	3.8/1.5/0.6
Played For: Cleveland Cavaliers				
Dennis Wuycik	Forward	1970–72	1972–75 (ABA)	4.4/2.1/0.8
Played For: Carolina Cougars, Spirits of St. Louis (ABA)				
Rich Yonakor	Forward	1976–80	1981–82	3.3/2.7/0.3
Played For: San Antonio Spurs				
Henrik Rodl	Guard-Forward	1989–93	(Olympics 1992)	N/A
Played For: Germany (Olympics)				

WOMEN

Despite being overshadowed by a century of success by the men's team, the University of North Carolina women's basketball program is now among the best in collegiate athletics. Coach Sylvia Hatchell is, quite simply, a legend. The home-state hero (born in Gastonia) had 907 career wins going into the 2013–14 season, which was her 28th in Chapel Hill. She was enshrined into the Naismith Memorial Basketball Hall of Fame in September 2013. "At North Carolina, there's a lot of men's players who have been inducted," she said. "To be the first woman, that's pretty special." Yes, it is—and well deserved.

While obviously one person doesn't make a program, we feel compelled to explain just how important Hatchell has been in the development of UNC women's basketball.

After graduating from Carson-Newman College in 1974, she then got a master's degree from the University of Tennessee, where she coached the junior varsity women's team, while a young Pat Summitt was just beginning her career as head coach of the Volunteers. The next season, though, Hatchell became head coach of Francis Marion College, where she went on to achieve a 272-80 record in 11 seasons. In 1986, Hatchell became just the third coach in the history of Tar Heel women's basketball, succeeding Angela Lumpkin (who coached three seasons) and Jennifer Alley (who coached nine seasons).

By the time Hatchell arrived, the bar for the program was already high, as Alley had just led the Heels to four consecutive 20-plus-win seasons. Hatchell rode that momentum to a 19-10 season in her first year, but she struggled after that. Four consecutive losing seasons followed. Hatchell's career in Chapel Hill was in question. She was definitely sitting on the hot

Sylvia Hatchell has had a legendary coaching career at the University of North Carolina, winning a national championship and more than 600 games while with the Tar Heels.

seat heading into her fifth season, when she broke out with a 22-9 year. Winning seasons became automatic thereafter. The program reached a pinnacle in 1994 with a 60–59 victory over Louisiana Tech, resulting in a National Championship. Hatchell has led UNC to six seasons of at least 30 victories. In the past decade, the Tar Heels have been known for high-powered offenses, ranking No. 1 nationally in 2006–07 and 2007–08 while finishing second in 2004–05 and 2008–09. Hatchell has also been successful with U.S. national teams, including serving as an assistant coach for the 1988 U.S. women's team that won a gold medal in the Seoul, South Korea, Olympic Games.

In 2013, Hatchell was diagnosed with leukemia and took a leave of absence to focus on treatment. Longtime assistant Andrew Calder has stepped in as interim coach while Hatchell is away, guiding a team that is full of talent.

Certainly Carolina would not have been so successful without great players, though. And the Heels have had plenty of talented basketball players. Five women scored at least 2,000 points in their Carolina careers: Ivory Latta (2,285), Tracy Reid (2,200), Tonya Sampson (2,143), Charlotte Smith (2,094), and Pam Leake (2,001). Two women have at least 1,200 rebounds: Bernadette McGlade (1,251) and Charlotte Smith (1,200). Two women have at least 300 blocked shots: LaToya Pringle (336) and Dawn Royster (329). And one woman has more than 700 assists: Nikki Teasley (728). Yes, great players have been a regular part of UNC women's basketball, and a few of them have gone pro.

Head Coaching Records

(In chronological order, including record and winning percentage; a tie counts as half a win, half a loss, per NCAA practice)

YEARS	COACH	RECORD	WINNING PCT.
1974–77	Angela Lumpkin	39-26	.600
1977–86	Jennifer Alley	179-104	.632
1987–2014	Sylvia Hatchell	636-241	.725

(Ranked by victories)

RECORD	COACH	YEARS	WINNING PCT.
636-241	Sylvia Hatchell	1987–2014	.725
179-104	Jennifer Alley	1977–86	.632
39-26	Angela Lumpkin	1974–77	.600

(Ranked by winning percentage; a tie counts as half a win, half a loss, per NCAA practice)

WINNING PCT.	COACH	YEARS	RECORD
.725	Sylvia Hatchell	1987–2014	636-241
.632	Jennifer Alley	1977–86	179-104
.600	Angela Lumpkin	1974–77	39-26

Player Bios

LA'TANGELA ATKINSON ■ 6' 1" 164 ■ *Guard / Forward*

COLLEGE: 2002–06 **WNBA:** 2006–09

In her four years as a Tar Heel, the South Carolina native was a consistent scorer, averaging 9.7, 9.8, 8.3, and 9.1 points per game respectively. She was the ACC Rookie of the Year as a freshman, a season in which she led Carolina in rebounding. In fact, she was known as a tenacious rebounder, usually ranking near the top of the ACC in rebounds per game. One of her most memorable performances came in a January 29, 2006, contest at Duke in her senior year. Atkinson tied her career high of 15 rebounds in the game (allowing her to pass 900 for her career) and sunk two free throws late to seal a 74–70 victory.

Atkinson was chosen in the first round of the 2006 WNBA Draft by the Indiana Fever. "She's a terrific athlete, she has great size, very long arms, [and is an] excellent defender and rebounder," said Indiana's then-coach Brian Winters. "We think her offensive game will develop over time." Atkinson had a relatively lackluster season, averaging just 3 points and 2.3 rebounds per game. She got in some off-season work playing in the Israeli League, and she was then traded to the Sacramento Monarchs for her second WNBA season. A similar season to that of her rookie year led to yet another off-season in the Israeli League. Her WNBA career, though, continued to fizzle. She played very little in 2008 and was picked up very late in the season by Seattle in 2009 to help fill an injury-depleted roster for the Storm.

JESSICA BRELAND ■ 6' 3" 170 ■ *Forward*

COLLEGE: 2006–11 **WNBA:** 2011, 2013

Jessica Breland has always been competitive, never backing down from a challenge While playing hoops at UNC, she didn't expect the challenge she ultimately faced. She missed the entire 2009–10 season while receiving treatment for Hodgkin's lymphoma. Prior to that, she had been the Gatorade Player of the Year in North Carolina as a high school senior and was a productive member of the Tar Heels in three

LAQUANDA BARKSDALE ■ 5' 10" 156 ■ *Guard / Forward*

COLLEGE: 1997–01 **WNBA:** 2001–03

LAQUANDA BARKSDALE. Former West Forsyth star LaQuanda Barksdale (now known as LaQuanda Quick) played in the WNBA and is now coaching at her high school alma mater.

Things have come full circle for LaQuanda Barksdale. She became known for her athletic prowess at West Forsyth High School (also the alma mater of NBA star Chris Paul) near Winston-Salem, where she lettered in basketball, volleyball, and track and field. She was known as one of the region's best hoops players, winning Central Piedmont Conference Player of the Year in 1996 and 1997. She signed with Carolina and had a fantastic career, leading the ACC in scoring as a senior (19 ppg) and a junior (17.6 ppg). She poured in 32 points against Elon in her senior season. But she was a prolific rebounder, too, especially for her size. She grabbed 19 rebounds twice as a Tar Heel—versus Holy Cross in 1998 and Radford in 1999.

She was the first-round choice of the Portland Fire in the 2001 WNBA Draft, but she played quite sparingly as a rookie and suffered a back injury that caused her to miss about half of the season. She played a bit more in her second season, averaging 5.9 points per game, but her season was again cut short due to injury. She played a final WNBA season with the San Antonio Silver Stars, playing in more games but only recording 2.3 points per game.

After her WNBA days, Barksdale went into teaching and coaching. She stayed at home for a few years with her son, Nicholas, but never gave up her love for basketball. Coach Quick, as she's now known to her students, is married and coaching girl's basketball at her old school, West Forsyth. Her teams are winning conference championships; she's also teaching Healthy Living at the school and has taught math in the past. "I enjoy every minute of coaching," Quick said recently. "It makes it even better that I'm coaching at my alma mater. West Forsyth played a major role in my success as a person and an athlete. I'm proud that I now get to pass on the tools, given to me, to the current student-athletes at West."

seasons in Chapel Hill. Her scoring and rebounding averages increased each season, going from 6.5 points per game as a freshman to 10.6 and then to 14.5. Her rebounding average went from 4.5 to 7.1 to 8.1. But all of a sudden her career was in doubt. She had bigger concerns than basketball.

"I've never really been a person who thought about death like that," she told the *New York Times* in 2011. "But I felt like death would be easier than going through [treatment]." She persevered, though, saying she was a different person. "I've always been mature, just not taking life for granted and things for granted. Now that I'm here on the court, I think about people who are in a wheelchair and can't run. That makes me push harder." She came back for a successful season, despite issues with conditioning and scar tissue on her lungs, which limited her playing time a bit. She was selected in the second round of the 2011 WNBA Draft by the Minnesota Lynx and was then traded to the New York Liberty. She was then waived by New York during the 2011 season and picked up by the Connecticut Sun, for which she played sparingly the rest of the year. In 2012, she went through training camp with the Washington Mystics before getting cut, so she spent time overseas refining her game. In 2013, she made it back to the WNBA with the Indiana Fever, settling in as a steady reserve player.

CORETTA BROWN ■ 6' 9" 150 ■ *Guard*

COLLEGE: 1999–2003 **WNBA:** 2003–06

An outstanding high school athlete and Georgia's Gatorade Player of the Year in her senior season, Coretta Brown attended the University of North Carolina and immediately made an impact on the court, starting 10 games as a freshman. She became a full-time starter after that, culminating in an outstanding senior season in which she led the team in scoring with 14.5 points per game. She also led the ACC in three-pointers per game (2.6) and three-point percentage (.395). Brown then was the 11th overall pick in the 2003 WNBA Draft. Chosen by San Antonio, she was then traded to the Indiana Fever.

Brown played three seasons with the Fever and a fourth with the Chicago Sky. Her best year as a scorer was her first, when she averaged 6.2 points per game. She poured in 26 points in a game against Connecticut that season. After the WNBA, she spent two seasons with Georgia Tech as an administrative coordinator before moving to the high school level as an assistant coach at Benjamin E. Mays in Atlanta. She then spent three seasons at Tennessee Tech as an assistant coach before becoming head coach at Thomas University in Thomasville, Georgia, in 2012.

SYLVIA CRAWLEY ■ 6' 5" 187 ■ *Forward*

COLLEGE: 1990–94 **ABL:** 1995–99 **WNBA:** 2000–03

Ohio native Sylvia Crawley came to Carolina as a high school star and didn't disappoint. Her fantastic collegiate career culminated as team captain on the 1994 championship Tar Heels team, and her #00 jersey now hangs in the rafters of the Carmichael Arena. After graduation, she played internationally with USA Basketball and played abroad in France and Spain before joining the new American Basketball League in 1995. She played three full seasons in the league and part of a fourth before it folded. Crawley began her ABL career with the Colorado Xplosion and after her rookie season starred for the Portland Power. She joined the WNBA's Portland Fire in 2000, turning in a nice season, averaging 11.5 points and 6 rebounds per game, which included a 25-point game against Utah that year.

SYLVIA CRAWLEY. Sylvia Crawley spent time playing in the ABL and the WNBA, in addition to being a member of USA Basketball. She has also been a collegiate coach.

Crawley was an assistant coach at UNC in 2000–02 and later an assistant at Fordham University. Her first head-coaching gig was with the Ohio Bobcats, followed by a stint with Boston College in 2008–12. In the midst of all that, she helped found *Monarch Magazine*, which is dedicated to reflecting affluent African American professionals and their lifestyles. She's a motivational speaker and a talk show host on Internet radio.

MARION JONES ■ 5' 10" 178 ■ *Guard*

COLLEGE: 1993–95, 1996–97 **WNBA:** 2010–11

The California-born Marion Jones has a profile in the Olympics chapter, but we thought we should at least give a mention to her basketball prowess. She was an excellent player for the Tar Heels, helping to lead the Tar Heels to a national championship in 1994 as a freshman point guard. She was also a vital cog on the 1994–95 Carolina team but then gave up the sport for a year to concentrate on track and field. She came back for one more season before giving up the sport again. Overall, Carolina was 92-10 in the three seasons that Jones was on the team.

IVORY LATTA ■ 5' 6" 138 ■ *Guard*

COLLEGE: 2003–07 **WNBA:** 2007–13

IVORY LATTA. Ivory Latta was the ACC Tournament MVP three times. She has gone on to a solid career in the WNBA.

As a highly decorated and recruited high school player from South Carolina, Ivory Latta headed to Chapel Hill with substantial expectations, and she did not disappoint. She was the all-time leading scorer in South Carolina high school history. A look now at the UNC basketball record books will find the name Ivory a lotta. (Sorry, couldn't resist.) Latta is Carolina's all-time leading scorer with 2,285 points, averaging 16.6 points per game throughout her Tar Heels career. She was the ACC Player of the Year in 2006 (being named as national player of the year by several organizations) and was the ACC Tournament MVP an amazing three times (2004–06). She holds UNC records for most three-pointers attempted and made in both a season and a career. Her career three-point percentage of 38.9 is also a school best. She was a winner too. Latta helped lead UNC to consecutive Final Four appearances in 2006–07.

She was drafted in the first round by the Detroit Shock in 2007 and struggled during her rookie season, averaging just three points per game. That was obviously a low scoring mark for someone who had always been a prolific scorer. She was dealt to the Atlanta Dream for her second season, in which she saw her pro career start clicking. She finished with 11.4 points per game, but had a bit of a setback her next year, which was her last with Atlanta. She has come on strong in three seasons for the Tulsa Shock (which had moved from Detroit) and one with the Washington Mystics, averaging in double digits for the past four seasons. She also got in a couple off-seasons playing overseas to help refine her game. In 2013, Latta was hired by her alma mater as an assistant coach, working with the Tar Heels during the WNBA off-season. Latta called her hire "a dream come true."

After her fall from grace in track and field for using performance-enhancing drugs, Jones decided she would make a sports comeback by trying out for the WNBA. She signed with the Tulsa Shock in 2010 and played for the team in 2010 and part of 2011 before she was waived. She had averaged a mere 2.6 points per game in her pro career.

ELANA LARKINS ■ 6' 1" 185 ■ *Forward*

COLLEGE: 2004–08 **WNBA:** 2008–09, 2012–13

One of UNC's most dominant post players, Florida native Elana Larkins was a star throughout her career in Chapel Hill. She made numerous all-conference teams and was named the MVP of the 2008 ACC Tournament. She ranks among the UNC career leaders in scoring (seventh), field goal percentage (second), total rebounds (third), rebounding average (sixth), steals (fifth), and blocked shots (seventh). Her scoring averages per game ranged from 14.6 as a freshman to 12.9 as a junior. She averaged at least nine rebounds per game in her final two seasons.

Elana Larkins was a 2008 first-round pick in the WNBA by the New York Liberty, where she played for two years. In those years, she averaged 4.8 and 2.4 points per game respectively. She found herself trying to catch onto another WNBA team for two years after being waived by the Liberty. In 2012, she finally latched on with the Indiana Fever. In between, she played in the Turkish League for Mersin. She helped lead Indiana to the WNBA Championship in the 2012 season.

CAMILLE LITTLE ■ 6' 2" 180 ■ *Forward*

COLLEGE: 2003–07 **WNBA:** 2007–13

Arriving at UNC at the same time as the aforementioned Ivory Latta, Little combined with her to lead the Tar Heels team to one of its most successful four-year periods, including NCAA appearances all four years, the last two of which were Final Four appearances. The native of Winston-Salem beat out Latta, and many others, for ACC Rookie of the Year honors as a freshman. Solid in all aspects of the game, Little could score, rebound, and play some serious defense. She finished her Carolina career with 12.8 points and 5.9 rebounds per game, while being named to the ACC All-Defensive Team her senior year. To illustrate her well-roundedness: Little tallied more than 1,700 points, 800 rebounds, 250 assists, and 250 steals at UNC.

Little was drafted by the San Antonio Silver Stars and made the WNBA's All-Rookie Team. The following year, Little was traded to Atlanta prior to the season and then to Seattle during the season. She has settled in and become a key cog for the Storm, helping to lead them to a WNBA title in 2010. She has started every game she's played in over the past five years and continues to put up good numbers for the Storm. And perhaps most importantly, Little has helped lead her teams to the playoffs in each of her seven WNBA seasons.

RASHANDA McCANTS ■ 6' 1" 163 ■ *Forward*

COLLEGE: 2005–09 **WNBA:** 2009–10

Rashanda McCants tagged along with big brother Rashad, who also went on to play basketball as a Tar Heel, on the playgrounds and in the gyms around Asheville, North

Carolina. By the time Rashanda was a senior at Asheville High, she was a highly recruited McDonald's All-American. She stayed in state and followed her brother to Chapel Hill. She made an immediate impact as a top reserve, scoring 5.8 points per game as a freshman. She started all 38 games of her sophomore year, setting a UNC record for most games started in a season. In her junior season, McCants scored a career high of 28 points in a November 29, 2007, matchup against Purdue. She finished her junior year averaging nearly 16 points per game. She finished her Carolina career as the ACC Player of the year, averaging 15 points and 6.5 rebounds per game.

McCants was then chosen in the 2009 WNBA Draft by the Minnesota Lynx. She only started one game in her rookie year for the Lynx, but, as in her rookie year at UNC, she proved to be an important reserve. During her second season, she was traded to the Tulsa Shock, where she finished the year. She was waived by the Shock prior to the 2011 season and has played some ball internationally since.

LATOYA PRINGLE ■ 6' 3" 170 ■ *Forward / Center*

COLLEGE: 2004–08 **WNBA:** 2008–09, 2011

LaToya Pringle has always had a knack for blocking shots. In fact, when asked a few years ago what she enjoys most about basketball, her answer was "Meeting new people and blocking shots." So there ya go. It's no surprise that she finished her four years at UNC as the school record-holder in shots blocked with 336, including 121 in her junior season. That season she recorded nine blocks in a single game against Wofford. Not known as a prolific scorer, she did average 14.6 points per game as a senior.

That led to her being drafted by the Phoenix Mercury in the 2008 WNBA Draft. She saw action in 29 games and was fifth in the league in blocked shots. In January 2009, she was traded to the Minnesota Lynx, played one season, and then signed with the Los Angeles Sparks in February 2010. Pringle didn't make the Sparks roster that year but came back and played for Los Angeles in 2011. She also married former UNC men's basketball player Byron Sanders in 2011.

TRACY REID ■ 6' 0" 175 ■ *Forward*

COLLEGE: 1994–98 **WNBA:**1998–03

Tracy Reid was a high school legend in Miami. While scoring nearly 2,800 points, she was a three-time Florida Player of the Year selection. When she moved up to Carolina, the accolades didn't stop. She was twice named ACC Player of the Year. As a senior, she had a 42-point performance in a losing cause against Virginia in January 1998.

Selected in the first round of the 1998 WNBA Draft by the Charlotte Sting, Reid went on to become the league's Rookie of the Year. The following year, she was beset with injuries and only played in 10 games. She bounced back in 2000, but her numbers were off from her great rookie season. She was then dealt to the Miami Sol, where she played the 2001 season. She played a full season in 2002 with the Phoenix

Mercury and then just a few games with Phoenix in 2003. Continuing to be plagued by injuries, Reid was waived by the Mercury just a couple games into the 2003 season. She later played for teams in Spain and Israel.

TIERRA RUFFIN-PRATT ■ 5' 10" 183 ■ *Guard*

COLLEGE: 2009–13 **WNBA:** 2013

Most Carolina players that have entered the WNBA have done so via the draft, typically in the first or second round. Tierra Ruffin-Pratt wasn't drafted. She instead tried out for the Washington Mystics and impressed the coaches enough to sign a free-agent contract. Prior to that, though, she was a two-time All-Met Player of the Year at T.C. Williams High School in Alexandria, Virginia. She chose to play her college ball at UNC and played in 30 games as a freshman, starting 19 of those. She was also a part-time starter in her sophomore year. Off-season shoulder surgery impeded her progress as a junior, as she missed the first 13 games. She finally got her chance to take over the team as point guard in her senior season.

In her senior year, Ruffin-Pratt led the Tar Heels in scoring, assists, steals, free throws attempted and made, and minutes played, while the team posted a 29-6 record. She then turned in a strong rookie season as a reserve for the Mystics. She was an every-game player who averaged 4.4 points per game. Her season high came in a July 16 game against the San Antonio Silver Stars, in which she scored 13 points in an 86–64 win.

NIKKI TEASLEY ■ 6' 0" 170 ■ *Guard*

COLLEGE: 1997–02 **WNBA:** 2002

High school phenom Nikki Teasley was ranked by most recruiting services as the top player in the nation after being named Player of the Year by *Parade* magazine and Gatorade. In the summer before she headed to Chapel Hill, the Maryland native captained the gold medal–winning USA Junior Basketball Team. She immediately made an impact for the Tar Heels, leading the ACC in assists and earning the ACC Rookie of the Year honors. As a sophomore, she led the ACC in assists and steals. Her junior season was highlighted by a 31-point performance, including seven three-pointers, in the ACC Championship game. As a senior, she ranked among the ACC's top five in scoring (fifth), assists (first), three-pointers (second), three-point percentage (second), free-throw percentage (first), steals (fourth), and assist-turnover ratio (second).

A first-round draft choice by the Portland Fire, she was then traded to the Los Angeles Sparks to begin her pro career. She was a starter in her first three seasons but missed nearly half of the 2005 season with a foot injury. Teasley was then traded to the Washington Mystics. She was a two-year starter for the Mystics before missing the 2008 season because she gave birth to her daughter in June. She then played in Spain for the winter. Teasley got back into the WNBA with the Atlanta Dream for 2009 but was waived 10 games into the season. Interestingly, her roster spot was given to fellow

CHARLOTTE SMITH ■ 6' 0" 148 ■ *Forward*

COLLEGE: 1991-95 **ITALY:** 1995–96 **ABL:** 1996–98
WNBA: 1999–05

CHARLOTTE SMITH. Charlotte Smith played in the ABL and the NBA, as well as internationally, after leading the Tar Heels to an NCAA championship in 1994.

If you know only one player from the rich, but fairly short, history of Carolina women's basketball, it could be Charlotte Smith, who remains its most decorated player. While most associate the number 23 with Michael Jordan, many associate it with Smith too. Hailing from Shelby, North Carolina, she was named the ACC Rookie of the Year in 1992 and finished her career with numerous All-ACC and All-America honors. She may be best remembered for her three-pointer as time expired in the 1994 national championship game, giving the Heels a 60–59 victory over Louisiana Tech. That was in addition to an amazing 23 rebounds. In her senior season, she became the second female collegiate player to dunk in a game.

She came out of Carolina before the WNBA even existed, so she played professionally in Italy for a couple of years before connecting with the American Basketball League, which was in existence from 1996 to 1999. In the ABL, she played a year for the Colorado Xplosion and another for the San Jose Lasers. When the league folded in 1999, she entered the WNBA draft and was selected by the Charlotte Sting, who were happy to get the Carolina legend from nearby Shelby on the team. Smith played six seasons for the Sting before playing a final year with the Washington Mystics.

Smith became an assistant coach at her alma mater while she was sill playing for the WNBA in the summer. She was an assistant at UNC until 2011 when she was named the sixth head coach in the history of Elon University women's basketball. In her first two seasons, she led the Phoenix to a 35-28 record.

Tar Heel Ivory Latta. Teasley was picked up by the Detroit Shock and finished out the 2009 season there. She made it to two WNBA All Star Games (being named MVP of one of those) and may be best remembered for her game-winning shot in the 2002 (her rookie year) WNBA Championship against the New York Liberty. She now operates the Teasley Assist Group, whose mission is to provide young females the opportunity to learn and enjoy the game of basketball at a highly competitive level.

FOOTBALL
FOOTBALL
FOOTBALL
FOOTBALL
FOOTBALL
FOOTBALL

While basketball, lacrosse, and women's soccer have brought a lot more championships to Chapel Hill than football, the Tar Heels still have a long history of success on the gridiron. And is there a better way to spend an autumn Saturday than under the Carolina blue skies in Kenan Memorial Stadium? It's a fantastic venue for football—and over the decades it has seen its share of marvelous athletes who went on to professional careers in the sport.

The first UNC coach to stick around more than a year, W. A. Reynolds, started to build a successful program at UNC. In four seasons, from 1897 to 1900, Reynolds went 27-7-4. After more than 120 seasons of football, North Carolina compiled a record of 670-503-54, a winning percentage of .568. The Heels won three Southern Conference titles back in the day and own five Atlantic Coast Conference championships, appearing in 29 bowl games over the years. The program even claims an 1895 championship in the long-defunct Southern Intercollegiate Athletic Association (SIAA).

Certainly some coaches have had success in Chapel Hill. In the modern era, Bill Dooley was one of the first to have a nice run at UNC. The brother of University of Georgia legendary coach Vince Dooley, Bill led the Tar Heels for 11 seasons, compiling a 69-53-2 record. His best season was in 1972, when Carolina finished with an 11-1 record and was undefeated in the ACC. He left the Tar Heels for the head job at Virginia Tech and later finished his career at Wake Forest. Dick Crum followed Dooley and had even more success, leading the Heels to a 72-41-3 record in 10 years. Crum also had an 11-1 season. His was in 1980. Carolina, led by sack-machine Lawrence Taylor on defense and superstar running back Amos Lawrence on offense, went undefeated in the ACC that year. He couldn't match that success thereafter, though, so Crum was fired in 1987 and replaced by Mack Brown.

At the time, Brown was a relative unknown. He had coached for a year at Appalachian State and then for three years at Tulane, where he failed to have a winning season. Many Carolina fans were skeptical of the hire. After consecutive 1-10 seasons, it seemed the skeptics were correct. The guy was proving to be a loser. Finally, a winning season in 1990 saved his job. Back-to-back 10-win seasons in 1996–97 made him a hot commodity, and he bolted for the newly vacant job at the University of Texas. Brown left with a 69-46-1 record in 10 seasons, and thus Dooley, Crum, and Brown remain the only coaches with at least 60 wins in Carolina football history.

In recent years, Carolina has found itself in some hot water with the NCAA. In July 2010, the NCAA launched an investigation into an array of issues with the football program at the University of North Carolina. The investigation uncovered financial ties between a sports agent and an assistant coach, a range of impermissible gifts accepted by football players, and improper academic assistance from a tutor. UNC self-imposed several penalties, including vacating all 16 wins for 2008 and 2009, reducing nine scholarships over the next three academic years, and putting the program on two years of probation. The NCAA, however, added to those penalties in 2012, finding that the school was responsible for violations including academic fraud, impermissible agent benefits, participation by ineligible players, and a failure to monitor the football program. The NCAA put the school on three years of probation and banned it from post-season play in 2012. The NCAA also issued a three-year show-cause penalty for former assistant coach John Blake, who had received personal loans from an NFL agent.

That post-season ban in 2012 actually turned out to be quite the bummer for the Tar Heels. New Head Coach Larry Fedora led UNC to an 8-4 season and tied for first in the ACC's Coastal Division. The Heels are putting the past behind them now, and Fedora is looking to lead Carolina to new heights on the gridiron.

We've pulled together some historical perspective on NCAA football in general and North Carolina football in particular. If that's not your thing, feel free to skip ahead to the player bios.

Divisions and Subdivisions

The National Collegiate Athletic Association splits its football-playing members into three divisions—or, depending on how you count, four. They are:

- **Division I, which generally consists of the major football schools. It is subdivided into:**
  - The Football Bowl Subdivision, formerly known as Division IA and commonly (if clumsily) called Division I FBS.
  - The Football Championship Subdivision, formerly known as Division IAA and commonly (if equally clumsily) called Division I FCS.
- **Division II, in which the schools tend to be smaller.**
- **Division III, in which the schools are usually smaller yet.**

The big-time programs play in Division I FBS—124 schools as of 2013, with one transitional team. That's North Carolina's subdivision. It's the only NCAA sport or subdivision that does not have a post-season playoff to determine its national champion, although that will change with the new four-team playoff plan that's scheduled to begin with the 2014 season. Division I FBS had not previously had a playoff out of deference to the post-season bowl games (35 of them, as of 2013, including the BCS National Championship Game) that have proliferated, especially in recent years, since the first Rose Bowl in 1902.

The NCAA anoints no official champion in this top division. Various ratings groups make their selections at the end of the year. Most prominent are the Associated Press poll of sportswriters and a coaches poll that has been conducted by several different entities (currently *USA Today*). Sometimes they agree; sometimes they don't.

Starting with the 1992 season, an alliance of post-season bowl games and major conferences, plus powerful independent Notre Dame, has attempted to create a de facto national championship, using various polls and computer ranking systems to pick what it thinks are that season's two best teams. Since 1998, the alliance has been known as the Bowl Championship Series.

The coaches poll agreed to vote the BCS champion number one in its final ranking. The AP poll did not. Since the BCS system started, it has differed only once, favoring Southern California in 2003 instead of BCS champion LSU. Still, because of arguments over its selection process, the BCS system seems to have made just partial progress toward the goal of crowning a universally acknowledged national champion. Beginning in 2014, a four-team playoff, with the teams chosen by a selection committee, will take place to determine a champion.

Division I FCS schools have a newly expanded (up from 20) 24-team championship playoff that begins in late November. The national championship game takes place in early January. FCS schools can offer up to 63 athletic scholarships, compared with the 85 scholarships allowed at FBS schools.

Some FCS conferences don't participate in the tournament, notably the Ivy League, which de-emphasized football in 1945 because of academic concerns.

Division II schools are allowed to offer up to 36 football scholarships. Their 24-team playoff begins in mid-November, with the championship in mid-December.

The members of Division III do not offer athletic scholarships. Their 32-team tournament also begins in mid-November and ends with the championship in mid-December.

Some smaller colleges and universities are members of the National Association of Intercollegiate Athletics. Of its 25 member conferences, 11 sponsor football. The NAIA puts on a 16-team post-season tournament, starting in late November and culminating in a December championship game.

And then there's the Collegiate Sprint Football League. Formerly known as the Eastern Lightweight Football League and before that the Eastern 150-pound Football League, it dates back to 1934. It currently has eight members: Penn, Princeton, Cornell, Navy, Army, Mansfield University, Post University, and Franklin Pierce University. At those schools, sprint football is a varsity sport. It follows the familiar college football rules, but players must weigh no more than 172 pounds and have a minimum body fat of 5 percent (to discourage excessive weight loss). Those with less than 5 percent body fat may weigh no more than 165 pounds. There's no post-season tournament. Regular-season records determine the league champion.

The Evolving Atlantic Coast Conference

Keeping up with changing conference affiliations has become a chore in recent years. After relative stability, conference hopping has taken on a new fervor. North Carolina's conference since 1953, the ACC, is no exception. For 2013, Pitt and Syracuse came to the ACC from the Big East while Notre Dame joined the conference in all sports except football. In 2014, Louisville will join the ACC, while Maryland will leave to join the Big Ten. North Carolina is in the Coastal Division of the ACC, along with Duke, Georgia Tech, Miami, Pitt, Virginia, and Virginia Tech. The Atlantic Division features Boston College, Clemson, Florida State, Maryland, North Carolina State, Syracuse, and Wake Forest. It's expected that Louisville will simply replace Maryland in the 2014 alignment.

Bowl Tie-ins

The ACC has tie-ins to the following bowl games: Orange, Chick-fil-A, Russell Athletic, Sun, Belk, Music City, Independence, Military, and Kraft Fight Hunger. The Kraft Fight Hunger Bowl, however, picks an ACC team only if its primary partners are not bowl eligible, and there are nine bowl-eligible ACC teams. If that happens, the Kraft Fight Hunger Bowl would pick the ninth ACC bowl-eligible team. Also, the Orange Bowl would be free to pick another BCS team if the ACC champion is selected for the newly devised four-team playoff.

Tailback U?

North Carolina has been called Tailback U for its number of quality tailbacks. Of course, the University of Southern California and even Georgia have also shared that moniker at times, so it's tough to say who the real Tailback U might be. That said, UNC has had a tailback to rush for at least 1,000 yards in a season on 25 occasions, which ain't bad. The first was Don McCauley, who rushed for 1,092 yards in 1969 and then increased his productivity in 1970 to gain 1,720 yards. Mike Voight and Kelvin Bryant each rushed for more than 1,000 yards in three consecutive seasons, while the great Amos Lawrence is the only Tar Heel to gain at least 1,000 yards in four seasons. In 1983, Carolina had two tailbacks to reach the 1,000-yard mark: Tyrone Anthony (1,063) and Ethan Horton (1,107).

Head Coaching Records

(In chronological order, including record and winning percentage; a tie counts as half a win, half a loss, per NCAA practice)

YEARS	COACH	RECORD	WINNING PCT.
1888	Hector Cowan	2-2	.500
1894	V.K. Irvine	6-3	.667
1895, 1913–15	Thomas Gawthrop "Doggie" Trenchard	26-9-2	.730
1896	Gordon Johnston	3-4-1	.438
1897–1900	William A. Reynolds	27-7-4	.763
1901	Charles Jenkins	7-2	.778
1902–03	Herman P. "Bo" Olcott	11-4-3	.694
1904	Robert R. Brown	5-2-2	.667
1905	William "Bill" Warner	4-3-1	.562
1906	William S. Kienholz	1-4-2	.286
1907	Dr. Otis Lamson	4-4-1	.500
1908	Edward Green	3-3-3	.500
1909–10	A.E. Brides	8 8	.500
1911	Branch Bocock	6-1-1	.812
1912	William C. Martin	3-4-1	.438
1916–19	Thomas J. Campbell	9-7-1	.559

YEARS	COACH	RECORD	WINNING PCT.
1920	Myron E. Fuller	2-6	.250
1921–25	Bob Fetzer & Bill Fetzer	30-12-4	.696
1926–33	Chuck Collins	38-31-9	.545
1934–35; 1945–52	Carl G. Snavely	59-35-5	.621
1936–41	Raymond Wolf	38-17-3	.681
1942; 1956–58	Jim Tatum	19-17-3	.526
1943	Thomas B. Young	6-3	.667
1944	Gene McEver	1-7-1	.167
1953–55	George Barclay	11-18-1	.383
1959–66	James Hickey	36-45	.444
1967–77	Bill Dooley	69-53-2	.565
1978–87	Dick Crum	72-41-3	.634
1988–97	Mack Brown	69-46-1	.599
1997–2000	Carl Torbush	17-18	.486
2001–06	John Bunting	27-45	.375

Coach Bill Dooley won three ACC titles and 69 games at the University of North Carolina.

YEARS	COACH	RECORD	WINNING PCT.
2007–10	Butch Davis	12-23	.343
2011	Everett Withers	7-6	.538
2012–14	Larry Fedora	15-10	.600

(Ranked by victories)

RECORD	COACH	YEARS	WINNING PCT.
72-41-3	Dick Crum	1978–87	.634
69-46-1	Mack Brown	1988–97	.599
69-53-2	Bill Dooley	1967–77	.565
59-35-5	Carl G. Snavely	1934–35; 1945–52	.621
38-31-9	Chuck Collins	1926–33	.545
38-17-3	Raymond Wolf	1936–41	.681
36-45	James Hickey	1959–66	.444
30-12-4	Bob Fetzer & Bill Fetzer	1921–25	.696
27-45	John Bunting	2001–06	.375
27-7-4	William A. Reynolds	1897–1900	.763
26-9-2	Thomas Gawthrop "Doggie" Trenchard	1895, 1913–15	.730
19-17-3	Jim Tatum	1942; 1956–58	.526
17-18	Carl Torbush	1997–2000	.486
15-10	Larry Fedora	2012–14	.600
12-23	Butch Davis	2007–10	.343
11-18-1	George Barclay	1953–55	.383
11-4-3	Herman P. "Bo" Olcott	1902–03	.694
9-7-1	Thomas J. Campbell	1916–19	.559
8-8	A.E. Brides	1909–10	.500
7-2	Charles Jenkins	1901	.778
7-6	Everett Withers	2011	.538
6-1-1	Branch Bocock	1911	.812
6-3	V.K. Irvine	1894	.667
6-3	Thomas B. Young	1943	.667
5-2-2	Robert R. Brown	1904	.667

RECORD	COACH	YEARS	WINNING PCT.
4-4-1	Dr. Otis Lamson	1907	.500
4-3-1	William "Bill" Warner	1905	.562
3-3-3	Edward Green	1908	.500
3-4-1	Gordon Johnston	1896	.438
3-4-1	William C. Martin	1912	.438
2-2	Hector Cowan	1888	.500
2-6	Myron E. Fuller	1920	.250
1-4-2	William S. Kienholz	1906	.286
1-7-1	Gene McEver	1944	.167

(Ranked by winning percentage; a tie counts as half a win, half a loss, per NCAA practice)

WINNING PCT.	COACH	YEARS	RECORD
.812	Branch Bocock	1911	6-1-1
.778	Charles Jenkins	1901	7-2
.763	William A. Reynolds	1897–1900	27-7-4
.730	Thomas Gawthrop "Doggie" Trenchard	1895, 1913–15	26-9-2
.696	Bob Fetzer & Bill Fetzer	1921–25	30-12-4
.694	Herman P. "Bo" Olcott	1902–03	11-4-3
.681	Raymond Wolf	1936–41	38-17-3
.667	Robert R. Brown	1904	5-2-2
.667	V.K. Irvine	1894	6-3
.667	Thomas B. Young	1943	6-3
.634	Dick Crum	1978–87	72-41-3
.621	Carl G. Snavely	1934–35; 1945–52	59-35-5
.600	Larry Fedora	2012–14	15-10
.599	Mack Brown	1988–97	69-46-1
.565	Bill Dooley	1967–77	69-53-2
.562	William "Bill" Warner	1905	4-3-1
.559	Thomas J. Campbell	1916–19	9-7-1
.545	Chuck Collins	1926–33	38-31-9

WINNING PCT.	COACH	YEARS	RECORD
.538	Everett Withers	2011	7-6
.526	Jim Tatum	1942; 1956–58	19-17-3
.500	A.E. Brides	1909–10	8-8
.500	Hector Cowan	1888	2-2
.500	Edward Green	1908	3-3-3
.500	Dr. Otis Lamson	1907	4-4-1
.486	Carl Torbush	1997–2000	17-18
.444	James Hickey	1959–66	36-45
.438	Gordon Johnston	1896	3-4-1
.438	William C. Martin	1912	3-4-1
.383	George Barclay	1953–55	11-18-1
.375	John Bunting	2001–06	27-45
.343	Butch Davis	2007–10	12-23
.286	William S. Kienholz	1906	1-4-2
.250	Myron E. Fuller	1920	2-6
.167	Gene McEver	1944	1-7-1

North Carolina's Complete List of Bowl Games

1947 Sugar Bowl: Georgia 20, North Carolina 10
1949 Sugar Bowl: Oklahoma 14, North Carolina 6
1950 Cotton Bowl: Rice 27, North Carolina 13
1963 Gator Bowl: North Carolina 35, Air Force 0
1970 Peach Bowl: Arizona State 42, North Carolina 26
1971 Gator Bowl: Georgia 7, North Carolina 3
1972 Sun Bowl: North Carolina 32, Texas Tech 28
1974 Sun Bowl: Mississippi State 26, North Carolina 24
1976 Peach Bowl: Kentucky 21, North Carolina 0
1977 Liberty Bowl: Nebraska 21, North Carolina 17
1979 Gator Bowl: North Carolina 17, Michigan 15
1980 Bluebonnet Bowl: North Carolina 16, Texas 7
1981 Gator Bowl: North Carolina 31, Arkansas 27
1982 Sun Bowl: North Carolina 26, Texas 10
1983 Peach Bowl: Florida State 28, North Carolina 3

1986	**Aloha Bowl:** Arizona 30, North Carolina 21
1993	**Peach Bowl:** North Carolina 21, Mississippi State 17
1993	**Gator Bowl:** Alabama 24, North Carolina 10
1994	**Sun Bowl:** Texas 35, North Carolina 31
1995	**Carquest Bowl:** North Carolina 20, Arkansas 10
1997	**Gator Bowl:** North Carolina 20, West Virginia 13
1998	**Gator Bowl:** North Carolina 42, Virginia Tech 3
1998	**Las Vegas Bowl:** North Carolina 20, San Diego State 13
2001	**Peach Bowl:** North Carolina 16, Auburn 10
2004	**Continental Tire Bowl:** Boston College 37, North Carolina 24
2008	**Meineke Car Care Bowl:** West Virginia 31, North Carolina 30
2009	**Meineke Car Care Bowl:** Pittsburgh 19, North Carolina 17
2010	**Franklin American Mortgage Music City Bowl:** North Carolina 30, Tennessee 27
2011	**Independence Bowl:** Missouri 41, North Carolina 24
2013	**Belk Bowl:** North Carolina 37, Cincinnati 19

All-Time North Carolina Bowl Game Records

Aloha Bowl: 0-1	**Cotton Bowl: 0-1**	**Music City Bowl: 1-0**
Bluebonnet Bowl: 1-0	**Gator Bowl: 5-2**	**Peach Bowl: 3-2**
Belk Bowl: 1-0	**Las Vegas: 1-0**	**Sugar Bowl: 0-2**
Carquest Bowl: 1-0	**Liberty Bowl 0-1**	**Sun Bowl: 2-2**
Continental: 0-1	**Meineke Car Care Bowl: 0-2**	**Overall: 14-16**

Player Bios

SAM AIKEN ■ 6' 2" 204 ■ *Wide Receiver*

COLLEGE: 1999–2003 **NFL:** 2003-10

At James Kenan High School in Warsaw, North Carolina, Sam Aiken was an all-around sports star. He received honors in football, basketball, and track and field. He was a productive receiver in Chapel Hill, including a sterling junior season in which he scored eight touchdowns and averaged 17.2 yards per catch. In his senior year, he set school records for catches (68) and yards (990). He was also a vital special teams player throughout his years at Carolina.

He parlayed those accomplishments into being a fourth-round selection in the 2003 NFL Draft by the Buffalo Bills, where he saw limited playing time in his five years there. After just 19 catches in Buffalo, he signed with New England in 2008 and had a career-best 20 catches during the 2009 season. Despite the best season of

ETHAN ALBRIGHT ■ 6' 5" 283 ■ *Long Snapper*

COLLEGE: 1989–93 **NFL:** 1995–10

Trivia: What former Tar Heel went on to the longest NFL career? Known as "The Red Snapper" due to his red hair and the fact that for most of his NFL tenure he specialized as a long snapper, Ethan Albright had a 16-year pro career, playing in 236 games. But before that, Albright starred in football, basketball, and baseball at Grimsley High School in Greensboro, North Carolina. He was recruited to UNC as a tight end but later moved to offensive tackle while also handling long snapping duties.

ETHAN ALBRIGHT. Ethan Albright found his niche in the NFL as a long snapper.

Albright went undrafted but signed as a free agent with the Miami Dolphins, where he played the 1995 season. He signed with the Buffalo Bills the next year and thus started a streak of most consecutive games played by an NFL long snapper. Playing for both Buffalo and the Washington Redskins, Albright played in 230 straight games between 1996 and 2010. He was selected to the Pro Bowl in 2007. In 2006, Albright gained notoriety for a letter supposedly written by him to former NFL coach and analyst and EA Sports football video game namesake, complaining about his player rating in the game. It was later revealed that the humorous, but profane, letter was a hoax and not written by The Red Snapper. But hey, it's hard for a snapper to get much love in a video game. He had plenty of respect, though, among his teammates and others in the league for such a steady and long-lasting pro career.

his career, he was cut by the Patriots in 2010. He was then picked up briefly by the Cleveland Browns but saw action in only three games in 2010 before being cut. He was recently a graduate assistant for the Tar Heels and ponders a career in coaching.

CARLTON BAILEY ■ 6' 3" 242 ■ *Linebacker*

COLLEGE: 1984–88 **NFL:** 1988–97

If you're reading this in order, you may think, "What's up with UNC players and the Buffalo Bills? Three player bios, three Bills players." We think it's just a coincidence. Nonetheless, Carlton Bailey was a ninth-round NFL Draft choice by the Buffalo Bills after a very productive career for the Tar Heels. Bailey played five seasons for the Bills, playing for three of the four Bills teams that made it to the Super Bowl, though each resulted in a loss. He signed with the New York Giants in 1993 and had his best NFL season: 136 tackles, 2 forced fumbles, 1.5 sacks, 1 fumble recovery. He played one more year for the Giants, followed by three with the Carolina Panthers before retiring with 562 total tackles in his career.

ROY BARKER ■ 6' 5" 287 ■ *Defensive End / Tackle*

COLLEGE: 1988–92 **NFL:** 1992–2000

Born in 1969 in New York, New York, Roy Barker grew up on Long Island and played high school ball at Central Islip before attending the University of North Carolina, where he starred on the defensive line. He was chosen in the fourth round of the 1992 NFL Draft by the Minnesota Vikings. Barker had four good, but not great, seasons and ended up with the San Francisco 49ers for the 1996 season, which proved to be a breakout year. Barker racked up 12.5 sacks and 36 total tackles. He played two more seasons with the 49ers but didn't match his 1996 numbers. In 1999, he spent most of the year with Cleveland but played one game for Green Bay and then finished his career back with Minnesota in 2000.

TOMMY BARNHARDT ■ 6' 2" 228 ■ *Punter*

COLLEGE: 1982–86 **NFL:** 1986–2000

You now know that Ethan Albright had the longest pro career of any former Tar Heel, but John Thomas Ray Barnhardt, known more commonly as Tommy, isn't far behind. Seems those specialists can eke out some long careers. Albright was a long snapper; Barnhardt a punter. After booting the ball for Carolina, he was chosen by the Tampa Bay Buccaneers in the ninth round of the 1986 NFL Draft. He was cut by the Bucs but came back in 1987 to log in time for both the Chicago Bears and the New Orleans Saints. That got his proverbial and literal foot onto NFL rosters, and Barnhardt continued from there. He ended up playing eight seasons with the Saints but did make it back to his draft team of Tampa Bay, plus stints with the Washington Redskins and Carolina Panthers.

Barnhardt's best year in terms of average was with Tampa in 1996 when he averaged 45 yards per punt. He averaged at least 43 yards per punt in seven seasons. The longest single punt of his career was a 65-yarder that came with New Orleans in 1990. In 1991, he led the NFL in punting yards with 3,743. Unfortunately, he also led the NFL three times in punts blocked and finished his career with 106 punts blocked, which is an NFL rank of third.

HARRIS BARTON ■ 6' 4" 286 ■ *Guard / Tackle*

COLLEGE: 1983–87 **NFL:** 1987–96

Harris Barton came from the Atlanta area to play center for the North Carolina Tar Heels. Fairly rare for an offensive lineman, Barton was a four-year starter in Chapel

Hill, changing positions to tackle. During his senior season, he helped lead an offensive squad that led the ACC in total offense and ranked sixth nationally.

He was a first-round NFL Draft choice by the San Francisco 49ers and played his entire career during a golden era there. He and the 49ers won three Super Bowls during Barton's playing days, which also included being named a First-Team All-Pro twice and to one Pro Bowl. A constant stalwart on the offensive line, Barton played with Hall of Famers Joe Montana, Jerry Rice, and Steve Young. After his playing days were over, he put his UNC finance degree to work, becoming a managing partner for Champion Ventures, which was taken over by Capital Dynamics. He now lives in Palo Alto, California, and owns H. Barton Asset Management.

BRIAN BLADOS ■ 6' 5" 300 ■ *Guard / Tackle*

COLLEGE: 1980–84 **NFL:** 1984–92

Hailing from Arlington, Virginia, Brian Blados became a top-notch offensive lineman for the North Carolina Tar Heels. He was so good, in fact, that he was a first-round NFL Draft choice by the Cincinnati Bengals. He played the majority of his career with the Bengals before finishing with the Indianapolis Colts and Tampa Bay Buccaneers respectively. At heart, he remained a Bengal and said years after his playing days that he still has tigers all over the place in his home. "They're in every room," he said. Blados ran a landscaping company for a while after his retirement and has since been a territory manager for US Foodservice in West Chester, Ohio. His daughter Gabby is just beginning her stint as a volleyball player for ACC rival Clemson.

ALGE CRUMPLER ■ 6' 3" 266 ■ *Tight End*

COLLEGE: 1997–2000 **NFL:** 2001–10

Carlester Crumpler had a favorite book: Flowers for Algernon. He liked it so much that he named his son Algernon Darius Crumpler. Little Alge's older brother, Carlester, Jr., was a star football player in Greenville and, like their father, went on to play for the hometown East Carolina University. Carlester, Jr., then played in the NFL as a tight end for Seattle and Minnesota. So the bar was set high for Alge, and he jumped right over it.

He attended high school in Wilmington, where he excelled at football (tight end and linebacker) and track and field (a state champion in the discus and shot put). The accolades continued to pile up for him as a tight end at the University of North Carolina, where he received all-ACC honors his final three seasons in Chapel Hill.

From there, he became a second round draft choice for the Atlanta Falcons in 2001, where he was an All-Pro in 2003 and played in four consecutive Pro Bowls 2003–06. His productivity dropped a bit in 2007, and he signed with the Tennessee Titans in 2008. After two years with the Titans, he played a final season with the New England Patriots before being released in 2011. For his career, though, Crumpler

DRÉ BLY ■ 5' 9" 185 ■ *Cornerback*

COLLEGE: 1996–99 **NFL:** 1999–2009

As a redshirt freshman in Chapel Hill, Donald André Bly led the nation (and set an ACC record) with 11 interceptions. That's quite a collegiate debut. He finished his three-year career at UNC with 20 interceptions, which was an ACC record at the time. The Tar Heels had a 28-8 record in Bly's three years under coaches Mack Brown and Carl Torbush.

After his junior season, he was a second-round NFL Draft choice by the St. Louis Rams and went on to a distinguished pro career. While with St. Louis, he helped the Rams to win Super Bowl XXXIV and reach Super Bowl XXXVI. He went on to play for Detroit, Denver, and San Francisco before his playing days were finished. He was twice named to the Pro Bowl and earned All-Pro honors once. In 11 years in the NFL, Bly totaled 419 tackles and 43 career interceptions. Bly currently resides in Charlotte.

DRÉ BLY. Dré Bly, an interception machine for the Tar Heels, went on to an 11-year NFL career, winning a Super Bowl with the St. Louis Rams.

played in 155 games and made 373 catches, including 39 touchdowns. He's considered one of the best tight ends in Falcons history.

BUDDY CURRY ■ 6' 4" 224 ■ *Linebacker*

COLLEGE: 1976–79 **NFL:** 1980–87

George Jessel Curry, better known as "Buddy," is a North Carolina native who received numerous accolades playing defense for the Tar Heels in the late 1970s. He went on to star for the Atlanta Falcons in a solid eight-year career. His NFL days began impressively as he was named the Associated Press NFL Rookie of the Year in 1980—a season in which he started all 16 games and had three interceptions, including one for a touchdown.

Curry has remained close to football since his retirement. In 2002, he helped found Kids and Pros, a series of camps in the Southeast, featuring noncontact instruction for children ages 7 to 13. He is also a master trainer in USA Football's Heads Up program, a series that offers coaches nationally accredited courses regarding proper fundamentals and techniques.

JOHN BUNTING ■ 6' 1" 220 ■ *Linebacker*

COLLEGE: 1969–71 **NFL:** 1972–82

JOHN BUNTING. After being a star linebacker for UNC, John Bunting came back to coach the Tar Heels after his NFL career.

The name John Stephen Bunting pops up a few times in Tar Heels history. As a player under Coach Bill Dooley, Bunting had three solid seasons at linebacker that included an ACC Championship in 1971. He had a high football IQ and was often thought of as a coach on the field. "John not only knew his assignment, but he knew the assignments of 10 other positions on the field," said former Tar Heel teammate and longtime ACC Commissioner John Swofford. Bunting parlayed his collegiate skills into an 11-year career with the Philadelphia Eagles. While never known as a top talent, he was a starter for basically his entire pro career and was once again known for his smarts on the field. "John Bunting as a player knew more about our defense than our coordinator, Marion Campbell, who was a defensive genius," Eagles linebacker Bill Bergey said.

After retiring from playing, Bunting got into coaching, first as an assistant in the United States Football League and then at Brown University before becoming head coach for Glassboro State (now Rowan University) in New Jersey after one season as an assistant there. His fifth and final season as head coach at Glassboro State saw his team achieve a 12-1 record and make it to the Division III Semifinal. This led him back to the NFL, where he was an assistant with the Chiefs, Rams, and Saints before landing his dream job of head coach of his alma mater.

Bunting's stint as the head man in Chapel Hill began well enough. In 2001, the Tar Heels had an 8-5 season that included a Peach Bowl victory over Auburn. Over the next five seasons, though, the Tar Heels didn't manage another winning season. He was fired near the end of the 2006 season but was allowed to finish out the schedule before being replaced by Butch Davis. Bunting's final Carolina team finished 3-9 but did end the season with consecutive victories over in-state rivals N.C. State and Duke. Since his coaching days ended, Bunting has often been found as a commentator for college football.

RONALD CURRY ■ 6' 2" 220 ■ *Wide Receiver*

COLLEGE: 1998–2001 **NFL:** 2002–08

A high school sports legend in Virginia, Ronald Curry took his athletic prowess to Chapel Hill, where he was a two-sport star. Curry was a starting point guard in 2000–01 and a four-year starter at quarterback for Carolina. He finished his football career for the Tar Heels with 6,236 yards of total offense and 4,987 passing yards. He was an excellent running quarterback, finishing first all-time among UNC quarterbacks with 13 rushing touchdowns and 1,249 rushing yards. He finished on a high note leading the Tar Heels to a 16–10 victory over Auburn in the Peach Bowl while being named Offensive MVP.

RONALD CURRY. Ronald Curry was a two-sport star in Chapel Hill before a short career in the NFL.

While considered one of Carolina's greatest athletes, his skills didn't necessarily translate into pro success. Curry was a seventh-round draft pick of the Oakland Raiders in 2002, and the effort was made to turn him into a wide receiver. By his third season, Curry was starting to click as a receiver and turned in a nice 679 yards and six touchdowns. He then missed most of the following season with an Achilles injury. Thereafter, he had more than 700 yards receiving in both 2006 and '07 before his productivity slacked again in 2008, and he was released by the Raiders after the season.

Curry spent three years at North Carolina's Morrisville High School as athletic director and head football coach before joining the San Francisco 49ers in 2013 as an offensive assistant.

REUBEN DAVIS ■ 6' 5" 300 ■ *Defensive Line*

COLLEGE: 1984–87 **NFL:** 1988–96

Sometimes those late-round draft choices turn out to be very productive players. Reuben Cordell Davis was one of those. The big Greensboro native was a stellar defensive lineman in Chapel Hill before being chosen in the 9th round of the 1988 NFL Draft by the Tampa Bay Buccaneers. He had very consistent stats in his first three seasons for the Bucs, recording 61, 61, and 62 tackles respectively. His productivity didn't stay at that level, but he remained a steady player throughout his 11-year career, which also included stints with Phoenix and San Diego. As a Charger in 1995, Davis made it to the Super Bowl, where San Diego was defeated by San Francisco.

TORIN DORN ■ 6' 0" 200 ■ *Cornerback*

COLLEGE: 1986–89 **NFL:** 1990–96

As a freshman in 1986, Torin Dorn averaged 6.2 yards per carry in limited action, and Dorn was expected to be the backup, again, to running back Derrick Fenner in the 1987 season. Things can change quickly. Fenner was arrested on murder charges in June before the season, so Dorn burst onto the scene with 165 yards on 15 carries as his sophomore season kicked off versus Illinois. Fenner, meanwhile, was exonerated on murder charges but was arrested later for cocaine possession and parted ways with UNC. Dorn's football career, though, turned out to be a bit baffling after that fantastic start.

TORIN DORN. Torin Dorn began his Carolina career as a running back before being moved to defense.

As a junior, Dorn put up solid numbers at running back but then was moved to defensive back as a senior. He was chosen in the fourth round of the 1990 NFL Draft by the Oakland Raiders, where he continued to develop as a cornerback. After very limited action in his first two seasons in Oakland, he began to see a bit more playing time in his next two years. He then finished his career with two seasons with the St. Louis Rams. In all, he played in 84 NFL games, starting just four games. His son, Torin Dorn, is a star basketball player in the class of 2014 for Zebulon B. Vance High School in Charlotte.

RUSSELL DAVIS ■ 6' 4" 310 ■ *Defensive Line*

COLLEGE: 1995–98 **NFL:** 1999–2007

A two-way lineman at Fayetteville's E.E. Smith High School, Russell Davis went to UNC, where he was part of a phenomenal defensive line that included future long-time pros Greg Ellis and Vonnie Holliday. Davis started 22 games at Carolina but only two as a senior due to an ankle sprain. He was then selected in the second round of the 1999 NFL Draft by the Chicago Bears.

He was cut after one year with Chicago but was picked up by the Arizona Cardinals, where he played the next six seasons. He played in 80 games, starting 75 for the Cardinals, before finishing his career with a season each for Seattle and the New York Giants. For his career, he recorded 215 tackles and 11.5 sacks.

KEVIN DONNALLEY ■ 6' 5" 310 ■ *Offensive Line*

COLLEGE: 1989–90 (at UNC) **NFL:** 1991–2003

Kevin Donnalley graduated from Athens Drive High School in Raleigh before beginning his collegiate experience at Davidson College and then transferring to UNC. He was drafted by the Houston Oilers in the third round of the 1991 NFL Draft. Playing mostly at guard, Donnalley played six years in Houston and then stayed with the franchise when it moved to Tennessee. He then finished his NFL career with three years in Miami and another three with the Carolina Panthers. Overall, he started 144 of the 193 pro games in which he played.

Donnalley is Director of the March Forth with Hope Foundation, an organization that helps families battling cancer and other life-threatening diseases. He is also on the National Advisory Board for Make-A-Wish and is actively involved in the Charlotte Make-A-Wish chapter. He and wife, Erica, have three children and live in Charlotte.

EBENEZER EKUBAN ■ 6' 4" 275 ■ *Defensive End*

COLLEGE: 1996–99 **NFL:** 1999–2008

Ebenezer Ekuban was an honor student who played both sides of the ball in high school. He came to Carolina with thoughts of playing tight end. Turns out he was everything you would want in a defensive end: strong, fast, smart, a beast on the field, but a great guy off the field. It took a couple years for everyone to understand that Ekuban's future was on the defensive side of the ball. He moved to defensive end his junior year with the Heels; by the end of the season, it was clear that the dude could flat-out play some defense. Finally a full-time starter as a senior, he recorded 96 tackles and seven sacks. Ekuban won UNC's Patterson Award in 1999, which is the school's top athletic honor.

His draft stock soared over the course of his senior year, and his performance at the NFL combine solidified him as a first-round choice. The Dallas Cowboys chose Ekuban as the 20th overall pick in the 1999 NFL Draft. In his third year, he had finally won a starting position, but a herniated disc in the first game caused him to miss the rest of the season. He bounced back with two nice years as a starter with Dallas but never quite fulfilled his role as a speed rusher as hoped. He signed with the Cleveland Browns as a free agent and had the most sacks (eight) of his NFL season in 2004. In 2005, he was traded to the Denver Broncos, where he finished his career as the primary starter there for three seasons. In 2010, Ekuban interned in player development at UNC and followed that with an internship with the NFL league office. That led to rejoining the Denver Broncos, this time working in player development.

DERRICK FENNER ■ 5' 11" 240 ■ *Running Back*

COLLEGE: 1985–86 (at UNC) **NFL:** 1989–97

If you're reading this straight through, you will remember the name Derrick Fenner mentioned along with Torin Dorn, who was the running back at UNC after Fenner.

GREG ELLIS ■ 6' 6" 275 ■ *Defensive End*

COLLEGE: 1994–97 **NFL:** 1998–2009

GREG ELLIS. Greg Ellis was a great defensive end for the Tar Heels who went on to record 84 sacks in his NFL career.

Like Ebenezer Ekuban, Greg Ellis is yet another in a long line of great defensive ends to play for the Tar Heels. Born in Wendell, North Carolina, and starring in football and basketball for East Wake High School, Ellis stayed close to home for his stellar collegiate career. By the end of his sophomore season in Chapel Hill, Ellis was already racking up accolades. When he graduated with a communications degree, he stood as UNC's all-time sack leader.

Selected in the first round of the 1997 NFL Draft by the Dallas Cowboys, Ellis became a mainstay during more than a decade on Dallas teams. An injury in 2006 could have ended his career, but his grit and determination had him back on the field in 2007 when he was named NFL Comeback Player of the Year, in a season in which he totaled 12.5 sacks (his career best) in just 13 games. That was also the best season Dallas had during Ellis's time there, as the Cowboys finished 13-3. He ended his career with one season with the Oakland Raiders, after which he was released and retired. For his career, though, Ellis finished with 84 sacks, 22 forced fumbles, 11 fumbles recovered, and four interceptions.

Ellis is the founder and CEO of Church Now Network, which strives to connect Christians and spread the word of God by providing affordable media for television and Internet to connect ministries to the world. He's married to his high school sweetheart, and they have three children.

The story of Derrick Fenner and the Tar Heels is complex. He came to Carolina from the Washington, D.C., area as a heralded running back and set an ACC single-game rushing record as a UNC sophomore when he rushed for 329 yards against Virginia. He finished that season, 1986, with 1,250 rushing yards and a 6.3 yards-per-carry average. Then he spent time in jail when he was charged with first-degree murder in a drug-related homicide. That charge was eventually dropped, but then he found himself in trouble for cocaine possession; in a separate incident, he was shot outside a nightclub. He and UNC parted ways, and he ended up at Gardner-Webb but didn't play football there. Still he had the talent to attract NFL scouts. The Seattle Seahawks took a chance on Fenner in the 10th round of the 1989 NFL Draft.

He had been out of the game for a couple years, and his start was slow with the Seahawks. Like his second year at UNC, though, Fenner had a great second year with Seattle: 859 yards and 14 touchdowns on the ground, with another 143 yards and a touchdown receiving. He never matched those numbers in another NFL season, though. Fenner played one more year with Seattle, three in Cincinnati, and another three in Oakland. He remains close to the game, though, as a trainer with Grassroots Youth Football.

WILLIAM FULLER ■ 6' 3" 275 ■ *Defensive End*

COLLEGE: 1980–83 **USFL:** 1984–85 **NFL:** 1986-98

Yes, another of the great Carolina defensive ends, William Henry Fuller, Jr., was a multisport athlete at Indian River High School in Chesapeake, Virginia. He attended UNC, where accolades and impressive play were the norm. As a senior, he had 81 tackles, a team-leading five sacks, and 22 tackles for a loss. He is still among the school leaders for sacks and tackles for a loss.

He was drafted by the NFL and the United States Football League, choosing to play initially for the Philadelphia Stars. Fuller helped lead the Stars to two consecutive championships in 1984-85 before the league disbanded. He was then acquired by the Houston Oilers, though he had a bit of a slow NFL start. After just one start in his first two years with Houston, Fuller suddenly became one of the league's top defensive linemen. He recorded at least 6.5 sacks per season over his next six years with the Oilers, peaking with 15 in 1991. In 1994, Fuller signed a free-agent contract with the Philadelphia Eagles and continued to soar. He netted 9.5 sacks his first season in Philly and followed that up with two seasons of 13 sacks each. He was named to the Pro Bowl in each of his three seasons with the Eagles (plus in his phenomenal 1991 season with Houston). He then signed a two-year contract with the San Diego Chargers, where his productivity greatly decreased, leading Fuller to retire at the end of the 1998 season. But he had made it to age 36 in pro ball, which is a rarity, and he is one of a handful of NFL players to record at least 100 career sacks. Fuller squeaked over that mark with 100.5.

Giving of his time and money, he hosts the William Fuller Celebrity Golf Tournament in Houston, Texas, for the Juvenile Diabetes Foundation and an annual golf tournament and auction event for the Chesapeake Care Free Clinic. He serves on several boards and is married with four children. He heads up the business-consulting firm Fuller Consulting Group based in Chesapeake, Virginia.

TIM GOAD ■ 6' 3" 280 ■ *Defensive Tackle*

COLLEGE: 1984–87 **NFL:** 1988–96

Not to be confused with the author and speaker of the same name, Carolina's Tim Goad was a member of some poor Patrick County High School football teams in

Stuart, Virginia. Playing on the offensive and defensive lines, Goad was one of the few bright spots on those teams—bright enough to attract major college attention. He went on to become a defensive star for the Tar Heels and even competed in track and field, where he was the ACC shot put champion in 1986.

Selected in the fourth round of the 1988 NFL Draft by the New England Patriots, Goad spent seven years anchoring the defense for the Pats. He was a model of consistency and stability in the middle of New England's defensive line, though this was prior to the run of success that New England has had in recent years. Quite frankly, the Patriots weren't very good for most of Goad's time there, though they finally made the playoffs in 1994, Goad's final year in New England. He then played the 1995 season with the Cleveland Browns, the franchise's final season in Cleveland before moving to Baltimore in 1996 to become the Baltimore Ravens. Goad then retired as a Raven after the 1996 season. For his career, he had played in 141 games, starting 123 of them, over nine years.

His sporting life after football has been quite colorful. Goad spent several years on the pit crew for various drivers in the Wood Brothers Racing team on the NASCAR circuit. (The Wood brothers shared the same hometown as Goad.) And most recently, Goad has tried his hand as a professional bass fisherman.

LARRY GRIFFIN ■ 6' 0" 197 ■ *Defensive Back*

COLLEGE: 1981–85 **NFL:** 1986

Larry Griffin was a star athlete in Chesapeake, Virginia, and then played as a receiver for UNC. As a freshman he averaged 19.1 yards per catch. But behind dominant runners, such as Kelvin Bryant, Ethan Horton, and Tyrone Anthony, the passing game in Chapel Hill wasn't particularly electric in those days. So while he caught only 39 passes for seven touchdowns as a Tar Heel, Griffin's talents were switched over to the defensive side of the ball as a defensive back and were sufficient for the Houston Oilers to choose him in the eighth round of the 1988 NFL Draft.

After very limited action in his first season with Houston, Griffin spent the rest of his career—seven more pro seasons—as a defensive back for the Pittsburgh Steelers. He finished his career with 13 interceptions. In 1992, he even ran an interception back for a touchdown, marking his only NFL TD.

DEE HARDISON ■ 6' 4" 274 ■ *Defensive Line*

COLLEGE: 1974–77 **NFL:** 1978–88

William David "Dee" Hardison was a high school running back who kept growing. After some time in the weight room, Hardison became a standout defensive lineman for the Tar Heels. Turns out, the move was good for Hardison and his Carolina teams, as he became a highly touted defensive player in Chapel Hill. By his junior season, he anchored a stout defense that helped UNC to a 9-3 record, including a

CHRIS HANBURGER ■ 6' 2" 218 ■ *Linebacker*

COLLEGE: 1961–64 **NFL:** 1965–78

CHRIS HANBURGER. Chris Hanburger is an NFL Hall of Famer who was selected to nine Pro Bowls while playing for the Washington Redskins.

All of these University of North Carolina football stars come with a story, but the one for Christian G. Hanburger, Jr., is special. His father was in the Army, so he was born in Fort Bragg, North Carolina. Hanburger was a running back in Hampton, Virginia, but he then spent two years in the Army immediately after high school. After that, he ended up in Chapel Hill and eventually became a center and linebacker for the Tar Heels. In his junior season, Hanburger helped lead a salty Carolina defense that allowed its opponents 10 or fewer points in seven games, including a 14–0 victory over Air Force in the Gator Bowl. Hanburger married his longtime girlfriend at the end of the regular season, and the Gator Bowl became their honeymoon.

At his NFL Hall of Fame induction, Hanburger's son, Chris Hanburger III, recounted his father's pro beginnings: "He came back from a weekend trip. I think he may have been visiting my mom. And when he got back to campus, some of his friends came up and said, 'Hey, you've been drafted by the Washington Redskins,' and he had no idea." Hanburger had indeed been selected in the 18th round of the 1965 NFL Draft by Washington, a team that had not had a winning season since 1955. He started just five games in his first season but then became a full-time starter and an NFL legend thereafter. One of his nicknames was "The Hangman," which he received due to his tendency to make clothesline tackles. Another nickname, "The General," he liked better. He was selected to the Pro Bowl nine times and was a First Team All-Pro four times. Twice he reeled in four interceptions in a season from his linebacker spot, and he scored five defensive touchdowns during his career. He played 187 games in his pro career, all of them with Washington. He was inducted into the Hall of Fame—finally—in 2011.

During NFL off seasons, he sold insurance and cars. He also was known to endorse a few products here and there. He opened Chris Hanburger Ford in the D.C. area. "I eventually sold it but stayed with Ford until I retired," he told a South Carolina newspaper a few years ago. "The hours were long, but working for Ford was very rewarding." He lived on 12 acres in Croon, Maryland, before retiring to Darlington, South Carolina, nearly a decade ago.

WILLIAM HENDERSON ■ 6' 1" 249 ■ *Fullback*

COLLEGE: 1991–94 **NFL:** 1995–2006

WILLIAM HENDERSON. Blocking for the likes of Natrone Means, Randy Jordan, Curtis Johnson, and Leon Johnson at UNC, William Henderson became one of the top fullbacks in the NFL from 1995 to 2006.

Remember when fullback was an integral position in just about every offense? William Henderson does, because he made a nice living as a fullback. The stout and strong Henderson ran for 750 yards as a fullback in Mack Brown's UNC offenses and scored eight rushing touchdowns at Chapel Hill. He also caught 14 passes as a Tar Heel, but he was best known as a punishing blocker for the likes of tailbacks Natrone Means, Randy Jordan, Curtis Johnson, and Leon Johnson.

He was then chosen by the Green Bay Packers in the third round of the 1995 NFL Draft. Henderson's arrival in Wisconsin came just after Green Bay's return to glory after many subpar seasons. Making the playoffs in 1993 and 1994 (after making the playoffs only once before that since 1973), the Packers made it to the NFC Championship in Henderson's first season, 1995. In his second year, the Packers won Super Bowl XXXII over the New England Patriots. Many successful seasons followed but no more Super Bowl wins. (The Packers made it to the Super Bowl in Henderson's third season but were beaten by the Denver Broncos.)

For his career, Henderson got a lot of time at fullback and on special teams. He only had 426 yards and five touchdowns running the ball but became known as an outstanding receiver out of the backfield. He reeled in 320 catches for 2,409 yards and 14 touchdowns over his career, being named to the Pro Bowl in 2004. "I came in with the desire to make enough money to go to grad school," Henderson told **foxsportswisconsin.com** a few years after his retirement. "I just wanted to keep my student loans down and sustain myself. I had no idea I'd spend 12 years with the most storied franchise in sports. I just happened to find a niche, and the Packers believed in me, and we worked well together."

Henderson has been active with as many as 150 charities throughout the state of Wisconsin and recently has been running four locations of sweetFrog Premium Frozen Yogurt. He's married and has two children.

DEE HARDISON *continued from page 101*

Peach Bowl loss to Kentucky. The team finished with an 8-3-1 record during Hardison's senior year, which included a tough loss to Nebraska in the Liberty Bowl.

He was selected in the second round of the 1978 NFL Draft by the Buffalo Bills. He started 15 games in his rookie season but never again got that many starts in his career. He was traded to the New York Giants for the 1981 season. He played five seasons for the Giants before finishing his career with two seasons for the San Diego Chargers and a season with the Kansas City Chiefs. After his playing days, he went into sales back in Fayetteville, North Carolina.

DWIGHT HOLLIER ■ 6' 2" 246 ■ *Linebacker*

COLLEGE: 1988–91 **NFL:** 1992–99

"Dwight Hollier is the perfect example of what a student-athlete should be," North Carolina coach Mack Brown said at the end of Hollier's UNC playing days, as part of an announcement that Hollier had won the school's Patterson Medal. "He's worked to be a success on the field and in the classroom and has succeeded at both." The Patterson Medal is awarded to the North Carolina senior who has demonstrated general excellence in athletics. Totaling 502 tackles in his time at UNC, Hollier was a four-year starter at linebacker who served as the Tar Heels' captain in 1990 and '91. He was a double major in speech communications and psychology and made the ACC's All-Academic team his final three years.

Hollier was chosen in the fourth round of the 1992 NFL Draft by the Miami Dolphins, where he played for eight seasons. In his second year, he recorded 94 tackles. By 1998, his productivity with the Dolphins had dropped precipitously, so he joined the Indianapolis Colts for the 2000 season. The change of scenery seemed to be just what he needed, as he had a sterling season with the Colts. Nevertheless, Hollier decided to retire after nine NFL seasons.

After pro football, Hollier became a licensed professional counselor and now is back with the NFL, based in Charlotte, as the director of transition and clinical services.

ETHAN HORTON ■ 6' 4" 235 ■ *Running Back / Tight End*

COLLEGE: 1981–84 **NFL:** 1985–8, 89–94

UNC has been blessed with a ton of great running backs over the years. Ethan Horton is yet another of those. Horton saw limited playing time in his first two seasons in Chapel Hill before rushing for more than 1,000 yards in his two final seasons—leading the ACC in rushing yards both those years. As a junior, he finished with eight rushing touchdowns, which led the ACC in 1983. As a senior, he was named ACC Player of the Year. In his four years at UNC, he ran for 3,104 yards and 22 TDs. He also added 506 yards receiving and another five TDs.

VONNIE HOLLIDAY ■ 6' 5" 290 ■ *Defensive Line*

COLLEGE: 1994-97 **NFL:** 1998–12

VONNIE HOLLIDAY. Vonnie Holliday enjoyed a long NFL career in which he recorded 62.5 sacks as a defensive lineman.

A native of Camden, South Carolina, Dimetry Giovonni Holliday decided early on he'd simply go by the name of Vonnie. He played football, basketball, and baseball for Camden High School. He then accepted a football scholarship to the University of North Carolina, where he appeared in 46 games, starting in 28, in four years. As co-captain his senior year, Holliday recorded 64 tackles and five sacks. He graduated from UNC with a bachelor's degree in communications.

He was then chosen in the first round of the 1998 NFL Draft by the Green Bay Packers, where he joined former Tar Heel (and just profiled) William Henderson. Unlike Henderson, who spent his entire career as a Packer, Holliday traveled around the NFL a bit. He immediately made an impact in Green Bay, recording 52 tackles, eight sacks, and two fumble recoveries as a rookie. He then joined the Kansas City Chiefs in 2003 as a free agent, where he played two seasons, the last riddled with injuries. He then spent four productive years with the Miami Dolphins before his career began to wind down. He spent 2009 in Denver, 2010 in Washington, and 2011–12 in Arizona before finally hanging up his cleats for good. He had played in 214 NFL games, starting 147. He recorded 62.5 sacks and 12 fumble recoveries in his career. He even managed a couple of interceptions.

Holliday supports the Boys and Girls Club and is currently working with the Boys and Girls Club of Midlands (South Carolina) to bring Boys and Girls Club programming to his hometown of Camden. He created The Vonnie Holliday Foundation in 2001, a 501(c)(3) organization with the purpose of improving the quality of life of citizens in underserved communities by donating time and monetary resources. He's married and has two children.

For his pro career, Horton was chosen in the first round of the 1985 NFL Draft by the Kansas City Chiefs as a running back, but he's most known as an Oakland Raiders tight end. Horton ran 48 times and scored three TDs as a rookie, but he was cut after just one season. Out of the league for a year, he got a chance with the Raiders but was cut again after a single season. He was out of the league for another year before he returned to the Raiders, but this time he was a tight end. He struggled to learn

KEN HUFF ■ 6' 4" 260 ■ *Guard*

COLLEGE: 1971–74 **NFL:** 1975–85

KEN HUFF. Ken Huff became a dominant offensive guard for the Baltimore Colts and Washington Redskins.

Ken Huff was a highly acclaimed fullback and defensive tackle at Coronado High School near San Diego, California. He then spent a postgraduate year at Deerfield Academy in Massachusetts, where he was also an excellent swimmer. He had ambitions of following his father's path into the Navy but discovered that his eyesight would keep him from ever being a fighter pilot. So he accepted a scholarship to play football in Chapel Hill. Coach Bill Dooley immediately turned him in to an offensive guard, a move that turned out pretty well. He was a dominant lineman during some prolific years for the Carolina offense.

Huff was a first-round draft choice for the Baltimore Colts in 1975. It took him a couple of years to break into the starting lineup, but then he became a dominant lineman for the Colts just as he had been for the Tar Heels. In 1983, he was traded to the Washington Redskins, where he was a member of the "Hogs" offensive line. In his first season in Washington, the team earned a 14-2 regular-season record and an appearance in the Super Bowl, though the D.C. football club ran into a buzzsaw called the Los Angeles Raiders and lost the game 38–9. But hey, the national anthem was sung by Barry Manilow, so at least Huff has that memory.

Huff played two more seasons with Washington before retiring after the 1985 season. He then founded Ken Huff Builders in Chapel Hill, a custom homebuilding and renovations company. "Building a home is a lot like building a championship football team," Huff says. "It takes the right players to put together a winning combination." He was a 2008 inductee of the North Carolina Sports Hall of Fame.

ETHAN HORTON *continued from page 105*

the new position in 1989; by 1990, Horton was the regular starter at tight end and in 1991 recorded 53 catches and five TDs in a Pro Bowl season. In 1994, Horton left the Raiders to play a season with the Washington Redskins before he retired.

Horton has had a few stints in broadcasting and is marketing director for Charlotte-based company The Best of Knowledge. He's a founder in the Charlotte area's Youth Development Football League and participates in a number of celebrity golf outings to raise funds for United Way affiliates and other community-based organizations. Horton and his wife, Lawanda, live in the Charlotte area with their two sons, Jay and Kyle.

LEON JOHNSON ■ 6' 0" 220 ■ *Running Back, Punt / Kick Returner*

COLLEGE: 1993–96 **NFL:** 1997–2003

Carolina native Leon Johnson burst into the hearts and minds of UNC football fans as a redshirt freshman in 1993. In the season debut, an upset over Southern Cal, he rushed for 94 yards on 10 carries and caught four passes for 35 yards. He racked up 1,012 yards and a league-leading 14 touchdowns rushing, while adding another 233 yards and two touchdowns receiving. Leon will be forever linked with another Johnson of no relation, Curtis. Johnson and Johnson shared carries in the Carolina backfield for much of their careers, as Curtis was a sophomore when Leon was a freshman. Leon never had another 1,000-yard rushing season in Chapel Hill and never matched that number of rushing touchdowns. He remained a top-notch back, though, and finished his career with 3,693 yards and 43 TDs on the ground. His pass-catching ability was one of his great attributes. Johnson finished with 1,288 yards and four TDs receiving, proving to be one of Carolina's all-time great all-around backs.

Johnson was a fourth-round draft choice by the New York Jets, for whom he had a nice rookie season as a return man (he led the NFL in punt return yards) but only modest results as a running back. Never matching his rookie-year stats as a return guy, and failing to become a major contributor at running back, Johnson was cut by the Jets in 2000. He then played for the Chicago Bears in 2001–02. Still used primarily on special teams, Johnson did manage 329 yards rushing, his career best, in 2001. He finished his NFL career in the 2003 season as a member of the San Diego Chargers, playing almost exclusively on special teams.

SAMMY JOHNSON ■ 6' 0" 223 ■ *Running Back*

COLLEGE: 1970–73 **NFL:** 1974–79

Carolina has had some great backs with the name Johnson, and Sammy was rocking the UNC backfield back in the early 1970s. But he wasn't always a running back. Johnson was an all-around athlete at High Point Central, playing offense and defense in football. He was recruited to UNC as a quarterback but played two seasons at linebacker before settling in as a running back. He was a solid contributor as a junior running back and then matured into a great runner as a senior. He carried the ball 183 times that year for 1,006 yards and seven touchdowns. He finished second in the ACC in plays from scrimmage, rushing attempts, rushing yards, and yards from scrimmage.

Johnson was drafted in the fourth round by the San Francisco 49ers. He found a home on special teams and got some time as a running back, mostly on third downs.

After two and a half seasons with the 49ers, he was dealt to the Minnesota Vikings, where he played another two and a half seasons before finishing his career with a season in Green Bay. He managed nine TDs rushing in his six NFL seasons.

In the fall of 1982, Sportscenter Fitness and Athletic Club was established in Concord, North Carolina, by Dr. William Burchfield, a local eye surgeon, and partners Dr. Frank Sellers, a local orthopedic surgeon, and the recently retired Sammy Johnson. The club has become a local institution. Johnson and the two other original owners sold the business a few years ago to Burchfield's children. Johnson, though, has two other Sportscenter locations, one in High Point and one in Greensboro.

RANDY JORDAN ■ 5' 10" 207 ■ *Running Back*

COLLEGE: 1989–92 **NFL:** 1993, 1995–2002

Hailing from Manson, North Carolina, Randy Jordan was sometimes known as "the other running back" during his Carolina days, most of which overlapped with Natrone Means, who had two 1,000-yard rushing seasons in Chapel Hill. But Jordan was a stellar back in his own right. His best season for the Tar Heels came in 1991 when he rushed for 618 yards and seven TDs (third-most rushing TDs in the ACC). That year, he also caught 11 passes for 160 yards and two more touchdowns. Jordan and Means formed a formidable tandem and Jordan went on to sign with the Los Angeles Raiders out of college.

He got only 12 carries in his rookie season and found himself out of the NFL in 1994. But Jordan refused to give up on his dream of playing in the League. In 1995, he joined the expansion Jacksonville Jaguars, where he mostly saw time on special teams for three seasons. In 1998, he landed back with the Raiders, who had moved back to Oakland. He continued to see time on special teams but got a few chances as a running back in his five years with Oakland. In 2000, he carried the ball 46 times for 213 yards and three touchdowns and added 27 catches for 299 yards and another score. It was easily his best year as a pro. He was the special teams captain for the 2002 Raider squad that reached Super Bowl XXXVII. Jordan was released after that season but spent 2003 as an assistant coach for the team.

That marked the beginning of his second pro football career, this time as a coach. Jordan coached running backs at Nebraska (2004–07) and at Texas A&M (2008–11) before returning to his alma mater to coach Carolina running backs. In 2013, he added special teams to his coaching responsibilities. He and his wife have three children.

BILL KOMAN ■ 6' 2" 229 ■ *Linebacker*

COLLEGE: 1952–55 **NFL:** 1956–67

When he was nine, William John Koman had a terrible bicycle accident—so bad, in fact, that doctors discussed amputating his leg. Fortunately, the leg was saved and

FREDDIE JONES ■ 6' 4" 265 ■ *Tight End*

COLLEGE: 1993–96 **NFL:** 1997–2004

The football career of Freddie Jones was a gradual process. In his first two years in Chapel Hill, Jones caught just 13 passes total. In his junior year alone, he had 16. He doubled that number his senior year, establishing himself as a top college tight end.

Chosen in the second round by the San Diego Chargers, Jones proved himself as one of the better tight ends in the NFL. He had at least 500 receiving yards and two TDs per season in each of his first four years. His production slipped a bit in his fifth year, and he signed with the Arizona Cardinals for the 2002 season. He had three solid years as the starting tight end with the Cardinals before signing with the Carolina Panthers after the 2004 season. He decided to retire, though, before the start of the 2005 season, having never played for the Panthers. He finished his career with 4,232 receiving yards and 22 TDs. Since 2010, Jones has been an assistant football coach for the Shelton School in Dallas, Texas.

FREDDIE JONES. Freddie Jones had a good run as one of the better NFL tight ends from 1997 through 2004.

little Bill Koman became a football star, first for Hopewell High School in Beaver County, Pennsylvania, then for the University of North Carolina Tar Heels. By the time he was finished in Chapel Hill, he was considered by most to be the best linebacker in UNC history and among the best in ACC history. The Tar Heels have had a lot of great linebackers since then, but Koman is still seen as one of the best, alongside such names as Lawrence Taylor, Chris Hanburger, Buddy Curry, and John Bunting.

Koman was drafted by Baltimore and played his rookie season with the Colts, followed by two seasons with the Philadelphia Eagles. He then settled in with the Cardinals. He joined the team in 1959, the club's final season in Chicago, and remained with the Cardinals in St. Louis until his retirement in 1967. He was named to Pro Bowl teams in 1962 and '64. He remained a fixture in St. Louis after his retirement with numerous business interests. His gift of $1 million to UNC provided for Koman Way, the walkway located between Fetzer Hall and the Stallings-Evans Sports Medicine Center that connects South Road to Stadium Drive.

CHARLIE JUSTICE ■ 5' 10" 176 ■ *Halfback*

COLLEGE: 1946–49 **NFL:** 1950, 1952–54

CHARLIE JUSTICE. Charlie "Choo Choo" Justice remains one of Carolina's most beloved players, though his pro career was cut short due to injuries.

It's tough to claim that any UNC player has topped Lawrence Taylor's performance as a pro. But it is equally tough to claim that any UNC player has bested the status of Asheville's Charlie "Choo Choo" Justice as a beloved player during his years in Chapel Hill. I mean, old No. 22 does have a statue on campus—located by the west entrance of the Frank H. Kenan Football Center, near the Sonja Haynes Stone Center. Plus, how many UNC players have a song written about them? Justice does: "All the Way, Choo Choo," by Benny Goodman.

His legendary status started as a schoolboy for Lee H. Edwards High School (now Asheville High), where he was part of two undefeated regular seasons and averaged 25 yards per carry as a senior. The 94–0 win over Hickory that year stands as the school's largest margin of victory. For the season, the team outscored opponents 441–6. But the United States was just entering World War II, so Justice went into the Navy after high school and earned his nickname while playing football at the Bainbridge Naval Center. An officer sitting in the stands

AMOS LAWRENCE ■ 5' 11" 181 ■ *Running Back*

COLLEGE: 1977–80 **NFL:** 1981–82

In a book about going pro, Amos Lawrence's accomplishments get lost among many more successful Tar Heels. In terms of his collegiate days at UNC, however, it would be tough to argue that there was ever a better Carolina running back. He certainly passed the eye test as an amazing athlete, and his stats back it up. He went to Chapel Hill as a highly acclaimed running back from Lake Taylor High School in Norfolk, Virginia, and burst onto the scene as a freshman rushing for 1,211 yards and 6 TDs with an average of 6.3 yards per carry. (He even threw four passes, completing one for a TD.) He never topped that season in terms of total yards on the ground or average per carry, but he did follow it with three more great seasons. He's the only UNC player to have four 1,000-yard rushing seasons, finishing his Carolina career with 4,391 yards and 28 touchdowns rushing. (We should add that in 1980, Lawrence said, "Look at that guy run. He looks like a runaway train. We ought to call him 'Choo Choo.'" It was picked up and used in the newspaper, and the name stuck.

"It was the perfect time," Justice told the *Charlotte Observer* in 2000 about his days running the single wing at UNC from 1946 to 1949. "Carolina needed a star. Everyone had been through a war. Confined. There had been gas rations. The war was over, and people wanted to turn it loose a little." And a star he was. Justice was exciting, talented, and a winner. He won the Maxwell Award as national player of the year in 1948 and finished second in Heisman voting in 1948 and '49. Meanwhile, the Tar Heels went 39-9-2 and played in the Cotton Bowl and two Sugar Bowls.

But this book is about going pro, which Justice did. For a college legend, it was somewhat surprising that Justice wasn't picked until the 16th round of the 1950 NFL Draft. His age may have played a part. He was 26 by the time his pro career got underway. Maybe the pro scouts knew he would be susceptible to injuries. He was. He played for the Washington Redskins, but his career was riddled with injuries. His best season came in 1953, when he ran for 616 yards and had another 434 yards receiving. He was also a punt and kick returner and handled punting duties for the Redskins.

Justice was in the insurance business for many years until he retired. He died in 2003 at the age of 79. The *New York Times* said this in his obituary: "Zigzagging through defenders in his No. 22 powder-blue jersey, Justice thrilled crowds during the spectator-sports boom after World War II. He ran, he passed and he punted superbly." Injuries diminished his pro career, but he remains a Carolina legend.

shared carries with Kelvin Bryant, who was in the first of three 1,000-yard rushing seasons. Carolina also finished 11-1 that year, including a win over Texas in the Bluebonnet Bowl.) Lawrence was never really known as much of a receiver but did add 35 catches, including six touchdowns, to his UNC totals.

Known as "Famous" Amos for his stunning collegiate feats, you would think he was a surefire early draft pick. Apparently, NFL management knew something. Lawrence was finally drafted in the fourth round by the San Diego Chargers, and problems began immediately. He couldn't work out a contract and was traded to the San Francisco 49ers. He only got 13 carries with the 49ers as a rookie but did return 17 kickoffs, one for a touchdown. It was the only TD for Lawrence as a pro. The following year his production on the field was even less, but the 49ers did make it to the Super Bowl. Lawrence fumbled away the opening kickoff. He was cut in training camp the next summer. He sat out the 1983 season and gave the USFL a try, but that didn't pan out either. Playing in Canada was an option, but by then Lawrence had lost the passion. He was ready to hang up the cleats.

DEEMS MAY ■ 6' 4" 263 ■ *Tight End*

COLLEGE: 1988–91 **NFL:** 1992–99

Deems May saw limited action playing backup quarterback as a freshman, completing 28 of 68 passes for 270 yards. He also threw five interceptions and zero touchdowns. And thus he was a tight end thereafter. He was still learning the position through college, making just two catches as a sophomore, five as a junior, and then 12 as a senior. His potential was strong enough for the San Diego Chargers to take a chance on May as a seventh-round draft pick.

May never got a lot of action as a tight end but did see the field quite a bit on special teams. His final season with San Diego, 1996, May started 12 games and had 19 catches, more starts and more catches than his other seven NFL careers combined. He finished with three years playing for the Seattle Seahawks, again mostly on special teams and as a backup tight end. May remains close to the UNC program, having done some radio work for UNC broadcasts. He is a partner at the financial firm of Solamere Advisors. He also oversees the Deems May Foundation, which benefits charities around his hometown of Lexington, North Carolina. He lives with his wife and two children in Charlotte.

KEITH NEWMAN ■ 6' 2" 248 ■ *Linebacker*

COLLEGE: 1995–98 **NFL:** 1999–2006

A high school standout in Tampa, Florida, Newman played offense and defense for Thomas Jefferson High School but was recruited to Carolina as a linebacker. He was a vital cog on some good teams. In his junior year, Mack Brown's final season as Carolina coach, Newman's outstanding play helped lead the Tar Heels to an 11-1 record, including a Gator Bowl blowout at Virginia Tech. Newman was selected in the fourth round of the 1999 NFL Draft by the Buffalo Bills. Here's what a publication that covers the Bills said about the young UNC prospect: "He has a lot of potential but is an inconsistent player. He has good speed and can get to the QB on blitzes but is not considered to be a good pass defender. . . . If he returns to his junior year form he could be a steal, if not, he could be out of Buffalo in a hurry or on the practice squad."

Apparently, Newman was at least close to his junior year form, as he spent four seasons with the Bills. He saw little playing time as a junior but then totaled eight sacks in his second season. His production dropped in his fourth year, and he found himself playing the 2003 season as an Atlanta Falcon. One season there was followed by two in Minnesota and then a final season with the Miami Dolphins. Overall, Newman saw 102 NFL games, starting 77 of those. Back in the Tampa area, Newman is now defensive coordinator for Strawberry Crest High School in Dover.

DON McCAULEY ■ 6' 1" 211 ■ *Running Back*

COLLEGE: 1968–70 **NFL:** 1971–82

DON MCCAULEY. Don McCauley is sometimes forgotten among the great running backs at UNC, but he was a star for Carolina and had a very solid NFL career with the Baltimore Colts.

Coach Bill Dooley and his staff gave Don McCauley the number 23 when he came to Chapel Hill, thinking he was the next closest thing to Charlie "Choo Choo" Justice, who wore the number 22. In an era when freshmen were ineligible to play football, Don McCauley made up for lost time rather quickly. He rushed for 360 yards and two TDs as a sophomore and showed great skill as a receiver, too, catching 23 passes and hauling in another TD. McCauley was poised to become another top-notch back for the Tar Heels. He went on to rush for 1,092 yards and eight TDs as a junior and then gained an amazing 1,720 yards and 19 TDs (both still a Carolina single-season record) as a senior, leading the ACC in rushing attempts, rushing yards, rushing yards per attempt, and rushing touchdowns. As a senior, he finished the season on fire, running for 183 yards vs. South Carolina, 184 vs. Clemson, and then 279 (and five TDs) against archrival Duke. He finished his Carolina career with 35 total touchdowns in just three years. And for good measure, he also returned punts and kicks and punted. He was twice ACC Player of the Year.

Coming off such a phenomenal senior year, McCauley was chosen in the first round of the 1971 NFL Draft by the Baltimore Colts, a year after they won the Super Bowl, and he remained a Colt his entire career. The Colts made the playoffs four of McCauley's first seven years, as he earned the reputation of being a great third-down back. He bounced back and forth between tailback and fullback and also played on special teams. He started most games in 1972–73 but started only a handful of games for the rest of his career. McCauley and the Colts suffered through a 2-14 season in 1981, after which he decided to call it quits. He finished his career with 59 total touchdowns: 40 rushing, 17 receiving, one passing, and one kickoff return.

After his playing days were over, he went back to UNC, where he is now the major gifts director for the Rams Club after serving in that same capacity for the Kenan-Flagler School of Business. He and his wife live in Hillsborough.

NATRONE MEANS ■ 5' 10" 245 ■ *Running Back*

COLLEGE: 1990–92 **NFL:** 1993–2000

NATRONE MEANS. Known as another great UNC running back, Natrone Means rushed for more than 5,000 yards in his NFL career.

Yep, another great running back. Natrone Means was powerful and fast. He could run over you or run past you, and he did both as a freshman at UNC. He immediately became a fan favorite with 849 rushing yards and 10 TDs as a freshman to go with 24 catches and another touchdown receiving. It was clear, as ESPN's Chris Berman would often say later, that "Natrone Means Business." He backed up his stellar freshman campaign with two 1,000-yard rushing seasons and 24 more rushing touchdowns. Perhaps the most remarkable feat, though, was his consistency in carrying the ball. Means averaged 5.1 yards per carry in each of his three seasons in Chapel Hill before opting to take his skills to the NFL.

Selected in the second round of the 1993 NFL draft by the San Diego Chargers, Means managed 645 yards and eight touchdowns as a rookie, despite not starting. He earned the starting job in his second season and had the best year of his pro career: 1,350 yards and 12 TDs, earning a trip to the Pro Bowl. He also led the Chargers to the Super Bowl that year. And while San Diego lost 49–26 to the San Francisco 49ers, the 22-year-old Means did score a touchdown. The next year, though, Means was a holdout in training camp, wanting a new contract and joining the team just before the season began. Between the holdout and injuries, Means' production drastically dipped in 1995, and he was waived by the Chargers at the end of the season. He never quite regained his mojo. He spent two seasons with the Jacksonville Jaguars and then ended up with the Chargers for two more seasons. He finally ended his career after playing a mere one game for the Carolina Panthers in 2000. He did tally 5,215 rushing yards for his career, though, and scored 45 rushing touchdowns.

Means has remained close to football. He has worked with Pop Warner leagues and various football camps, participated in the NFL Minority Coaches Program, worked a season as a high school referee, and served as an assistant coach at Livingstone College and West Charlotte High. He is now an assistant football coach at Hopewell High School near Charlotte.

HAKEEM NICKS ■ 6' 0" 210 ■ *Wide Receiver*

COLLEGE: 2006–08 **NFL:** 2009–13

Born in Charlotte, Nicks was considered one of the top players in North Carolina in his senior season at Independence High School. He was there during an incredible 109-game winning streak, which means he never lost a game in high school. In his freshman season, Nicks led the team in receptions (39) and receiving yards (660)—both Carolina records for freshmen. While his best game that year came in a loss to Notre Dame (six catches, 171 yards, two TDs), many fans remember his vital role in the 45–44 victory over Duke that year, which included an 83-yard TD catch in the first quarter. After a remarkable freshman season, Nicks just continued to get better: nearly 1,000 yards receiving as a sophomore and then 1,222 yards and 12 TDs as a junior. He even carried the ball five times for 39 yards and a TD as a junior. He may be best remembered for his final game at Carolina. In the Meineke Car Care Bowl, he hauled in eight catches for 217 yards and three TDs. One of those catches was an amazing behind-the-back grab that was named by ESPN the No. 1 play of the bowl season. The post-season accolades poured in, and Nicks decided to go pro, becoming the first Tar Heel since Julius Peppers to forgo his senior season for the NFL.

Selected by the New York Giants in the first round of the 2009 NFL Draft, Nicks started in six games as a rookie and had a very productive season: 47 catches, 790 yards, six TDs. In his second season, he recorded his most touchdowns as a pro (11), and in his third season he recorded his greatest number of yards (1,192). Perhaps it shouldn't be a surprise that the Giants won the Super Bowl in Nicks's third season, a 21–17 victory over the New England Patriots. Nicks was clutch in the game, grabbing 10 passes from Eli Manning for 109 yards. But before that, Nicks and Manning were the talk of the NFL after a Hail Mary pass at the end of the first half of the Giants' playoff game against the Green Bay Packers.

Unfortunately, this all-time great Carolina receiver comes with an asterisk. In 2012, it was discovered that Nicks had been guilty of academic fraud in his junior season. He was one of the players connected with Jennifer Wiley, a former athletic department tutor who had assisted players beyond her role. Nicks was also one of five players found to funnel more than $27,000 in cash and other "impermissible assistance" to former teammates with eligibility remaining in 2009–10.

ROBERT PRATT ■ 6' 3" 255 ■ *Guard*

COLLEGE: 1971–74 **NFL:** 1974–85

Robert Pratt was a star fullback and defensive end at St. Christopher's School in Richmond, Virginia. He was quickly moved to guard at UNC. "It was one of the toughest days I've had when I traded that fullback's helmet with two facebars for a lineman's

WILLIE PARKER ■ 5' 10" 209 ■ *Running Back*

COLLEGE: 2000–03 **NFL:** 2004–09

Willie Parker attended UNC out of Clinton High School in Clinton, North Carolina, where he was a star player, rushing for 1,801 yards and 18 TDs as a senior. He averaged an amazing 12.3 yards per carry. At Carolina, though, he never really rose to the level of star. He played well, but he didn't lead the team in rushing in any of his four seasons. He had a few great games. As a freshman, he carried the ball 21 times for 158 yards against Maryland. He rushed for 131 yards on 19 carries, including one touchdown, against Auburn in the Peach Bowl his sophomore year. He definitely had his moments, but the consistency just wasn't there, plus his senior year was his worst: only 181 rushing yards.

WILLIE PARKER. Willie Parker may be best known for his 75-yard TD run for the Pittsburgh Steelers to help seal a victory in Super Bowl XL.

So when the NFL Draft came along in 2004, Parker never got a call. He did sign as a free agent with the Pittsburgh Steelers, though. As a rookie, it was questionable whether Parker would make it as a pro. He played in just eight games, carrying the ball for 186 yards and no touchdowns. But then Parker had three glorious years. In 2005, Pittsburgh running

ROBERT PRATT *continued from page 115*

'cage' style helmet," Pratt said in a 2013 interview. "But it was the best move that ever happened for me." Intelligent, athletic, durable, Pratt was a dream of an offensive guard.

He helped lead the team to ACC championships in his sophomore and junior seasons; as a senior, he received numerous All-ACC and All-American honors while also receiving the UNC Educational Foundation Award. He received his business administration degree and became a third-round draft choice for the Baltimore Colts.

Pratt started in 105 consecutive games for the Colts from 1975 to 1981, helping the team win three straight AFC East Division titles (1975–77). In 1977, he even scooped up a fumble in a game against the New York Jets and then used his old fullback skills to run it 21 yards into the end zone for a touchdown. He was traded to the Seattle Seahawks in 1982, where he quickly made an impact as a player and team leader. The Seahawks made the playoffs in 1983–84. After the 1985 season, Pratt retired, having played in 170 NFL games, starting 151 of them.

backs Jerome Bettis and Duce Staley were injured to start the season. Parker was the running back by default. He exploded for 161 yards in his first start against the Tennessee Titans and finished the year with 1,202 yards on the ground. The Steelers made it to Super Bowl XL, where they beat the Seattle Seahawks 21–10. Parker's 75-yard run for a touchdown in the third quarter gave Pittsburgh all the cushion it needed to take the win.

In 2006, Parker had a dream season: 1,494 yards and 13 TDs rushing, with another 222 yards and three TDs receiving. He ran for 213 yards against the New Orleans Saints and 223 yards, a Steelers single-game record, against the Cleveland Browns. In 2007, he was racking up yards again, leading the league in rushing, before a late-season broken leg finished his year. He was named to the Pro Bowl, though, in both 2006 and '07. He bounced back from the injury and started well in 2008 before a knee injury caused him to miss five games. Though his production was down, the Steelers once again made it to—and won—the Super Bowl. This time, however, Parker only managed 53 yards on 19 carries. In 2009, Parker had problems with turf toe. While he was missing games, Reshard Mendenhall was playing quite well and took the starting spot at running back. Parker's contract was not renewed after the season ended. He was signed by the Washington Redskins in 2010 but was cut before the season began, and thus his pro career came to a close.

Parker was an assistant coach at West Virginia Wesleyan College in 2012 before rejoining the Steelers in 2013 as a coaching intern during training camp. Parker is looking for opportunities to get back into coaching.

His father, Robert Pratt Sr., was a venture capitalist and taught his son the value of saving and investing. In the NFL off-season, Pratt worked in investment businesses in Richmond, Virginia. Pratt and a business partner own Mid-Atlantic Golf, which operates the Sycamore Creek Golf Course in Richmond.

JEFF REED ■ 5' 11" 226 ■ *Kicker*

COLLEGE: 2001–02 **NFL:** 2002–10

With a long field goal of 54 yards for East Mecklenburg High School in Charlotte, Jeff Reed walked on as a kicker at Carolina. He finally saw his first game action in his junior season, and he made it count. He was one of 20 finalists for the Lou Groza Award, which goes to the nation's top kicker, after he made 16 of 20 field goals and all 30 extra-point attempts. He led the ACC that year in field goals made, attempted, and percentage made. He was third in the ACC in points scored. As a senior, he made 12 of 16 field goal attempts and hit 36 of 36 extra-point tries. Against East

JULIUS PEPPERS ■ 6' 6" 283 ■ *Defensive End*

COLLEGE: 1998–2001 **NFL:** 2002–13

JULIUS PEPPERS. Julius Peppers has been one of the NFL's most dominant defensive ends since being drafted by the Carolina Panthers.

It would be tough to say any former Carolina football star has had a better pro career than Lawrence Taylor, but Julius Peppers isn't too far behind. Peppers is a true Carolina legend, even more so than Taylor. How's that, you ask? Here's how. First, while Taylor was from Virginia, Peppers was born in Wilson, North Carolina, and raised in nearby Bailey, which is just east of Raleigh. He was a schoolboy legend at Southern Nash Senior High School, where he starred in football (as a running back and defensive lineman), basketball, and track. In his senior season he was named Male Athlete of the Year by the North Carolina High School Athletic Association. So he was a home-state hero even before he stepped onto the campus at Chapel Hill. But once he did, he played football and basketball for UNC, capturing the hearts of Tar Heels everywhere.

In basketball, he was a walk-on after the football season was over. He played the 1999–2000 season, in which Carolina made it to the Final Four, and the 2000–01 season, in which the team finished 26-7, with Peppers scoring 21 points and grabbing 10 rebounds in an NCAA Tournament loss to Penn State. It seemed like he was really coming into his own as a star basketball player, but he decided to concentrate only on football after that season. In football, meanwhile, he got off to a bit of a slow start. He was redshirted as a true freshman, which was the 1998 season. It's still sort of amazing that Pepper was redshirted. He

JEFF REED *continued from page 117*

Carolina he made a career-best 49-yard field goal with just 2:48 remaining in a game; that field goal led to a 24–21 Tar Heel victory.

With a good collegiate showing as the kicker for two years, Reed signed a free agent contract with the Pittsburg Steelers in 2002 after Todd Peterson suffered an injury. Reed kicked so well that Peterson didn't get his job back and was released after the season. Reed became the regular kicker for the Steelers through 2009. In 2004, he had career bests in field goals made (28) and attempted (33). Reed had the privilege of being the Steelers' kicker in Super Bowl XL and Super Bowl XLIII, both of which Pittsburgh won. In 2010, Reed was cut by the Steelers during the season. A took advantage of sitting out the year, though, to get bigger, stronger, and faster, and to gain more overall practice experience. The result was quite grand.

In 1999, as a redshirt freshman, Peppers started in all 11 games and led the team in tackles for loss and sacks. A 10-tackle performance, which included four sacks, against Wake Forest convinced Carolina fans that they had a special player. As a sophomore, Peppers had 15 sacks, which was just one short of Lawrence Taylor's record of 16. And who can forget his fantastic over-the-head interception against Duke that year when Peppers then took the ball 27 yards for a touchdown. He also had two sacks in that game. As a junior, the opponents' offensive game plan was to not let Peppers beat them. He was double- and even triple-teamed but still finished the year with 63 tackles, including 19 tackles for loss and 9.5 sacks. He also intercepted three passes, which is amazing for a defensive lineman. Projected as a high draft choice, Peppers decided to forgo his senior season and enter the NFL Draft.

He was chosen as the second overall pick in 2002 by the Carolina Panthers, cementing his legendary status in his home state. He was a starter from the beginning and was named NFL Defensive Rookie of the Year by the Associated Press. He was named to five consecutive Pro Bowls (2004–09) while at Carolina, and his 81 sacks with the Panthers (2002–09) stand as a franchise record. Also a franchise record, and a career highlight, is the longest interception return in Panthers history: Peppers snagged a Denver Broncos pass in 2004 and went 97 yards for a touchdown. After the 2009 season, Peppers was the best defensive end in the league. And then he was an unrestricted free agent. Carolina fans had that sinking feeling that their longtime Tar Heel would finally leave the state. He did. In March 2010, the Chicago Bears gave Peppers a six-year deal worth more than $90 million. He has continued to excel in Chicago, making the Pro Bowl in each year there and having double-digit sack years in 2011–12. Peppers has proven to be a reliable, consistent, and durable player as a pro, and he continues to rack up accolades. When his career is finished, Peppers will be looked upon as one of the all-time greats at defensive end.

few weeks later, he signed with the 49ers, whose kicker Joe Nedney had been injured. That season was Reed's last as a pro. He signed with the Seahawks in training camp of 2011 but was cut before the season started.

Reed continued training with hopes of landing another kicking gig. He has also been a coach at kicking camps. He was known as an eccentric player, sometimes showing up with spiked or bleached hair, and he seemed to lead a fairly colorful lifestyle, being charged with a couple of misdemeanors during his playing days. But he wasn't just a wacky, eccentric kicker; he did a lot of charity work in the Pittsburgh area too. And who knows, perhaps we haven't seen the last of Jeff Reed.

JEFF SATURDAY ■ 6-2" 292 ■ *Center*

COLLEGE: 1994–97 **NFL:** 1999–2012

To call Jeff Saturday an overachiever might not be fair. Perhaps we'll just say he made the most of his opportunities. Although he was a standout player on offense and defense for Shamrock High School in Decatur, Georgia, he got few scholarship offers. His high school coach, though, had a friendship with UNC defensive coordinator Carl Torbush, which helped lead to an offer from Carolina. He was known as a model player. He was a leader who pushed those around him to excel. Meanwhile, he was excelling on the field and in the classroom. He was an All-ACC center in 1996–97 and an Academic All-ACC choice in 1997. He was also a team captain in 1996–97. Despite all that, he went undrafted after his senior year.

Saturday, though, wanted to play on Sundays. He was signed by the Baltimore Ravens as a free agent in 1998 but failed to make the team. He found himself in Raleigh working at an electrical supply store. He didn't give up, though. Nate Hobgood-Chittick, a teammate at UNC was a defensive

JEFF SATURDAY. Jeff Saturday was selected to six Pro Bowls and won a Super Bowl with the Indianapolis Colts. He is now an NFL analyst for ESPN.

GERALD SENSABAUGH ■ 6' 1" 210 ■ *Defensive Back*

COLLEGE: 2001–04 (only 2004 at UNC) **NFL:** 2005–12

A football, basketball, and track star for Dobyns-Bennett High School in Kingsport, Tennessee, Gerald Sensabaugh stuck close to home and attended East Tennessee State University. He made an immediate impact, as he started all 11 games his freshman season. He continued his fine play through his junior season, which was highlighted by three punt blocks against Georgia Southern, tying an NCAA record for the most in a game. But after his junior year, ETSU disbanded its football program, so Sensabaugh transferred to Carolina.

A solid year at UNC, plus an NFL combine in which he measured an amazing 46 inches in the vertical jump, caught the eye of the Jacksonville Jaguars, who selected Sensabaugh in the fifth round of the 2005 NFL Draft. He played four years with Jacksonville; his final year was his best. In 2008, he recorded four interceptions. He then signed a contract with the Dallas Cowboys and played four more seasons before retiring in

lineman with the Indianapolis Colts and helped grease the skids for a Saturday tryout. Saturday signed a free agent contract with the Colts in 1999. He made the team and made a couple starts at guard as a rookie. He was moved to center in the off-season and started all 16 games there in 2000, snapping the ball to Peyton Manning. The combo of Manning and Saturday played more snaps together than any other quarterback-center duo in NFL history—and they won a championship ring together, defeating the Chicago Bears 29–17 in Super Bowl XLI. In all, Saturday played 13 years with the Colts, starting 188 of 197 games played with the team. He finished his career with one season as a Green Bay Packer, retiring after 2012.

His accomplishments on the field are numerous: six Pro Bowls, twice a first-team All-Pro, and 19 playoff games. But perhaps it's his other awards that better indicate Saturday's greatness: Ed Block Courage Award, Walter Payton Man of the Year, Chaucies Place Kids Service Award, and the Sagamore of the Wabash Award (Indiana's Order of the Long Leaf Pine). Some would also suggest that he saved football in 2011: He was given credit as the key negotiator in a labor dispute between NFL players and owners. Since his retirement, Saturday has been a football analyst for ESPN.

2013. His best season with the Cowboys came in 2010 when he had five interceptions. He finished his career with 14 interceptions in eight years. Sensabaugh went back to ETSU in the fall of 2013 to finish his degree, with his eyes on getting into coaching.

RYAN SIMS ■ 6' 4" 315 ■ *Defensive Tackle*

COLLEGE: 1998–2001 **NFL:** 2002–10

Although a native of South Carolina, Ryan Sims said in a 2008 interview, "I always wanted to go to North Carolina. I was a big Lawrence Taylor and Michael Jordan fan. But, at first, it was looking like I'd go to Clemson. I never liked the (South Carolina) Gamecocks for whatever reason. At that time, North Carolina was No. 4 in the nation and everything was clicking. I had to go there." He did go there, and he played well. He was a three-year starter and an All-ACC selection as a senior. He finished his Carolina playing days as Defensive MVP in UNC's 16–10 win over Auburn in the Peach Bowl.

Sims began his pro career as a first-round draft choice by the Kansas City Chiefs, for whom he played his first five seasons. His best season there was his second, when he recorded three sacks, forced a fumble, recovered a fumble, and even had an interception. He was traded to Tampa Bay in 2007. He played three full seasons there and then suffered a knee injury in 2010 that put him on the inactive roster for the Buccaneers, who cut him three years later. He joined the Seattle Seahawks during the 2011 off-season but was released before the season.

BRIAN SIMMONS ■ 6' 3" 244 ■ *Linebacker*

COLLEGE: 1994–97 **NFL:** 1998–2007

Another all-around athlete, Brian Simmons lettered in football, basketball, baseball, and track while at New Bern High School in North Carolina. He stayed in state to play football for the Tar Heels. As a senior, he was a team captain and received numerous All-ACC and national honors.

Quiet, unassuming, and humble aren't necessarily traits of NFL players, but they describe Simmons quite well. He was chosen in the first round of the NFL Draft by the Cincinnati Bengals and played nine seasons there. In 2004, he was selected for the Good Guy Award by the Cincinnati chapter of the Pro Football Writers of America. He played his final year as a pro with the New Orleans Saints. He finished in the NFL with some nice numbers: 137 games played, 118 started, 11 interceptions, 24 sacks, and three touchdowns. Since 2009, Simmons has been a college scout for the Jacksonville Jaguars.

BRIAN SIMMONS. A dominant linebacker and team captain at Carolina, Brian Simmons went on to play nine NFL seasons with the Cincinnati Bengals and another for the New Orleans Saints.

THOMAS SMITH ■ 5' 11" 188 ■ *Defensive Back*

COLLEGE: 1989–92 **NFL:** 1993–2001

Thomas Smith arrived in Chapel Hill as a walk-on and left as a first-round NFL draft pick. He was known as a great cover guy who would have had a lot more interceptions if he could catch the ball better. Nonetheless, he was a first-round draft choice by the Buffalo Bills. He played sparingly as a rookie but did make it to the Super Bowl as the Bills lost to the Dallas Cowboys. He was then a starter in every game he played for the next six seasons for the Bills. He then played a season with the Chicago Bears, where he was also a starter in every game. He finished his nine-year NFL career with the Indianapolis Colts, finishing like he started by playing sparingly. He retired after the 2001 season.

He put his degree from UNC's Kenan-Flagler Business School to work after retiring from football. Smith is currently president of TR Transportation Network in Bel Air, Maryland.

LAWRENCE TAYLOR ■ 6' 3" 237 ■ *Linebacker*

COLLEGE: 1977–81 **NFL:** 1981–93

LAWRENCE TAYLOR. Lawrence Taylor seemed like Superman at times during his NFL tenure, with quarterbacks being his arch enemies. He totaled 132.5 sacks in his Hall of Fame career.

Most Tar Heels would say that the greatest NFL football player from the University of North Carolina is Hall of Fame linebacker Lawrence Taylor. He was one of the most intense and feared defensive players of his day and is considered to be among the top linebackers in NFL history. But before his days of NFL greatness, the native of Williamsburg, Virginia, was a terror to Tar Heel opponents. Taylor didn't start playing high school football until 11th grade, so he was lightly recruited, resulting in quite a coup for Carolina. He continued to improve on the football field, being named ACC Player of the Year for his senior year, in which he recorded 16 sacks.

Taylor was taken by the New York Giants as the second pick of the 1981 NFL Draft. Then all he did was win back-to-back AP Defensive Player of the Year awards. But L.T., as he was commonly known, was far from finished. He won another Player of the Year award in 1986, when he recorded a career-best 20.5 sacks, and was an All-Pro 10 times. He also won two Super Bowls with the Giants and finished with 132.5 sacks in his career officially, though sacks weren't recognized in Taylor's rookie season. Former NFL coach and color analyst (known more by the youth of today for his EA Sports football video game) John Madden said of Taylor, "Lawrence Taylor, defensively, has had as big an impact as any player I've ever seen. He changed the way defense is played, the way pass-rushing is played, the way linebackers play, and the way offenses block linebackers."

As good as he was on the football field, Taylor had his difficulties off the field. Substance abuse plagued him for years to the point where he failed NFL drug tests twice and was suspended both times. His life after football has been fraught with arrests, financial woes, and other personal problems. He's also had a few business successes and was in the public spotlight back in 1995 when he wrestled Bam Bam Bigelow (and won!) in a WrestleMania event and then in 2009 when he was a contestant on *Dancing with the Stars*. In addition, he has had a few minor acting roles and added his voice to a couple of video games. Always a colorful personality, Lawrence Taylor has certainly had his share of ups and downs off the field but will forever be recognized as a Tar Heel great on the field.

DONNELL THOMPSON ■ 6' 4" 270 ■ *Defensive End*

COLLEGE: 1977–80 **NFL:** 1981–91

Looking back, it's a wonder that Donnell Thompson isn't better known. He was one of North Carolina's top defensive linemen coming out of Lumberton High School. He was a major contributor for the Tar Heels, helping to lead the team to an 11-1 record, including 6-0 in the ACC, as a senior in 1980. A first-round draft choice by the Baltimore Colts, Thompson was an All-Rookie selection in the NFL and remained a rock-solid performer for the Colts in Baltimore and in Indianapolis. He had a few highlights, such as a safety back in 1983 and a fumble return for a TD in 1987, but the best part about Thompson was that he was such an amazingly consistent and dependable player. He started 143 of his 146 games with the Colts. And even in his final season before retirement, he was fifth on the team in tackles and tied for the team lead in sacks. In March of 1992, he announced he was leaving the game. "I've played for such a long time and I've been fortunate to have not sustained any serious injuries," he said at the time. "I feel this is the right time." He finished his career with 40 sacks.

While still in his playing days, Thompson had become the owner/operator of some McDonald's restaurants in the Atlanta area. He ended up selling those restaurants back to McDonald's and branching out his business into hospitality and construction. He has also remained a strong supporter of the University of North Carolina and received the Harvey E. Beech Outstanding Alumni Award. Eventually, he added restaurants to his business portfolio again. He joined with former UNC football player Ron Wooten to open a Zaxby's in Durham, and the two have teamed to open a series of Denny's restaurants in various North Carolina locations.

DAVID THORNTON ■ 6' 2" 230 ■ *Linebacker*

COLLEGE: 1998–2001 **NFL:** 2002–10

In terms of playing time and star quality at Carolina, David Thornton is a rags–to-riches story. Before he became a Tar Heel, he was an all-around student-athlete at Goldsboro High School, playing quarterback and safety in football, pitcher in baseball, and point guard in basketball. Meanwhile, he was student body president, a National Honor Society member, and an honors graduate. Even with all those accomplishments, he had to walk on to play football in Chapel Hill. He didn't see the field as a freshman and then saw just a small amount of action as a sophomore and junior, mostly on special teams. But for his dedication, hard work, and role model attitude, he was awarded a scholarship heading into his senior season. He proved he was worth it in the first game of the season when he recorded 15 tackles against Oklahoma in his first start. He became one of the ACC's top linebackers in 2001, leading Carolina in tackles. He ended his dream year with eight tackles, a sack, and a tipped pass that led to an interception in UNC's 16–10 win over Auburn in the Peach Bowl.

BRACY WALKER ■ 6' 0" 202 ■ *Defensive Back*

COLLEGE: 1990–93 **NFL:** 1994–2005

BRACY WALKER. In addition to his skills as a defensive back, Bracy Walker was also known to block a few kicks in his career.

Bracy Walker may be best remembered for the 1993 Peach Bowl, a 21–17 win over Mississippi State at the end of his junior year. Trailing 14–0 at the half, Walker blocked a pair of kicks, including one for a touchdown, and he forced an interception that was returned 44 yards by Cliff Baskerville for the winning touchdown. Walker earned Defensive MVP honors for his efforts. He was tough and played smart, parlaying that into an All-American-type senior season. Walker finished his Carolina career with 263 tackles, four interceptions, five forced fumbles, two fumble recoveries, and six blocked kicks. It may be no coincidence that Carolina's record improved each season that Walker was there, finishing with a 10-2 regular season before falling to Alabama in the Gator Bowl on the final day of 1993.

A few months later, he was chosen in the fourth round of the 1994 NFL Draft by the Kansas City Chiefs, and thus began a long and winding pro career. Just a couple games into his career, he found himself suddenly with a new team, playing seven games with the Cincinnati Bengals. He had a career-high four interceptions with the Bengals in 1995 and the following year had his best season as a pro when he started all 16 games at strong safety and ended the year with a career-high 116 total tackles. He also added two interceptions for 35 yards and a forced fumble. That was his last year as a Bengal, though, as he then played a year with the Miami Dolphins, four seasons back with the Chiefs, and then a final four with the Detroit Lions. He's best remembered in Lions lore as the man who saved the day in 2004 against the Chicago Bears with a 92-yard touchdown return, following a blocked field goal and an interception in the end zone, to seal the win with 18 seconds remaining. That victory ended a 24-game road losing streak.

The former walk-on became the fourth-round draft choice of the Indianapolis Colts in 2002. He didn't start as a rookie but did get in some quality playing time and finished the year with 36 solo tackles and nine assists. He won the starting job heading into his second year and blew up for an outstanding season, recording the most tackles

DAVID THORNTON *continued from page 124*

of his career and adding two interceptions. He played a total of four seasons for the Colts; then he was picked up as a free agent by the Tennessee Titans in 2006 and played four seasons in Nashville. In 2009, injuries cut his season short, and he had surgery in the off season. He then remained inactive throughout the 2010 season. In 2011, after a career that totaled 809 tackles, five sacks, five interceptions, 11 forced fumbles, and one fumble recovery in 121 games, he made his retirement official. He had won the Ed Block Courage Award in 2007 and was the Titans' Man of the Year in 2008.

After retirement, Thornton first joined the player development staff at UNC in 2011, then he joined the football operations staff of the Indianapolis Colts in 2012, and he is currently its director of player engagement.

GREG WARREN ■ 6' 3" 252 ■ *Long Snapper*

COLLEGE: 2001–04 **NFL:** 2005–13

We love those stories where perseverance pays off. Greg Warren was a capable player at Southern Wayne High School in Dudley, North Carolina, where he was also on the track and field team. He ended up having to walk on to play football at the University of North Carolina but earned a job as the team's starting long snapper as a redshirt freshman and held the job for four years. His consistency and athleticism attracted pro scouts. "Immediately after the draft, the Steelers called and said they wanted me to compete with their guy for the job," Warren said in a 2011 interview. "Even then, I didn't know how much chance I had. I decided to take the opportunity and just do my best. I had a good summer and had a good training camp, and they decided that they were going to make the move and change long snappers. The rest has been an awesome ride."

As of 2013, Warren was still a Steeler. A couple of knee injuries limited his playing time in 2008 and '09, but otherwise he has been a rock-solid long snapper for Pittsburgh and, in the process, has played in three Super Bowls, earning victories over Seattle and Arizona while falling to Green Bay.

MIKE WILCHER ■ 6' 3" 238 ■ *Linebacker*

COLLEGE: 1979–82 **NFL:** 1983–91

Perhaps best known as the guy who tried to fill Lawrence Taylor's shoes at UNC, Wilcher proved to be a decent football player in his own right. Picking up where Taylor left off, Wilcher stormed the edges and wreaked havoc on opposing offenses.

He was a second-round pick of the Los Angeles Rams in the 1983 NFL Draft. He saw very little action as a rookie and then started the final five games the following year before exploding for his best pro season after that. In 1985, Wilcher became a full-time starter at right outside linebacker and recorded 12.5 sacks for the year, by far his most in a single season, and he added an interception for good measure. And

KEN WILLARD ■ 6' 1" 219 ■ *Running Back*

COLLEGE: 1962–64 **NFL:** 1965–74

Trivia: Who was the University of North Carolina's first player to be chosen in the first round of an NFL Draft? You guessed it: Ken Willard. Willard came to Carolina from Richmond, Virginia, where he lettered in football, baseball, basketball, and track while also being an excellent student. He continued playing baseball and football for the Tar Heels. In 1963, he led the ACC in rushing attempts and yards and was named MVP of the Gator Bowl as the Heels beat Air Force 35–0. That was UNC's first-ever bowl victory. In 1964, his senior season, his numbers were even better: 835 yards on 228 carries with eight touchdowns. He even added 219 receiving yards and a TD reception. He was also the first UNC player to be honored as an Academic All-American.

KEN WILLARD. Ken Willard was chosen in the first round of the 1965 NFL Draft by the San Francisco 49ers.

Willard was the second overall pick in the 1965 NFL Draft by the San Francisco 49ers. He proved to be a solid pro, reliable and consistent. His best individual years were in the 1960s when he was named to the Pro Bowl in 1965, '66, '68, and '69, and his best individual game was a 162-yard rushing performance against Atlanta in the final game of the 1968 season. His 967 yards on the ground that year were his best in a single season. He was a durable back, missing only one game in his years in San Francisco. He was traded to the St. Louis Cardinals in 1974 and suffered a knee injury that essentially ended his career. In ten seasons, Willard recorded 6,105 yards and 45 touchdowns. He had another 2,184 yards receiving, adding 17 more TDs. He sold life insurance for a while and is enjoying retirement in Midlothian, Virginia. He and his wife, Bonnie, have four children and several grandchildren.

it wasn't just a good year for Wilcher, it was the best Rams team in his career too. Los Angeles finished the regular season with an 11-5 record, winning the NFC West. They made it to the NFC Conference Championship Game before running into the Chicago Bears, who were having a dream season of their own. The Bears won 24–0 and then went on to blow out the New England Patriots, the Super Bowl. Wilcher remained a productive, consistent member of the Rams through 1990. After that, he was released and ended up playing a couple of games for the San Diego Chargers in 1991, finishing his career with a total of 400 tackles, 38.5 sacks, four interceptions, and six fumbles recovered.

RON WOOTEN ■ 6' 4" 274 ■ *Guard*

COLLEGE: 1977–80 **NFL:** 1981–88

Initially from Massachusetts, Ron Wooten had a great career as an offensive guard for North Carolina before heading back to his home state to play for the Patriots. He was recruited by Coach Bill Dooley and played as a freshman for Dooley before finishing his career with three seasons under Coach Dick Crum. While in Chapel Hill, he won the Jacobs Trophy, which annually goes to the most outstanding blocker in the ACC. That same year, his senior season, the Tar Heels enjoyed an 11-1 season and a 16–7 victory over Texas in the Bluebonnet Bowl.

Wooten is a founding partner of NovaQuest Capital Management, a company that manages product and company investments in the global healthcare industry. Prior to that, he served as a managing director of investment banking with First Union Securities. In recent years, he has also joined with former UNC football player Donnell Thompson to open Zaxby's and Denny's restaurants in North Carolina. Married to UNC grad Ann, the couple have two children who are also UNC grads. His nephew, Carson Wooten, is currently on the Carolina football team.

Other Pro Players

NAME | POSITION | COLLEGE | PRO | PLAYED FOR
Tyrone Anthony *Running Back* | 1980–83 | 1984–85 | New Orleans Saints
Frank Aschenbrenner *Running Back* | 1944 | 1949 | Chicago Hornets
Marvin Austin *Defensive Line* | 2007–09 | 2011–13 | New York Giants, Dallas Cowboys, Miami Dolphins
Kentwan Balmer *Defensive Tackle* | 2005–07 | 2008–12 | San Francisco 49ers, Seattle Seahawks, Washington Redskins
Troy Barnett *Defensive Line* | 1990–93 | 1994–96 | New England Patriots, Washington Redskins
Connor Barth *Kicker* | 2004–07 | 2008–13 | Kansas City Chiefs, Tampa Bay Buccaneers
Hank Bartos *Guard* | 1935–37 | 1938 | Washington Redskins
Giovani Bernard* *Running Back* | 2011–12 | 2013 | Washington Redskins
James Betterson *Running Back* | 1973–75 | 1977–78 | Philadelphia Eagles
Terry Billups *Defensive Line* | 1994–97 | 1998–99 | Dallas Cowboys, New England Patriots
Phil Blazer *Guard* | 1955–58 | 1960 | Buffalo Bills
Eric Blount *Wide Receiver* | 1988–91 | 1992–93 | Phoenix Cardinals
Brian Bollinger *Guard* | 1988–91 | 1992–94 | San Francisco 49ers

* *pictured at right*

GIOVANI BERNARD. After two years with 1,200 yards rushing in Carolina, Giovani Bernard is now hoping that success will carry over into the NFL.

KELVIN BRYANT. Kelvin Bryant rushed for 1,000 yards in three consecutive seasons for the Tar Heels. Afterward, he played in the USFL and won a Super Bowl in the NFL with the Washington Redskins.

NAME	POSITION	COLLEGE	PRO	PLAYED FOR
Travis Bond	*Guard*	2011	2013	Carolina Panthers, Minnesota Vikings
Sean Boyd	*Defensive Back*	1992–95	1996	Atlanta Falcons
Bucky Brooks	*Defensive Back*	1989–93	1994–98	Buffalo Bills, Jacksonville Jaguars, Green Bay Packers, Kansas City Chiefs, Oakland Raiders
Jason Brown	*Center*	2002	2005–11	Baltimore Ravens, St. Louis Rams
Na Brown	*Wide Receiver*	1995–98	1999–2001	Philadelphia Eagles
Omar Brown	*Defensive Back*	1994–97	1998–99	Atlanta Falcons
Zach Brown	*Linebacker*	2008–11	2012–13	Tennessee Titans
Kelvin Bryant*	*Running Back*	1979–82	1986–90	Washington Redskins
Danny Burmeister	*Defensive Back*	1983–86	1987	Washington Redskins
Tom Burnette	*Blocking Back*	1936–37	1938	Pittsburgh Pirates, Philadelphia Eagles
Ron Burton	*Linebacker*	1983–86	1987–90	Dallas Cowboys, Phoenix Cardinals, L.A. Raiders
Alan Caldwell	*Defensive Back*	1975–77	1979	New York Giants
Jim Camp	*Quarterback*	1944–47	1948	Brooklyn Dodgers
Carl Carr	*Linebacker*	1982–85	1987	Detroit Lions

* *pictured above*

GREG DELONG. Tight end Greg DeLong was an undrafted free agent who went on to play for the Minnesota Vikings, Baltimore Ravens, and Jacksonville Jaguars.

MIKE MORTON. Linebacker Mike Morton may have knocked a few of his opponents' teeth loose in his football days. After a seven-year NFL career, he now fixes them. He's a dentist in Kannapolis, North Carolina.

NAME	POSITION	COLLEGE	PRO	PLAYED FOR
Bruce Carter	*Linebacker*	2007–10	2011–13	Dallas Cowboys
Reggie Clark	*Linebacker*	1987–88	1994–96	Pittsburgh Steelers, Jacksonville Jaguars
Henry Clement	*Tight End*	1958–60	1961	Pittsburgh Steelers
Joe Conwell	*Tackle*	1980–83	1986–87	Philadelphia Eagles
Jonathan Cooper	*Offensive Guard*	2009–12	2013	Arizona Cardinals
Quinton Coples	*Defensive End*	2008–11	2012–13	New York Jets
Calvin Daniels	*Linebacker*	1978–81	1982–86	Kansas City Chiefs, Washington Redskins
Bill Darnall	*Wide Receiver*	1964–66	1968–69	Miami Dolphins
Paul Davis	*Linebacker*	1978–80	1981–83	Atlanta Falcons, New York Giants, St. Louis Cardinals
Greg DeLong*	*Tight End*	1991–94	1995–2000	Minnesota Vikings, Baltimore Ravens, Jacksonville Jaguars
Jimmy DeRatt	*Defensive Back*	1971–74	1975	New Orleans Saints
Rick Donnalley	*Center/Guard*	1977–80	1982–87	Pittsburgh Steelers, Washington Redskins, Kansas City Chiefs

* *pictured above*

NAME	POSITION	COLLEGE	PRO	PLAYED FOR
Dave Drechsler	*Guard*	1979–82	1983–84	Green Bay Packers
Mike Dulaney	*Running Back*	1989–92	1995–98	Chicago Bears, Carolina Panthers
Deon Dyer	*Fullback*	1996–99	2000–02	Miami Dolphins
Bill Erickson	*Guard*	1943	1948–49	New York Giants, New York Yankees
Howard Feggins	*Defensive Back*	1984–87	1989	New England Patriots
Arnold Franklin	*Tight End*	1982–85	1987	New England Patriots
Frank Gallagher	*Guard*	1962–64	1967–73	Detroit Lions, Minnesota Vikings, Atlanta Falcons
Alan Goldstein	*End*	1957–59	1960	Oakland Raiders
Antonio Goss	*Linebacker*	1985–88	1989–96	San Francisco 49ers, St. Louis Rams
Cecil Gray	*Defensive Line*	1986–89	1990–95	Philadelphia Eagles, Green Bay Packers, Indianapolis Colts, Arizona Cardinals
George Grimes	*Defensive Back*	1943	1948	Detroit Lions
Darrell Hamilton	*Tackle*	1985–88	1990–91	Denver Broncos
James Hamilton	*Linebacker*	193–96	1997–98	Jacksonville Jaguars
Roscoe Hansen	*Tackle/Defensive Tackle*	1949–50	1951	Philadelphia Eagles
Bernardo Harris	*Linebacker*	1990–93	1995–2002	Green Bay Packers, Baltimore Ravens
Vic Harrison	*Wide Receiver*	1980–82	1987	New Orleans Saints
Rip Hawkins	*Linebacker*	1958–60	1961–65	Minnesota Vikings
Jeff Hayes	*Punter*	1978–81	1982–87	Washington Redskins, Cincinnati Bengals, Miami Dolphins
Ted Hazelwood	*Tackle/Defensive Tackle*	1945–48	1949–53	Chicago Hornets, Washington Redskins
Madison Hedgecock	*Fullback*	2001–04	2005–10	St. Louis Rams, New York Giants
Tom Higgins	*Lineman*	1950–52	1953–55	Chicago Cardinals, Philadelphia Eagles
Zachary Hilton	*Tight End*	1999–2002	2003–05	New Orleans Saints
Jimmy Hitchcock	*Defensive Back*	1991–94	1995–2002	New England Patriots, Minnesota Vikings, Carolina Panthers, New England Patriots
Nate Hobgood-Chittick	*Defensive Tackle*	1996–97	1999–2002	St. Louis Rams, San Francisco 49ers, Kansas City Chiefs
Sedric Hodge	*Linebacker*	1997–2000	2001–05	New Orleans Saints
Jesse Holley	*Wide Receiver*	2003–06	2010–11	Dallas Cowboys
Corey Holliday	*Wide Receiver*	1990–93	1995–97	Pittsburgh Steelers
Jason Horton	*Defensive Back*	1999	2004–05	Green Bay Packers

NAME	POSITION	COLLEGE	PRO	PLAYED FOR
Bill Jackson	*Defensive Back*	1979–81	1982	Cleveland Browns
Don Jackson	*Tailback/Defensive Back*	1933–35	1936	Philadelphia Eagles
Ray Jacobs	*Linebacker*	1990–93	1994–95	Denver Broncos
Brian Johnston	*Center*	1981–84	1986–87	New York Giants
Lewis Jolley	*Running Back*	1969–71	1972–73	Houston Oilers
Marcus Jones	*Defensive Line*	1992–95	1996–2001	Tampa Bay Buccaneers
Rondell Jones	*Defensive Back*	1989–92	1993–97	Denver Broncos, Baltimore Ravens
Eddie Kahn	*Guard*	1932–34	1935–37	Boston Redskins, Washington Redskins
Ken Keller	*Halfback*	1952–55	1956–57	Philadelphia Eagles
Bob M. Kennedy	*Halfback/Defensive Back*	1946–68	1949	L.A. Dons
John Kerns	*Tackle*	1944	1947–49	Buffalo Bills
Bob Lacey	*Wide Receiver*	1961–63	1964	Minnesota Vikings
Jonathan Linton	*Running Back*	1994–97	1998–2000	Buffalo Bills
Greg Little	*Wide Receiver*	2007–09	2011–13	Cleveland Browns
James Magner	*Back*	1928–30	1931	Frankford Yellow Jackets
Steve Maronic	*Tackle*	1936–38	1939–40	Detroit Lions
Eddie Mason	*Linebacker*	1993–94	1995–2002	New York Jets, Jacksonville Jaguars, Washington Redskins
Kivuusama Mays	*Linebacker*	1994–97	1998–99	Minnesota Vikings, Green Bay Packers
Andy Miketa	*Center*	1950–51	1954–55	Detroit Lions
Quincy Monk	*Linebacker*	1998–2001	2002–04	New York Giants, Houston Texans
Bill Moore	*End/Defensive End*	1933–35	1939	Detroit Lions
Tim Morrison	*Defensive Back*	1983–85	1986–87	Washington Redskins
Mike Morton*	*Linebacker*	1991–94	1995–2001	Oakland Raiders, St. Louis Rams, Green Bay Packers, Indianapolis Colts
Chase Page	*Defensive Tackle*	2001–03	2007	Miami Dolphins
Riddick Parker	*Defensive Line*	1991–94	1997–2003	Seattle Seahawks, New England Patriots, Baltimore Ravens
Doug Paschal	*Running Back*	1976–79	1980	Minnesota Vikings
Zach Pianalto	*Tight End*	2007–10	2011	Minnesota Vikings
Chris Pike	*Defensive Tackle*	1982	1989–91	Tampa Bay Buccaneers
Barney Poole	*Defensive End/End*	1943	1949–54	New York Yankees, Dallas Texans, Baltimore Colts, New York Giants

* *pictured, page 130*

NAME	POSITION	COLLEGE	PRO	PLAYED FOR
Ollie Poole	*Defensive End/End*	1943	1947–49	New York Yankees, Baltimore Colts, Detroit Lions
Ray Poole	*Defensive End/End*	1943	1947–52	New York Giants
Mike Pringley	*Defensive End*	1995–98	1999–2001	Detroit Lions, San Diego Chargers
Jack Protz	*Linebacker*	1966	1970	San Diego Chargers
Andre Purvis	*Defensive Tackle*	1994–96	1997–99	Cincinnati Bengals
Richard Quinn	*Tight End*	2005–08	2009–12	Denver Broncos, Washington Redskins, Cincinnati Bengals
Robert Quinn	*Defensive End*	2008–11	2011–13	St. Louis Rams
Kevin Reddick	*Linebacker*	2009–12	2013	New Orleans Saints
Dexter Reid	*Defensive Back*	2000–04	2004–06	New England Patriots, Indianapolis Colts
Garrett Reynolds	*Tackle*	2005–08	2009–13	Atlanta Falcons
Mike Richey	*Tackle*	1966–68	1969–70	Buffalo Bills, New Orleans Saints
Austin Robbins	*Defensive Tackle*	1990–93	1994–2000	L.A. Raiders, Oakland Raiders, New Orleans Saints, Green Bay Packers
Shelton Robinson	*Linebacker*	1979–81	1982–88	Seattle Seahawks, Detroit Lions
Hosea Rodgers	*Fullback*	1945–48	1949	L.A. Dons
Da'Norris Searcy	*Defensive Back*	2007–10	2011–13	Buffalo Bills
Jonas Seawright	*Defensive Tackle*	2002–04	2006	New York Giants
Dave Simmons	*Linebacker*	1976–78	1979–83	Green Bay Packers, Detroit Lions, Baltimore Colts, Chicago Bears
Bill Smith	*Tackle*	1946–47	1948	L.A. Dons, Chicago Rockets
Brandon Spoon	*Linebacker*	1997–2000	2001	Buffalo Bills
Don Stallings	*Defensive Line*	1957–59	1960	Washington Redskins
Harry Stanback	*Defensive End*	1978–80	1982	Baltimore Colts
Scott Stankavage	*Quarterback*	1980–83	1984–87	Denver Broncos, Miami Dolphins
Eric Streater	*Wide Receiver*	1983–86	1987	Tampa Bay Buccaneers
Quan Sturdivant	*Linebacker*	2007–10	2011–12	Arizona Cardinals, Kansas City Chiefs
Oscar Sturges	*Defensive End*	1991–94	1995	Dallas Cowboys
Ed Sutton	*Halfback/Defensive Back*	1954–56	1957–60	Washington Redskins, New York Giants
Len Szafaryn	*Tackle/Guard/Linebacker/ Defensive Tackle*	1945–48	1949–58	Washington Redskins, Green Bay Packers, Philadelphia Eagles

T. J. YATES. T. J. Yates has followed a prolific Carolina career as a backup quarterback for the Houston Texans.

NAME	POSITION	COLLEGE	PRO	PLAYED FOR
George Tandy	*Center/End*	1913–16	1920–21	Rochester Jeffersons, Cleveland Indians
Brandon Tate	*Wide Receiver*	2005–08	2009–13	New England Patriots, Cincinnati Bengals
Hilee Taylor	*Linebacker*	2004–07	2008–09	Carolina Panthers
Ryan Taylor	*Tight End*	2006–10	2011–13	Green Bay Packers
Jeb Terry	*Guard*	2001–03	2004–06	Tampa Bay Buccaneers
Rick Terry	*Defensive Tackle*	1994–96	1997–99	New York Jets, Carolina Panthers
Cam Thomas	*Defensive Tackle*	2006–09	2010–13	San Diego Chargers

NAME	POSITION	COLLEGE	PRO	PLAYED FOR
Dave Truitt	*Tight End*	1983–86	1987	Washington Redskins
Mike Voight	*Running Back*	1973–76	1977	Houston Oilers
Michael Waddell	*Defensive Back*	2000–03	2004–08	Tennessee Titans, Oakland Raiders
Art Weiner	*End/Defensive End*	1946–49	1950	New York Yankees
Johnny White	*Running Back*	2007–10	2011–12	Buffalo Bills, Green Bay Packers
Brennan Williams	*Tackle*	2009–12	2013	Houston Texans
Brooks Williams	*Tight End*	1975–77	1978–83	New Orleans Saints, Chicago Bears, New England Patriots
Robert Williams	*Defensive Back*	1995–97	1998–99	Kansas City Chiefs, Seattle Seahawks
Sylvester Williams	*Defensive Tackle*	2009–12	2013	Denver Broncos
Ernie Williamson	*Tackle*	1946	1947–49	Washington Redskins, New York Giants, L.A. Dons
E. J. Wilson	*Defensive End*	2006–09	2010–11	Tampa Bay Buccaneers, Seattle Seahawks
Bo Wood	*Defensive End*	1964–66	1967	Atlanta Falcons
Tito Wooten	*Defensive Back*	1990	1994–99	New York Giants, Indianapolis Colts
Victor Worsley	*Linebacker*	2003–06	2007	Indianapolis Colts
Wallace Wright	*Wide Receiver*	2002–05	2006–09	New York Jets
T. J. Yates	*Quarterback*	2007–10	2011–13	Houston Texans

* *pictured at left*

BASEBALL

BASEBALL

It's tough to argue North Carolina's success on the baseball diamond. Through the 2013 season, the Tar Heels have made nine College World Series appearances, including an impressive recent showing (2006, 2007, 2008, 2009, 2011, and 2013). In addition, the Tar Heels have been ACC tournament champions six times, regular season conference champions 10 times, and have made it into the NCAA's post-season tournament 28 times.

Baseball teams have taken the field at UNC since the 1860s, but teams were officially recognized beginning in 1891 under coach Perrin Busbee. A lot of coaches came and went in the early days, but long tenures became a hallmark of UNC coaches as early as the 1930s. Bunny Hearn coached the team in 1917–18 and then came back for a lengthy stint from 1932 to 1946. Then came Walter Rabb (1947–77), Mike Roberts (1978–98), and Mike Fox from 1999 to the present. That's only four coaches in more than 80 years!

As for standout players, North Carolina has had its share. The aforementioned Mike Roberts has a son who has done well in the sport. Brian Roberts began his college career at UNC but finished it at South Carolina after his dad was fired as UNC's coach. He has battled injuries in recent years, but the two-time All-Star is once again on the field for the Baltimore Orioles. Walt Weiss was a longtime Major League shortstop and is now manager of the Colorado Rockies. During B. J. Surhoff's versatile and long career in Major League Baseball, he played every position except pitcher.

Mike Roberts (father of Brian Roberts) played for the Tar Heels in the early 1970s and then went on to coach the team from 1978 through 1998.

Top 25 All-Time College Teams

(Ranked by wins through 2012)

RECORD	TEAM	WINNING PCT.	SEASONS PLAYED
4,320-2,164-48	Fordham	.665	152
3,276-1,155-31	Texas	.738	116
2,721-1,514-28	Southern California	.642	118
2,703-1,562-36	Michigan	.633	139
2,696-1,692-35	Stanford	.613	119
2,672-1,289-7	Arizona State	.674	101
2,621-1,387-23	Arizona	.653	107
2,618-966-11	Florida State	.730	65
2,601-1,444-30	Clemson	.642	115
2,576-1,531-37	**North Carolina**	**.626**	**123**
2,564-1,589-6	Washington State	.617	117

RECORD	TEAM	WINNING PCT.	SEASONS PLAYED
2,445-1,375-42	Texas A&M	.639	110
2,435-1,490-25	Minnesota	.620	124
2,428-1,816-21	California	.572	121
2,424-1,646-23	Harvard	.595	145
2,424-1,463-35	Alabama	.623	119
2,409-1,398-8	Fresno State	.633	84
2,409-1,418-27	Mississippi State	.629	123
2,406-1,566-38	Illinois	.605	133
2,386-1,209-4	Oklahoma State	.664	101
2,385-1,549-40	Ohio State	.605	129
2,369-1,425-11	South Carolina	.624	120
2,369-1,364-17	Oklahoma	.634	107
2,355-956-18	Miami (Florida)	.710	68
2,324-1,419-21	Notre Dame	.620	120

(Ranked by winning percentage through 2012)

WINNING PCT.	TEAM	RECORD
.738	Texas	3,276-1,155-31
.730	Florida State	2,618-966-11
.710	Miami (Florida)	2,355-956-18
.684	Wichita State	2,074-957-8
.674	Arizona State	2,672-1,289-7
.667	Southern	1,442-720-4
.665	Fordham	4,320-2,164-48
.664	Oklahoma State	2,386-1,209-4
.663	Grambling	1,711-868-3
.662	Oral Roberts	1,691-861-3
.658	St. John's (New York)	1,917-995-9
.654	East Carolina	1,706-899-11
.653	Coastal Carolina	1,343-713-0
.653	Arizona	2,621-1,387-23
.651	Cal State Fullerton	1,849-987-14

.642	Clemson	2,601-1,444-30
.642	Southern California	2,721-1,514-28
.640	South Alabama	1,644-926-3
.639	Texas A&M	2,445-1,375-42
.634	Oklahoma	2,369-1,364-11
.633	Michigan	2,703-1,562-36
.633	Fresno State	2,409-1,398-8
.632	Florida International	1,471-856-1
.629	Mississippi State	2,409-1,418-27
.626	**North Carolina**	**2,576-1,531-37**

North Carolina in the College World Series

YEAR	RECORD	YEAR	RECORD
1960	**0-2**	**2007**	**4-3** (Runner-up)
1966	**0-2**	**2008**	**3-2**
1978	**2-2**	**2009**	**1-2**
1989	**0-2**	**2011**	**1-2**
2006	**4-2** (Runner-up)	**2013**	**2-2**

College World Series Appearances

(Through 2013; teams with 10 or more appearances)

34 Texas	**19** Oklahoma State	**12** Clemson
23 Miami	**16** Arizona	**11** South Carolina
22 Arizona State	**16** Cal State Fullerton	**10 North Carolina**
21 Florida State	**16** LSU	**10** Northern Colorado
21 Southern California	**16** Stanford	**10** Oklahoma

Atlantic Coast Conference Championships

(Tournament, through 2013)

9 Clemson	**5** Florida State	**3** Virginia
8 Georgia Tech	**4** NC State	**1** Miami
6 North Carolina	**4** Wake Forest	

Head Coaching Records

(In chronological order)

YEARS	COACH	RECORD	WINNING PCT.
1891–93	Perrin Busbee	9-6-0	.600
1894	William R. Robertson	10-4-0	.714
1895	Jesse M. Oldham	6-4-0	.600
1896–97	Benjamin E. Stanley	14-8-1	.630
1898–99	William A. Reynolds	21-5-1	.796
1900, 1905–06, 1910	Robert B. Lawson	47-23-2	.667
1901	Ernest Graves	11-4-2	.706
1902	Edward M. Ashenback	7-6-0	.538
1903	John Curran	13-2-2	.824
1904	John Donnelly	5-8-0	.385
1907	Floyd Simmons	10-9-2	.524
1908–09	Otis Stockdale	31-14-0	.689
1911–12	Charles M. Clancey	26-14-0	.650
1913	Coach Bowers	7-11-0	.389
1914	Earl Mack	8-11-0	.425
1915–16	Charles A. Doak	19-15-0	.559
1917–18, 1932–46	Bunny Hearn	214-132-2	.618
1919–20	William Lourcey	19-16-4	.538
1921–25	Bill Fetzer	70-37-4	.649
1926	Duke Duncan	9-16-0	.360
1927–31	Jim Ashmore	72-39-3	.645
1947–77	Walter Rabb	540-358-9	.600
1978–98	Mike Roberts	780-428-3	.645
1999–2012	Mike Fox	635-262-1	.708

(Ranked by victories)

RECORD	COACH	YEARS
780-428-3	Mike Roberts	1978–98
635-262-1	Mike Fox	1999–2012

RECORD	COACH	YEARS
540-358-9	Walter Rabb	1947–77
214-132-2	Bunny Hearn	1917–18, 1932–46
72-39-3	Jim Ashmore	1927–31
70-37-4	Bill Fetzer	1921–25
47-23-2	Robert B. Lawson	1900, 1905–06, 1910
31-14-0	Otis Stockdale	1908–09
26-14-0	Charles M. Clancey	1911–12
21-5-1	William A. Reynolds	1898–99
19-16-4	William Lourcey	1919–20
19-15-0	Charles A. Doak	1915–16
14-8-1	Benjamin E. Stanley	1896–97
13-2-2	John Curran	1903
11-4-2	Ernest Graves	1901
10-4-0	William R. Robertson	1894
10-9-2	Floyd Simmons	1907
9-6-0	Perrin Busbee	1891–93
9-16-0	Duke Duncan	1926
8-11-0	Earl Mack	1914
7-6-0	Edward M. Ashenback	1902
7-11-0	Coach Bowers	1913
6-4-0	Jesse M. Oldham	1895
5-8-0	John Donnelly	1904

(Ranked by winning percentage; a tie counts as half a win, half a loss, per NCAA practice)

WINNING PCT.	RECORD	COACH	YEARS
.824	13-2-2	John Curran	1903
.796	21-5-1	William A. Reynolds	1898–99
.714	10-4-0	William R. Robertson	1894
.708	635-262-1	Mike Fox	1999–2012
.706	11-4-2	Ernest Graves	1901
.689	31-14-0	Otis Stockdale	1908–09

WINNING PCT.	RECORD	COACH	YEARS
.667	47-23-2	Robert B. Lawson	1900, 1905–06, 1910
.650	26-14-0	Charles M. Clancey	1911–12
.649	70-37-4	Bill Fetzer	1921–25
.645	780-428-3	Mike Roberts	1978–98
.645	72-39-3	Jim Ashmore	1927–31
.630	14-8-1	Benjamin E. Stanley	1896–97
.618	214-132-2	Bunny Hearn	1917–18, 1932–46
.600	540-358-9	Walter Rabb	1947–77
.600	9-6-0	Perrin Busbee	1891–93
.600	6-4-0	Jesse M. Oldham	1895
.559	19-15-0	Charles A. Doak	1915–16
.538	19-16-4	William Lourcey	1919–20
.538	7-6-0	Edward M. Ashenback	1902
.524	10-9-2	Floyd Simmons	1907
.425	8-11-0	Earl Mack	1914
.389	7-11-0	Coach Bowers	1913
.385	5-8-0	John Donnelly	1904
.360	9-16-0	Duke Duncan	1926

Player Bios

RUSS ADAMS ■ 6' 0" 200 ■ *Infield*

COLLEGE: 2000–02 **MLB:** 2004–09

A three-sport star at Scotland High in Laurinburg, North Carolina, Russ Adams decided to go with his best sport and play baseball at UNC. "Since I was a young kid, Carolina was the place I wanted to go," he said at the end of his time in Chapel Hill, where he played third base, shortstop, and second base in three years. In his senior year, he led the Tar Heels in batting average, walks, and stolen bases and finished second on the team in runs scored, hits, doubles, and triples.

Never known as a power guy, Adams used his good glove, versatility, and consistent hitting to impress the Toronto Blue Jays enough to make him a first-round draft choice in 2002. He made it to big-time baseball by the end of the 2004 season and hit

DUSTIN ACKLEY ■ 6' 1" 195 ■ *Second Base / Center Field / First Base*

COLLEGE: 2007–09 **MLB:** 2011–13

Dustin Ackley is a true North Carolina success story. While just finishing his third Major League Baseball season, Ackley has long been a legend in the Tar Heel State. Born in Winston-Salem, he was a star player at South Stokes High School through his junior year, where he led the team to two state titles, before playing for North Forsyth High School as a senior. He was a pitcher and played third base in high school, earning Louisville Slugger All-American honors.

DUSTIN ACKLEY. Dustin Ackley made quite a splash as an all-around player wearing Carolina blue. Now he's trying to make that same kind of impact in Major League Baseball.

He stayed in state to play in Chapel Hill, where he became a first baseman and immediately made his mark on Tar Heels baseball. Ackley was the consensus national freshman of the year, setting UNC single-season records and leading the nation with 119 hits, 296 at-bats, and 73 games played. He hit .402, drove in a Tar Heels rookie record 74 runs, and had 10 home runs. He finished his freshman season among the ACC's top 10 in 10 different offensive categories.

We said the guy made quite a splash in Carolina blue. In his sophomore year, Ackley continued where

RUSS ADAMS *continued from page 143*

.306 in limited action. His official rookie season was in 2005, but his numbers were lackluster. Adams hit .256 in 139 games with 8 home runs and 63 RBI, meanwhile committing 26 errors. Afterward, he never could stick with the Blue Jays' MLB roster. Playing mostly in the minors into the 2009 season, he signed with the Padres organization during that season but never made it to the bigs as a Padre. He spent another couple seasons in the minors playing for the Mets-affiliated Buffalo Bisons before officially retiring in 2011.

NATE ANDREWS ■ 6' 0" 195 ■ *Pitcher*

COLLEGE: 1933–34 **MLB:** 1937–46

Born in Pembroke, North Carolina, Nate's father, the senior Nathan Andrews, was a country doctor who often accepted eggs, a ham, or whatever else his patients could afford as payment for his services in and around the community of Rowland. The

he left off as a freshman. He earned All-America honors again as he hit .417 with a school-record 82 runs scored, seven home runs, 51 RBI, and 19 stolen bases. He ranked among the ACC's top 10 in 13 offensive categories. He followed that up with a stellar junior season in which he was named **rivals.com** National Player of the Year and was a consensus first-team All-America selection. He was also ACC Player of the Year and a first-team All-ACC pick. As he would go pro after his junior year, he finished his playing days as the top hitter in North Carolina history with a .412 career average, 346 hits, 227 runs, and 544 total bases.

He was picked by the Seattle Mariners as the second player in the 2009 MLB Draft, just behind Stephen Strasburg of the Washington Nationals. After playing for the Peoria Javelinas in the Arizona Fall League in 2009, Ackley started 2010 for the AA West Tennessee Diamond Jaxx before moving up to AAA Tacoma Rainiers. He also made a position move to second base that year. A full season with the Rainiers in 2010 had Ackley seasoned, accustomed to his new position, and ready for the majors in 2011. His rookie year with the Mariners saw Ackley getting some quality time on the field, batting .276 with six home runs and 36 RBI. As an everyday player in 2012, Ackley struggled, only batting .226 for the year. In 2013, he tried to settle into the role as the regular second baseman for the Mariners. Weak hitting got him sent down to the minors. Nonetheless, Ackley saw action in 113 Major League games.

young Nate learned to play an array of musical instruments from his mom but always preferred playing baseball. Nate Andrews became a pitching star at Rowland High School, then went on to Presbyterian Junior College, and finally landed at UNC. He was dominant in the Southern League and recorded a no-hitter versus Wake Forest.

Andrews signed with the St. Louis Cardinals in 1934, which was good and bad. On the good side, the Cardinals were a very successful Major League team. In fact, you may know the '34 Cardinals by their nickname, the Gashouse Gang, a group that won 95 regular season games and beat the Detroit Tigers in the World Series. On the bad side, they had a lot of great pitchers, which meant that Andrews struggled to see any playing time. Pitchers on that 1934 team, for instance, included the likes of Dizzy and Paul Dean, Tex Carlton, Bill Hallahan, and Bill Walker. He finally got a peak at the Major League club in 1937; by the end of 1939, he was dealt to the Cleveland Indians. A couple more lackluster seasons saw Andrews then go to the Boston Braves, where his career finally gained a bit of traction.

He found himself in the starting rotation for three seasons with the Braves, where he even made the All-Star team in 1944, though he didn't see game action. After those three years with the Braves, Andrews's career began to fizzle. He played for the Cincinnati Reds and the New York Giants in 1946 and then just walked away.

He later said, "I came home . . . of my own accord. I decided I had had enough of the Big Show, and the time had come for me to return to North Carolina, where I could be with my family. I had a lot of years up there and too many away from home." He played some minor league ball closer to home before working in the family drugstore and then later opening a dry-cleaning business. He died in 1991 at the age of 77.

SCOTT BRADLEY ■ 5' 11" 185 ■ *Catcher*

COLLEGE: 1979–81 **MLB:** 1984–92

Sure Scott Bradley is the answer to the trivia question: "Who caught the first no-hitter in Seattle Mariners franchise history?" (That no-hitter was thrown by Randy Johnson in 1990.) In fact, he's also the answer to this trivia question: "Who was the second player chosen by the New York Yankees in the 1981 MLB Draft after John Elway?" So, there's that. But Bradley has plenty more baseball highlights. For one, he was named the ACC Player of the Year back in 1980. He made it to the majors with the Yankees in 1984, playing in just a few games with the Yankees over two seasons. He began 1986 with the Chicago White Sox but was dealt to the Mariners in what proved to be a good career move. In his first full season with the Mariners, Bradley hit .302 in a part-time role. He played in at least 100 games per year for the Mariners from 1987 through 1990. His number dropped precipitously in 1991 and 1992, when he was dealt to the Cincinnati Reds. He saw action in just five games with the Reds before his Major League career was over. Overall, though, Bradley played 604 games in the big leagues, hitting .257 with 18 home runs and 184 RBIs.

A native of New Jersey, Bradley went back to the Garden State after his Major League career to get into college coaching. After a year as an assistant at Rutgers, he's been the head baseball coach at Princeton ever since. He's closing in on 300 wins as the Princeton coach.

HAL BROWN ■ 6' 2" 180 ■ *Pitcher*

COLLEGE: 1943–45 **MLB:** 1951–64

Hal Brown was a bit chunky as a kid in Greensboro, North Carolina, and thus came the family nickname "Skinny," which stuck with him his whole life. But Skinny Brown had another nickname that he probably enjoyed more: "The Yankee Killer." It's a nickname he got playing for six seasons with the Baltimore Orioles and beating the great Yankee teams of that era with regularity. His string of 36 scoreless innings in one season (1961) remains a club record.

After playing for UNC in the 1940s, Brown made it to Major League Baseball in 1951, appearing in three games for the Chicago White Sox. He appeared in 24 games with the Sox the following year before heading to Boston, where he turned in a fine year in terms of record (11-6) but had a 4.65 ERA. Brown really found his stride after

SCOTT BANKHEAD ■ 5' 10" 185 ■ *Pitcher*

COLLEGE: 1982–84 **MLB:** 1986–95 **OLYMPICS:** 1984

To get in 10 years of Major League Baseball is quite an accomplishment, and thus Scott Bankhead has to rank among the most successful UNC baseball players to go pro. A Tar Heel through and through, Bankhead was born in Raleigh and went to high school in Reidsville, where he was a good player on an average team. That combination didn't get him noticed by a whole lot of programs, though. He went to Carolina and had an average season on the mound as a freshman. But then he developed a slider and had a 9-0 sophomore season. After developing a split-finger change-up he went 11-0 and was almost unhittable. His 20-game winning streak remains a record. Fans still look back with awe at that ACC tournament win against Maryland in which Bankhead, in his junior year, struck out 14 Terrapins in just six innings.

SCOTT BANKHEAD. Scott Bankhead won Olympic Gold for Team USA in the 1984 Olympics and then had a 10-year career as a Major League pitcher.

His battery mate for a couple seasons at UNC was B. J. Surhoff, who went on to join Bankhead on the U.S. Olympics baseball team in 1984. Baseball was just a demonstration sport that year, but the United States fielded a great team. A few of the other players on that '84 team included Barry Larkin, Ken Caminiti, Will Clark, and Mark McGwire.

After being picked in the 1984 MLB Draft by the Kansas City Royals, he made it up to the majors in '86. Over the next decade, he saw action with the Royals, Seattle Mariners, Cincinnati Reds, Boston Red Sox, and New York Yankees. He played five seasons with the Mariners, and his best season was with them in 1989. He pitched more than 200 innings for the only time in his career and finished with a 14-6 record. His ERA was 3.34 while he recorded 140 strikeouts and just 63 walks. He proved to be a very successful reliever in 1992 with the Reds, posting a 10-4 record and a 2.93 ERA. He also had one save.

In 1998, Bankhead founded the North Carolina Baseball Academy in Greensboro. The NCBA covers all aspects of baseball instruction from hitting and pitching to weight training and team dynamics.

he was traded to the Orioles during the 1955 season. He got double-digit wins in three consecutive years (1959–61) and had a career-best 3.06 ERA in 1960. He had good control and tossed a knuckleball on occasion that would really baffle opponents if Brown had it working. He was dealt to the Yankees during the 1962 season, perhaps because the guys in pinstripes were tired of facing The Yankee Killer. They passed him along to the Houston Colt .45s at the end of the season, though. Brown finished his long Major League career with Houston. In 1963, he accomplished one of his more impressive feats. He walked just eight batters in 141.1 innings pitched.

In all, Brown totaled 85 wins and 92 losses along with 11 saves as a Major League pitcher. His career ERA was 3.81. After he left baseball, he joined fellow Greensboro sports star Edgar McBane to start McBane-Brown Heating and Air Conditioning in Greensboro. The company was bought in 2013 by Berico Heating and Cooling.

TOM BUSKEY ■ 6' 3" 200 ■ *Pitcher*

COLLEGE: 1967–69 **MLB:** 1973–80

Hailing from Harrisburg, Pennsylvania, Tom Buskey traveled south to become an outstanding pitcher for the Tar Heels in the late 1960s, culminating in an All-ACC season in 1969. He then signed a free agent contract with the New York Yankees and made it into just a few games in relief in 1973 and '74 before being traded to the Cleveland Indians early in the 1974 season. In 1975, he had the best season of his Major League career in terms of ERA (2.57) while also recording a 5-3 record with seven saves. He couldn't match those numbers in two more years with the Indians, after which he was traded to the Texas Rangers but was released before the 1978 season started. He got picked up by the Toronto Blue Jays, where he pitched in 1979 and then was released in August 1980.

Buskey retired from baseball after being released from the Jays. He won 21 Major League games and saved 34 more, pitching 479.1 innings in 258 games with a 3.66 career ERA. He died in 1998 back in his hometown of Harrisburg of injuries sustained in an auto accident.

JOHNNY HUMPHRIES ■ 6' 1" 185 ■ *Pitcher*

COLLEGE: 1936 **MLB:** 1938–46

Johnny Humphries, from Clifton Forge, Virginia, came to Carolina as a hard-throwing right-hander. He broke into Major League Baseball in 1938 with the Cleveland Indians. It was no part-time warm-up year, either. He saw action in 45 games, starting six and saving six and leading the league in appearances by a pitcher. He saw his productivity dwindle in the next two seasons with Cleveland and was traded to the Chicago White Sox. He did record a first, though, for the Indians. On May 16, 1939, Humphries was the winning pitcher in the American League's first night game. The Indians defeated the Philadelphia Athletics 8–3 in 10 innings in Philadelphia.

MATT HARVEY ■ 6' 4" 225 ■ *Pitcher*

COLLEGE: 2008–10 **MLB:** 2012–13

MATT HARVEY. Pitcher Matt Harvey was stellar for the Tar Heels and was the National League starter in the 2013 Major League Baseball All-Star Game.

Many younger readers may not know the names of Carolina baseball stars of the past, but baseball fans across the country have quickly learned the name of Matt Harvey. A native of Connecticut, Harvey decided to play ball at UNC rather than start his pro career straight out of high school. It seemed to turn out well for all parties. Harvey got in some great games, beginning with his freshman season when he went 7-2 with a 2.79 ERA. He continued to pitch well for the Tar Heels and spent two summers with the Chatham Anglers of the Cape Cod League. By the time the 2010 MLB Draft came along, Harvey was viewed as a hot prospect with a professional attitude and was chosen by the New York Mets as the seventh overall pick.

Harvey started 10 games for the Mets in 2012. While his record of 3-5 wasn't particularly impressive, his 2.79 ERA was, especially for a rookie. The Mets expected a big season from Harvey in 2013, and they got it. He ended up starting the All-Star Game in New York, finished third in National League ERA (2.27), and led the NL in home runs given up per nine innings. He finished fourth in the NL for the Cy Young Award. But then there was the bad news. In late August, Harvey was diagnosed with a partial ligament tear in his elbow. He and the Mets hoped for the best but feared the worst. In late October 2013, the inevitable finally happened and Harvey had Tommy John surgery to repair his elbow. It is expected that he will miss the entire 2014 season.

Humphries played five seasons for the Sox, and his fortunes almost changed in the middle of all that. Filmmaker Samuel Goldwyn was looking for someone to play Lou Gehrig in the movie *The Pride of the Yankees*. Several baseball folks suggested Humphries, who had a resemblance to Gehrig and who could obviously play a convincing baseball player. Ultimately, Goldwyn went with an actor with no baseball experience: Gary Cooper.

But back to his days with the White Sox. Humphries recorded a remarkable 1.84 ERA in his first year with the team, though he pitched just 73.1 innings. The following year, he pitched the most innings of his career (228.1) and still recorded a highly

CHRIS IANNETTA ■ 6' 0" 230 ■ *Catcher*

COLLEGE: 2002–04 **MLB:** 2006–13

CHRIS IANNETTA. Chris Iannetta was one of the great catchers in Tar Heel history and is now making his mark as a pro, most recently with the Los Angeles Angels.

Born in Rhode Island, Chris Iannetta grew up as a fan of the Boston Red Sox. He attended the University of North Carolina with the hopes of one day becoming a big-league ballplayer. He made an immediate impact for the Tar Heels, starting 47 games and being named a second-team Freshman All-American by Baseball America. Iannetta went on to better stats and more accolades in two more years with the Tar Heels before finally pursuing his dream of playing in the Major Leagues. He was selected, not by the Red Sox, but by the Colorado Rockies, in the fourth round of the 2004 MLB Draft.

After some impressive play in the minors, Iannetta made it to the Rockies fairly quickly, making his MLB debut with Colorado in 2006, playing in 21 games that season. He was a part-time catcher for the Rockies the following year, making 54 starts, and then jumped up to 96 starts in his third year. His offensive production also increased that third season, as Iannetta worked his batting average up to .264 and belted 18 home runs, still his Major League best. He began getting some looks at first base, third base, and even as a designated hitter, but his offensive production seemed to suffer with all the defensive experimentation. In late 2011, he was traded by the Rockies to the Los Angeles Angels and went back to his normal position as catcher. In 2013, he played the most games of his professional career (115). He's known as an excellent defensive catcher, leading the league at his position in fielding in 2008, double plays in 2009, and assists in 2011. His younger brother, Matt, played baseball for two seasons at UNC before transferring to Georgetown.

JOHNNY HUMPHRIES *continued from page 149*

respectable ERA of 2.68. From there, his ERA went up and his innings pitched went down, allowing the Philadelphia Phillies to purchase Humphries's contract in 1946. He only saw action in 10 games for the Phillies and was released by the team in the spring of 1947. He died in New Orleans in 1965.

CLYDE KING ■ 6' 1" 175 ■ *Pitcher*

COLLEGE: 1942–43 **MLB:** 1944–53

The newspaper headline read "Former Major League manager Clyde King dies." From his obituary: "GOLDSBORO, N.C.—Clyde King, whose baseball career as a player, coach, manager and front-office man spanned six decades, has died in North Carolina. He was 86." That's a quick summary of a former great for the Tar Heels who could truly be described as "a baseball man."

The Goldsboro native was a hotshot baseball player who played briefly for the Tar Heels in the early 1940s and even played basketball too. He had his Major League debut at age 20 for the Brooklyn Dodgers. The year was 1944, and rosters were difficult to fill because of World War II. King posted a respectable 2-1 record with a 3.09 ERA in limited action. After the war ended, King was sent to the minors for a bit more seasoning in 1946 but returned to the Dodgers in 1947. That season he posted his best Major League ERA (2.77). He had become a solid reliever who was known for his curveball but could pitch with some heat too. The Dodgers won the pennant that year but lost to the crosstown-rival New York Yankees in the World Series.

Health issues started to plague King thereafter: an infection on his finger, shoulder problems, arm issues. He had a good year in 1951, recording a 14-7 record with 6 saves, but those physical issues continued to mount in 1952. King and his Dodgers did make it back to the World Series, although the result was similar to that of 1947: They lost to the New York Yankees. At the end of the 1952 season, King was traded to the Cincinnati Reds for Dixie Howell. King saw limited action with the Reds and retired from baseball a few months short of his 30th birthday. Still with a passion for the game, King became a manager, first in the minors and then for brief stints with the San Francisco Giants and Atlanta Braves. In 1976, he latched on with the New York Yankees and became a key cog in the organization, performing the duties of scout, pitching coach, manager, and general manager, among other roles with the team.

"Clyde was a loyal and dedicated friend and advisor to my father, our family and the Yankees organization," said Yankees managing general partner Hal Steinbrenner, son of George Steinbrenner, in King's obituary. "Although his baseball achievements were impressive and deserving, he also lived a rich and fulfilling life away from the game. Clyde was a man of great faith who cared deeply about his friends and family, and he served as a role model to so many of us."

MATT MERULLO ■ 6' 2" 200 ■ *Catcher / First Base / Designated Hitter*

COLLEGE: 1984–86 **MLB:** 1989, 1991–95

Lennie Merullo played for the Chicago Cubs from 1941 to 1947 and scouted for the Cubs from 1950 to 1972. His son, Leonard, played several seasons of minor league baseball. Leonard's son, Matt, became the third generation to play the game

JESSE LEVIS ■ 5' 9" 180 ■ *Catcher*

COLLEGE: 1987–89 **MLB:** 1992–2001

JESSE LEVIS. Catcher Jesse Levis had an up-and-down journey in pro baseball with his most productive seasons coming with the Milwaukee Brewers in the late 1990s.

Jesse Levis (whose last name, by the way, is not pronounced like the popular denim jeans but rather LEV-iss) grew up in Philadelphia and was a baseball standout at Northeast High School. He became an All-American catcher for the Tar Heels during the late 1980s and was selected by the Cleveland Indians in the fourth round of the MLB Draft.

The good news is that Levis had one season in which he batted 1.000. OK, we'll get to that explanation. Levis struggled throughout his career to make it to, and stay in, Major League Baseball. After a few years of toiling in the minors, he had his big league debut in 1992 with the Indians, playing in 28 games and batting .279. While he did see at least some Major League action in the next three years with Cleveland, he spent most of his time in the minors. And as for that Major League action in 1994? It was one game, one at bat, one hit. His MLB batting average for the year: 1.000.

Levis was then traded to the Milwaukee Brewers and had a couple seasons as the team's primary catcher. He played in 104 games in 1996, and 99 in 1997. He batted a very respectable .285 in '97, so it was a disappointment that he spent most of '98 back in the minors. He found himself back in Cleveland briefly for the '99 season before returning to the minors for all of 2000. In an up-and-down career, Levis had his final "up" playing for Milwaukee briefly in 2001. He then played in the minor league organizations of the Cincinnati Reds, Philadelphia Phillies, and New York Mets until 2004, when he finally decided to hang up the cleats. In recent years, he has been a scout for the Boston Red Sox and Philadelphia Phillies.

MATT MERULLO *continued from page 151*

professionally. You might say that baseball runs in the blood of the Merullo family. Of that family connection to baseball, the younger Merullo said in 2013, "I would say that it was both a blessing and a curse at the same time, because I got great information, but at the same time, probably knew a little too much about things—about things that I could improve upon."

He proved to be an outstanding player for the Tar Heels in the mid-1980s and ended up being drafted in the seventh round by the Chicago White Sox in 1986. He spent some time in the minors. With baseball legend Carlton Fisk holding down the catcher spot at the big league level, there was little pressure on Merullo to make the team. But funny things happen in sports. Fisk broke his hand just a few days into the 1989 season, and Merullo found himself as the starting catcher for the team's home opener. He still has the lineup card from that game.

Merullo saw action in 31 games that season, but then it was back down to the minors for all of 1990. In 1991, though, he saw action in 80 games with the Sox, batting .268 with five home runs. Despite that effort, he saw much more time in the minors than the majors in the next two seasons and was traded to the Cleveland Indians. He was brought up to Cleveland for barely more than a cup of coffee in 1994 and was released by the team, allowing him to sign as a free agent in 1995 with the Minnesota Twins. He had more at bats with the Twins that season than ever before in his Major League career. He batted .282 in 76 games. But injuries had taken their toll. He had elbow surgery three times during his career. Merullo decided to retire from playing but to stay in baseball.

Merullo was a scout for the Arizona Diamondbacks for a while and then in 2013 became the manager for Class A Aberdeen IronBirds. Merullo led the team to the McNamara Division championship. His philosophy is simple: Have fun and play hard for all nine innings. He wears the number 27 as a reminder for his team to play all 27 outs. And baseball still runs through the family's blood. His son Nick plays baseball for James Madison University.

ANDREW MILLER ■ 6' 7" 210 ■ *Pitcher*

COLLEGE: 2004–06 **MLB:** 2006–13

Growing up in Gainesville, Florida, Andrew Mitchell left the shadow of the Florida Gators to play baseball in Chapel Hill. He had been the Florida Gatorade Player of the Year and was a highly rated left-handed hurler. He didn't disappoint at UNC. After his junior season, he was the *Baseball America* National Player of the Year and Roger Clemens Award winner. He also racked up plenty of school records, finishing as the single-season strikeout leader (133) and the career strikeout leader (325). His 27 wins with the Tar Heels ranks third all-time. Miller was then drafted sixth overall by the Detroit Tigers in 2006.

Miller made it into eight games in his first year as a pro and 13 in his second. In what has proved to be a historic trade, Miller was sent to the Florida Marlins along with five other little-known guys in the Marlins organization for Miguel Cabrera and Dontrelle Willis. Willis (who was 22-10 in 2005 for the Marlins) didn't really pan out, but Cabrera became known as the game's best hitter. Meanwhile, Miller, who showed great flashes of pitching brilliance in a 6-7 frame, continued to struggle to consistently get batters out. (At least he was playing for his childhood-favorite team.) He pitched more innings with the Marlins, but his ERA remained high and he was traded to the Boston Red Sox for the 2011 season. His best pitching has come with

BRIAN ROBERTS ■ 5' 9" 175 ■ *Second Base*

COLLEGE: 1997–98 (at UNC) **MLB:** 2001–13

Brian Roberts's decision to play baseball for the University of North Carolina was an easy one. His father, Mike Roberts, was the head coach. The younger Roberts was signed as a shortstop and then exploded for a phenomenal freshman season. He finished with the second-highest batting average in the ACC (.427), led the ACC in stolen bases (42), and led the Tar Heels in nine offensive categories. That batting average of .427, by the way, shattered the previous Carolina record batting average of .400 held by Tar Heels great B. J. Surhoff. In 1998, the father-son Roberts tandem led Carolina to within one game of the College World Series. Brian hit .353 with 13 homers and 49 RBIs and led college baseball with 63 steals. He was a first-team All-America and the ACC Player of the Year. After that, Mike Roberts was either fired by or resigned from UNC, depending on which story you believe, and Brian declared that he would transfer to South Carolina, where he had another All-America season, and was then drafted by the Baltimore Orioles in the first round.

BRIAN ROBERTS. Second baseman Brian Roberts has enjoyed a long tenure in pro baseball with the Baltimore Orioles.

ANDREW MILLER *continued from page 153*

the Red Sox, although he's found it difficult to keep a roster spot and missed the roster for the team's 2013 World Series victory. A 2.64 ERA in 2013, though, indicates that Miller is headed in the right direction.

JOHNNY PEACOCK ■ 5' 11" 165 ■ *Catcher*

COLLEGE: 1929–33 **MLB:** 1937–45

Always athletic, Johnny Peacock played baseball, football, and basketball for the University of North Carolina. In football, he was known for an 85-yard punt return against Wake Forest in 1930 and an 85-yard kickoff return, also against Wake Forest, in 1931. Baseball, though, was his primary sport. He played second base, right field, and occasionally catcher for the Tar Heels. Solid defensively but never a long-ball guy, Peacock spent some time playing semi-pro and minor league ball before making his Major League debut with the Boston Red Sox in 1937.

By the time Roberts made it to his Major League debut in 2001, all-time Oriole great Cal Ripken Jr. had been playing third base for a few years. Still, the thought of playing shortstop alongside a legend was daunting. (The aforementioned Surhoff had been traded to Atlanta the year before Roberts made it to the big-league team, but the two former Carolina stars played together for three seasons when Surhoff returned to the Orioles.) Roberts got into 75 games in 2001, which was Ripken's last season, and mostly played second base for an injured Jerry Hairston Jr. Roberts made quite an impression by belting a grand slam in his second game.

Roberts eventually became the regular second baseman for the Orioles, the team for which he has played his entire career. He had a string of very good seasons before injuries started taking their toll on his playing time. In 2004 and '09, he led the American League in doubles. In 2007, he led the American League in stolen bases. He was twice named to the All-Star Team. A herniated disc during 2010's training camp was the first of Roberts's injury woes. He hasn't played a full season since, due to the disc injury, an abdominal strain, and injuries to his head, hip, and knee. His 77 games in 2013 were the most he had played since 2009.

In an age where few players stick with one team throughout their careers, Roberts has become the face of the Orioles. Many players have made stops in Baltimore since Roberts debuted as a rookie in 2001. Nearing the end of his career, his future is somewhat in the air as of the end of the 2013 season. Through 2013, Roberts had played in 1,327 MLB games, batting .278 and hitting 351 doubles and 92 home runs. He also has 521 RBI. Off the field, he married his wife, Diana, in 2009, and the couple had a son in 2013.

Peacock got into nine games that season, getting three hits in 10 at bats. He had a part-time role on the team through the 1943 season before being purchased by the Philadelphia Phillies early in the 1944 season. Peacock played in Philadelphia in 1944 and the first half of 1945 before being traded to the Brooklyn Dodgers, prompting this headline in *The Sporting News:* "Peacock Added to Flock, All Brooklyn Preening." The article's evaluation was that "Peacock is what ballplayers call a good receiver. He hasn't any terrific plate punch, but he will hit for you in the clutch." He finished the season with the Dodgers and ended his career. And it's true, he had no terrific plate punch. In 1,743 Major League at bats, Peacock hit one home run—and that came in his second season. His .262 career batting average wasn't half bad, though, and he walked more than twice as much as he struck out. Defensively, he finished with a very nice .983 fielding percentage.

In 1946, he had been named the player-manager for the New Orleans Pelicans in the Southern Association. He kept that gig for a season, but his non-baseball business took precedence and he decided to go back to Carolina to his tobacco farms.

He also owned Peacock Builders Supply back in his hometown of Fremont. He had a couple of area sawmills and even a grain dealership. As a successful businessman, he was named to the boards of Wayne County Memorial Hospital and Wayne County Community College. Peacock died of a heart attack in 1981 at the age of 71.

PAUL SHUEY ■ 6' 3" 215 ■ *Pitcher*

COLLEGE: 1990–92 **MLB:** 1994–2003, 2007

You may know Paul Shuey as the assistant coach for women's soccer at Barton College in Wilson, North Carolina. OK, that's probably unlikely, but the former Carolina great and longtime Major League relief pitcher is indeed coaching soccer these days. But before this new career, Shuey was known for his baseball prowess. He attended Milbrook High School in Raleigh, North Carolina, where he was a star pitcher and right fielder. He then took his skills on the diamond the short distance to Chapel Hill, where he proved to be a dominant closer for the Tar Heels.

Shuey was chosen second overall by the Cleveland Indians in the 1992 MLB Draft with the idea that he would be a shutdown closer. As it turns out, he spent most of his career as a setup guy. He had his Major League debut with the Indians in 1994 but struggled in 14 appearances. In 1995, he played even fewer games at the big league level. His third season, though, was one of his best. He pitched in 42 games, went 5-2, recorded four saves, and had a 2.85 ERA. His career best in strikeouts came in 1999 with 103. Shuey remained a steady contributor to the Indians until late July 2002, when he was traded to the Los Angeles Dodgers. He had a 3-0 record and an ERA under 2.50 at the time of the trade. He initially struggled in LA but then settled down to finish with an overall solid performance in 2002. A steady year with a 6-4 record and 3.00 ERA followed, but then injuries sustained in 2004's training camp caused Shuey to miss the entire year.

What followed was more injuries, minor league play, retirement, hip replacement surgery, and more minor league play. He had a final Major League comeback in 2007, nearly four years after he had last played in a big league game. Shuey saw appearances in 25 games but realized that he just didn't have the stuff he used to, so he retired again, this time for good. Since then he, his wife, and three daughters have settled into Wake Forest, North Carolina, where he spent some time dabbling in pro fishing, doing baseball clinics, and getting involved in the greater Raleigh area's soccer scene, the last of which led to his current role with the Barton College women's soccer team.

KYLE SNYDER ■ 6' 8" 230 ■ *Pitcher*

COLLEGE: 1997–99 **MLB:** 2003, 2005–08

Hailing from Texas, perhaps it shouldn't be a surprise that Kyle Snyder is big. At 6-foot-8, he was an imposing figure on the mound for the Tar Heels, impressing scouts as a rangy right-hander. Moving into the pros, Snyder had a world of potential. He was selected as the seventh overall pick of the 1999 MLB Draft by the Kansas City Royals. Like many a professional athlete, however, injuries derailed a promising career. Early in the 2000 minor league season, he pitched only two games before requiring Tommy John surgery, which forced him to miss the entire 2001 season. He finally saw Major League action in 2003 but only in 15 games. He missed the entire 2004 season due to injury. It seemed that Snyder's career might be over.

In 2005, he battled back, appearing in 13 games with the Royals, posting a 1-3 record and a 6.75 ERA. In 2006, he was brought up to the Royals again and pitched in one game: one start, two innings, an ERA of 22.50. The Royals finally gave up on Snyder and released him. He was picked up by the Boston Red Sox and found his way into 16 Major League games during the rest of the season. In 2007, he became a reliever for the Red Sox and appeared in 46 games, a remarkable number compared to the rest of his Major League career. He even made it to the World Series roster for the Sox that year and earned a championship ring. He started one game for the Sox in 2008 and got bombed, thus he was sent back down to the minors. After toiling in the minor leagues the rest of that season and in 2009, Snyder gave up the game. Most recently, he has been in the Tampa Bay Rays organization as a pitching coach.

GEORGE "SNUFFY" STIRNWEISS ■ 5' 8" 175

■ *Second Base / Third Base / Shortstop*

COLLEGE: 1937–40 **MLB:** 1943–52

New York native George Stirnweiss, known to most as "Snuffy," was an excellent football player. He became an All-American halfback for the Tar Heels and was drafted by the Chicago Cardinals. He was also a top-notch baseball player for the Tar Heels, though, and seemed to enjoy baseball just a bit more than football—or basketball, in which he was a good player too. So he signed with the New York Yankees organization after graduating from the University of North Carolina in 1940.

Stirnweiss spent a couple seasons in the minors before making it up to the Yankees. In his rookie year of 1943, he got into 83 games, and it became clear that he was going to be a big-league star. He played mostly at shortstop that first year but became the regular second baseman for the Yankees in 1944, a year that saw him lead the American League in plate appearances, hits, triples, runs scored, and stolen bases. But it wasn't just offense at which he excelled. He also led the league in assists, putouts, and fielding percentage by a second baseman. His productivity in 1945 was just as good, and he led the league in batting average. He had become one of *the* top players of the World War II era. A lot of top-notch players returned from the war for the 1946 season and Stirnweiss never repeated the amazing numbers he put up in 1944–45. Still, he was an infield mainstay for the Yankees until 1950, when he was traded to the St. Louis Browns early in the season. The following year, the Browns traded him to the Cleveland Indians, with whom he finished his career.

B. J. SURHOFF ■ 6' 1" 185 ■ *Left Field / Catcher / Third Base*

COLLEGE: 1983–85 **MLB:** 1987–2005 **OLYMPICS:** 1984

No Carolina player had a longer pro career than William James Surhoff. Known to most as B. J., he had a legendary career as a hitter and catcher in Chapel Hill that included being on the 1984 Olympics U.S. baseball team (along with UNC teammate Scott Bankhead). In 1985, Surhoff was named the ACC's Male Athlete of the Year and was chosen by the Milwaukee Brewers as the first player in the MLB Draft.

B.J. SURHOFF. B.J. Surhoff, with an appearance in the Olympics and nearly a 20-year Major League career, ranks as one of the most successful Carolina baseball players.

He made it up to the Brewers in 1987 and had a nice rookie season, batting .299 with seven homers and 68 RBI in just 115 games. He could play just about anywhere on the diamond, was a good athlete, and had decent speed. After all, he came from an athletic family. His father, Dick, played in the NBA for a couple of seasons. His brother, Rick, played in the minors and very briefly for both the Texas Rangers and the Philadelphia Phillies.

It looked like Surhoff was about to burst into superstar status, but it wasn't an overnight process by any means. From 1988 through 1994, he posted solid numbers but nothing particularly impressive. In 1995, he finally had the season that everyone had expected. He batted .320, with a slugging percentage of .492 and 13 home runs—all career bests. That success allowed him to sign a fat free-agent deal with the Baltimore Orioles at the end of the season.

GEORGE "SNUFFY" STIRNWEISS *continued from page 157*

After leaving the game as a player, Stirnweiss stayed close to baseball for a while by managing minor league teams in Schenectady and Binghamton. Afterward, he became solicitor of new accounts for the Federation Bank & Trust Co. and then a foreign freight agent for Caldwell & Co. Stirnweiss died in 1958 at the age of 39 when a Central Railroad of New Jersey commuter train slid off the open Newark Bay lift bridge. He was one of 48 people who died in that tragic accident. Known as a family man, Stirnweiss was survived by a wife and six children.

In 1996, Surhoff played mostly third base beside Orioles legend Cal Ripken Jr., who was at shortstop. Surhoff hit .292/.352/.482 with 21 homers and 82 RBI and helped lead the Orioles to the playoffs. In 1997, Ripken moved from short to third, sending Surhoff to left field, where he continued his great play. Surhoff had an All-Star year in 1999, batting .308/.347/.492 with 28 homers and 107 RBI. He also led the league in at bats. In 2000, the Atlanta Braves were in the midst of their run of first-place division finishes and in a tight race with the New York Mets. They needed another strong batter and veteran leadership and made a trade to get Surhoff. He played for the Braves the rest of that season and for the next two—all of which were division-winning years for Atlanta. In 2003, as a free agent, Surhoff chose to go back to the Orioles. By then he was in his late 30s but was still putting up good numbers. In fact, he hit over .300 for the final time in his career in 2004, batting .309.

Surhoff was elected to the Orioles Hall of Fame in 2007.

Still a Baltimore-area resident, Surhoff and his wife, Polly, helped found Pathfinders for Autism, which is a 501(c)(3) organization that has grown into Maryland's largest autism group. B. J. Surhoff currently serves as the organization's president.

BURGESS WHITEHEAD ■ 5' 10" 160
■ *Second Base / Third Base / Shortstop*

COLLEGE: 1929–32 **MLB:** 1933–37, 1939–41, 1947

Born in Tarboro, North Carolina, Burgess Whitehead is best remembered as a member of the 1934 St. Louis Cardinals, known as the Gashouse Gang, who won the World Series that year. After attending the University of North Carolina, the versatile athlete took his skills to professional baseball. He made it to the Cardinals in 1933, playing in only 12 games, but setting the stage for becoming a regular infielder for the team. In 1934, a dream season for the Cards, Whitehead, or "Whitey" as he was often called, played in 100 games, batting .277. He played another solid year with St. Louis before being traded to the New York Giants.

He was an everyday second baseman for the Giants in 1936, batting .278/.317/.356 with four home runs in his first year with the club. It seemed Whitey might prove to be a star, as he helped lead the team to the World Series, though the Giants lost to the New York Yankees. His second season with the team was similar, also ending to a loss to the Yankees in the World Series, but then his career began to take some curious turns. In February 1938, Whitehead had an appendectomy that proved to be a traumatic experience—so much so that he suffered a nervous breakdown afterward. He refused to play baseball in the 1938 season and instead stayed at home in North

WALT WEISS ■ 6' 0" 175 ■ *Shortstop*

COLLEGE: 1983–85 **MLB:** 1987–2000

A Carolina teammate of the just-profiled B. J. Surhoff, Walt Weiss was an All-ACC player all three of his seasons in Chapel Hill. He was known for his work ethic and smooth play in the field. He had a quiet passion for the game and he was selected 11th overall in the 1985 MLB Draft by the Oakland Athletics. He had his Major League debut in 1987 in a handful of games but then won American League Rookie of the Year honors in 1988 playing in 147 games, batting .250, and turning in a fielding percentage of .979. His performance was one factor that got the A's to the World Series, which they eventually lost to the Los Angeles Dodgers. Weiss was never known as a great hitter, nor did he have a lot of pop in his bat. He was better known as a defenseman and as a leader with a high baseball IQ. In six years of Major League action with the A's, he never had more than three home runs or 40 RBIs in a season. He did win a World Series ring with the A's in 1989 as Oakland defeated its fellow Bay Area team, the San Francisco Giants. The A's were back in the Series in 1990, though Weiss had suffered an injury that kept him from playing and Oakland lost to the Cincinnati Reds. After the 1992 season, Weiss was traded to the Florida Marlins, where he played for a season before signing a free-agent contract with the Colorado Rockies.

WALT WEISS. After his days in Chapel Hill, Walt Weiss found success as a Major League player and manager.

It was at Colorado that Weiss really hit his stride as a player. In four years with the Rockies, he had an overall batting average of .266 and even hit a career-high eight home runs in 1996. He finished his career with three years playing for the Atlanta Braves, helping them get to the playoffs each season and finally making an All-Star Game in 1998. After his playing days were over, he went back to the Rockies, where he worked as special assistant to the general manager for seven seasons and then as an assistant coach before becoming the head baseball coach for Regis Jesuit High School in Aurora, Colorado. He led the high school team to a 20-6 record and a trip to the 5A semifinals. In November 2012, Weiss was named manager of the Colorado Rockies. He and his wife, Terri, and sons Blake, Brody, Bo, and Brock reside in Franktown, Colorado.

Carolina. He finally returned to the Giants in 1939 and had a subpar year by his standards. His 1940 season was back to normal, but his productivity dipped again in '41 amid the backdrop of the war in Europe.

By 1942, the United States was now involved in the war, and Whitehead joined the Army. By the time he got back to big-league baseball, it was 1946 and he was 36 years old. He played in 55 games for the Pittsburgh Pirates, hitting only .220. He was released by the Pirates and played a couple years of minor league ball before finally hanging up his cleats. Whitehead died in Windsor, North Carolina, back in 1993, as the last remaining member of the Cardinals' old Gashouse Gang. He was 83. He was survived by his wife, Ruth Madre Lyon Whitehead, and two children, Charles Lyon Whitehead and Susan Whitehead Harrell.

LARRY WOODALL ■ 5' 9" 165 ■ *Catcher*

COLLEGE: 1914–15 **MLB:** 1920–29

During the 1920s, Larry Woodall was one of the regular catchers of the Detroit Tigers. After playing college ball for both Wake Forest and the University of North Carolina, Woodall had his Major League debut in 1920 and shared time at the catcher spot with other guys, such as Oscar Stanage, Clyde Manion, and Johnny Bassler. And yes, these were the Tigers of legendary outfielder and hitter Ty Cobb, who played in Detroit from 1905 until 1926. Woodall didn't have much pop at the plate. He only had one home run in a decade in the bigs. He was a solid defenseman, though. In 1927, he led the American League in fielding percentage by catchers.

Throughout his career, his batting average was inconsistent. He batted over .300 in three seasons, including an outstanding .363 in 1921. On the other hand, he batted a mere .205 in 1925 and not much better in 1928 (.210). In 1929, he played in just one Major League game, failing to get a hit in his one at bat. Woodall loved the game too much to give it up after 10 Major League seasons, so he played another 10 years in the Pacific Coast League for the Portland Beavers, Sacramento Senators, and San Francisco Seals. After his playing days were finally over, he stayed in the Pacific Coast League briefly as a manager before joining the Boston Red Sox organization. Woodall served in several capacities with the Sox, scout and coach among them, until his death in 1963 at the age of 68.

Other UNC Major League Players

PLAYER	POSITION	COLLEGE	MLB	STATS	PLAYED FOR:
Daniel Bard	*Pitcher*	2004–06	2009–11	10-19, 3.67, 5 saves	Boston Red Sox
Mike Bynum	*Pitcher*	1997–99	2002–04	2-5, 7.73	San Diego Padres
Claude Crocker	*Pitcher*	1944	1944–45	0-0, 6.75, 1 save	Brooklyn Dodgers
Jim Dougherty	*Pitcher*	1987–90	1995–99	8-8, 5.99	Houston Astros, Oakland A's, Pittsburgh Pirates
Vern Duncan	*Outfield, Third Base*	1909–10	1913–15	.279/.357/.347	Philadelphia Phillies, Baltimore Terrapins
Tyrell Godwin	*Pinch Hitter*	1998–2000	2005	.000/.000/.000	Washington Nationals
Moonlight Graham	*Right Field*	1900–02	1905	.000/.000/.000	New York Giants
Adam Greenberg	*Pinch Hitter*	2000–02	2005, 2013	.000/1.00/.000	Chicago Cubs, Miami Marlins
Bill Haywood	*Pitcher*	1963–64	1968	0-0, 4.70	Washington Senators
Harry Hedgpeth	*Pitcher*	1909–10	1913	0-0, 0.00, 1 save	Washington Senators
Garry Hill	*Pitcher*	1967	1969	0-1, 15.43	Atlanta Braves
Herm Holshouser	*Pitcher*	1925	1930	0-1, 7.80, 1 save	St. Louis Browns
Tommy Irwin	*Shortstop*	1934–35	1938	.111/.333/.111	Cleveland Indians
Mike Jerzembeck	*Pitcher*	1993	1998	0-1, 12.79	New York Yankees
Fred Johnston	*Second Base, Third Base*	1922	1924	.250/.250/.250	Brooklyn Robins
Bob Lawson	*Pitcher, Left Field, Third Base*	1897–99	1901–02	2-4, 3.66; .152/.176/.273	Boston Beaneaters, Baltimore Orioles
Dave Lemonds	*Pitcher*	1968	1969, 1972	4-8, 2.99	Chicago Cubs, Chicago White Sox
Clem Llewellyn	*Pitcher*	1917–22	1922	0-0, 0.00	New York Yankees
Dwight Lowry	*Catcher*	1977–80	1984, 1986-88	.273/.343/.374	Detroit Tigers, Minnesota Twins
Jim Mallory	*Outfield*	1939–40	1940, 1945	.268/.301/.289	Washington Senators, St. Louis Cardinals, New York Giants
Bill Paschall	*Pitcher*	1973–76	1978–79, 1981	0-2, 5.32, 1 save	Kansas City Royals
Chris Pittaro	*Third Base, Second Base, Shortstop*	1980–82	1985–87	.333/.385/.333	Detroit Tigers, Minnesota Twins
Mule Shirley	*First Base*	1921–23	1924–25	.210/.240/.280	Washington Senators
Ryan Snare	*Pitcher*	1998–2000	2004	0-0, 10.80	Texas Rangers

Pitcher Brad Woodall saw Major League stops with the Atlanta Braves, Milwaukee Brewers, and Chicago Cubs during the 1990s.

PLAYER | POSITION | COLLEGE | MLB | STATS | PLAYED FOR:
Buck Stanton *Right Field* | 1925 | 1931 | .200/.200/.333 | St. Louis Browns
Fred Stem *First Base* | 1904–07 | 1908–09 | .224/.263/.265 | Boston Doves
Shaq Thompson *Center Field* | 1913 | 1914–16 | .203/.357/.253 **Played For:** Philadelphia Athletics
Alex White *Pitcher* | 2007–09 | 2011–12 | 5-13, 6.03 | Cleveland Indians, Colorado Rockies
Marsh Williams *Pitcher* | 1914–16 | 1916 | 0-6, 7.89 | Philadelphia Athletics
Brad Woodall* *Pitcher* | 1988–91 | 1994–96, 1998–99 | 10-14, 5.31 | Atlanta Braves, Milwaukee Brewers, Chicago Cubs

* *pictured above*

SOFTBALL

Softball at the University of North Carolina dates back to the spring of 1977. It had been a club sport on campus but finally achieved varsity status and, led by coach Dolly Hunter, the Tar Heels won their first game against North Carolina Central. The game looked different then, as the team played slow-pitch ball. The Tar Heels, under the tutelage of Susan Clark, switched to fast-pitch play in 1984, which was also the year that the Tar Heels moved to Finley Field. In 1986, Carolina hired Donna Papa, who had been the head volleyball and softball coach at Susquehanna University. In the Carolina tradition of keeping coaches for a long time, Papa has been there ever since. Now approaching 30 years of coaching experience, including 27 in Chapel Hill, she has built the Tar Heels into a perennial power. In 1992, the Tar Heels officially joined the ACC in softball. In 2002, the program moved into its new home, which has evolved as the UNC Softball Complex.

Papa won her 1,000th career game in a 4–0 victory over Florida State in 2011. She is one of just 11 Division I softball coaches to achieve 1,000 wins. She has been named ACC Coach of the Year on five occasions: 1996, 1998, 2000, 2008, and 2012. She was inducted into the National Fastpitch Coaches Association Hall of Fame in 2012. And while Papa had won numerous accolades, she couldn't have achieved them without the help of some great Carolina Tar Heels along the way. She has five times coached ACC Player of the Year recipients: Beverly Smith (1994), Brandy Arthur (1998), Michelle Semmes (2000), and Danielle Spaulding (2008–09).

As for pro softball, the International Women's Professional Softball Association began in 1976 with 10 teams from across the country, each playing

Coach Donna J. Papa was inducted to the National Fastpitch Coaches Association Hall of Fame in 2012. She's been the ACC Coach of the Year five times.

a 120-game schedule consisting of 60 doubleheaders. The league ran out of money after four seasons.

The current National Pro Fastpitch league has its roots in Women's Pro Fastpitch, which began league play in 1997. It started out with six teams in the eastern half of the country. It changed its name to the Women's Professional Softball League for the 1999 season, contracted to four teams in 2000, tried an 11-city Tour of Fastpitch Champions in 2001, and finally suspended play in 2002.

The league relaunched in 2004 with six teams. Many additions and subtractions followed, and today the league continues with four teams: USSSA Pride of Kissimmee, Florida; Chicago Bandits; Akron (Ohio) Racers; and Carolina Diamonds of Charlotte, North Carolina.

NCAA Championships

(Through 2013)

12 UCLA	**2** Texas A&M	**1** Fresno State
8 Arizona	**1** Alabama	**1** Michigan
2 Arizona State	**1** Cal State Fullerton	**1** Washington
2 Oklahoma	**1** California	

ACC Team Appearances in the NCAA Tournament

(Through 2013)

26 Florida State	**6** Virginia Tech	**3** NC State
11 Georgia Tech	**4** Maryland	**3** NC State
11 **North Carolina**	**3** Boston College	**1** Virginia

Atlantic Coast Conference Championships

(Tournament, through 2013)

11 Florida State	**2** Virginia Tech	**1** Virginia
5 Georgia Tech	**1** Maryland	**1** Virginia
2 North Carolina State	**1** **North Carolina**	**1** Virginia

Head Coaching Records

(In chronological order)

YEARS	COACH	RECORD
1979	Beth Miller	18-11
1980–85	Susan Clark	211-119-1
1986–2013	Donna Papa	1,062-575-2

Natalie Anter was a four-year starter at catcher for the Tar Heels who went on to represent Italy in the 2004 Olympic Games.

University of North Carolina Athletes Who Have Played Pro Softball

Natalie Anter* *(represented Italy in the 2004 Olympic Games in Athens, Greece)*

Brandy Arthur	**Victoria Huff**	**Emily Price****
Sonya Bright	**Christie Knauer**	**Lorin Slade**
Amy Cole	**Radara McHugh****	**Beverly Smith**
Yvette Davis	**Brittany McKinney**	**Danielle Spaulding**
Jeanine Gunther	**Lisa Norris**	

* *pictured above* ** *other notes below*

RADARA MCHUGH
Pitcher Radara McHugh helped lead the Akron Racers to the National Pro Fastpitch championship in 2005.

EMILY PRICE
After setting a single-season record for home runs (16), Emily Price played in the Ladies Professional Fastpitch Association before getting into coaching.

SOCCER

Soccer is still catching on in much of the United States. That's not the case in Chapel Hill, though, where soccer is held in high esteem and success, at the highest level is the norm. That's especially true for UNC's women's soccer program, which has been one of the most triumphant of any collegiate program in any sport.

"The University of North Carolina women's soccer is special in so many ways," says former Tar Heel star Mia Hamm in her foreword to the book *The Vision of a Champion.* At the center of UNC soccer success—and the author of that book—is Anson Dorrance, whose feats as a head coach are legendary. Hamm adds, "When I was there, we all shared the feeling that it is an honor and a privilege to play in the program. Every single day you earn the right to be there, and to wear that uniform. Your commitment to yourself, to your teammates, and to that program, is a constant renewal process."

Some casual fans might not know that Dorrance began his long tenure at UNC as the men's soccer coach. After playing soccer for the Tar Heels, Dorrance was recruited by his former coach, Marvin Allen, to succeed him as the men's coach. Just a quick word about Allen before we proceed: He must be recognized as the father of Carolina soccer. He was the coach when men's soccer was raised to varsity status in 1947. In 28 seasons at the helm, Allen's teams combined for a 174-81-23 record. That's pretty darn successful. But between 1977 and 1988, Dorrance actually won one more game than his mentor, compiling a 175-65-21 record. Dorrance's most successful year was in 1987, when he led the team to an Atlantic Coast Conference Championship and an NCAA Final Four appearance while being named NCAA Men's Soccer Coach of the Year.

Meanwhile, in 1979, Dorrance was also asked to coach the women's team at UNC. For someone to juggle both tasks with aplomb is commendable. Dorrance, though, put up jaw-dropping numbers with the women's team. Through 2012, Dorrance's teams won 21 of 31 NCAA championships and 20 ACC championships. His team also won the Association for Intercollegiate Athletics for Women (AIWA) championship in 1981 before UNC (and basically the rest of women's intercollegiate programs) joined the NCAA. His teams once had a streak of 101 games without a loss.

One of the great testaments to Dorrance's tutelage lies in the fact that 17 different Tar Heels have been named national players of the year during Dorrance's tenure: April Heinrichs in 1984 and 1986, Shannon Higgins in 1988–89, Kristine Lilly in 1990–91, Mia Hamm in 1992–93, Tisha Venturini in 1994, Debbie Keller in 1995–96, Staci Wilson in 1995, Cindy Parlow in 1996–98,

Anson Dorrance is simply the most successful collegiate soccer coach in U.S. history.

Robin Confer in 1997, Lorrie Fair in 1999, Meredith Florance in 2000, Lindsay Tarpley in 2003, Catherine Reddick in 2003, Heather O'Reilly in 2006, Yael Averbuch in 2006, Casey Nogueira in 2008, and Whitney Engen in 2009.

The point is that Dorrance is a coaching legend, and the UNC women's program is nothing short of remarkable. Let's not forget the men, though. Without the large shadow of the women's program, the men would be the amazing success story. Three ACC championships and two NCAA championships are solid accomplishments. In 2011, Coach Carlos Somoano became the fifth head coach in the history of UNC men's soccer. He did pretty well—if you consider an ACC Championship, National Championship, and being named National Coach of the Year by Soccer America as pretty well. Somoano served as an assistant to Elmar Bolowich for nine seasons. Bolowich is the winningest coach in the history of the men's program.

"After nine years with the team and in the ACC, it's the smoothest transition it can be to take over a team on which he recruited many of the players," Bolowich said upon the hire of Somoano. "He has all the ingredients for him to be successful as a head coach." Apparently, Bolowich knew what he was talking about.

As for professional soccer, the distinction in this sport is much more unclear than in football, for example. Soccer has had a handful of professional leagues and also has national and club teams. And, of course, there's the Olympic Games as well. In women's soccer, the Women's Premier Soccer League (WPSL) has been in existence since 1998 as a pro-am league. It is sanctioned by the United States Adult Soccer Association (USASA) as an affiliate of the United States Soccer Federation (USSF). That pro-am makes it tricky, however, as a player in this league might be a pro who is getting paid or might not. The first real professional league in the United States, in which all of the players were paid as professionals, was the Women's United Soccer Association (WUSA), which was around from 2000 to 2003. Women's Professional Soccer (WPS) was a league that was around from 2007 to 2013. The National Women's Soccer League (NWSL) began play in the spring of 2013.

For the men, the situation is similar, with national, international, and Olympics teams. Major League Soccer has emerged as the dominant pro league, but you also have the North American Soccer League (NASL), which began play in 2011 after taking its name from a league that existed from 1968 to 1984, and the United Soccer Leagues (USL), organizer of several soccer leagues both pro and amateur. One of those is the Major Indoor Soccer League, founded in 2008 and known to even the most casual soccer fan.

It can definitely be a bit confusing as players wend through the ranks and hop from one level to the next. But we'll do our best to give you some idea of what your favorite soccer stars have done since leaving UNC.

First, let's take a look at the UNC soccer players who made it to the Olympic Games.

Men

Eddie Pope (Atlanta 1996)	**Ken Harnden** (Sydney 2000)	**Eddie Neufville** (Sydney 2000)	**Dominic Demeritte** (Sydney 2000)
Allen Johnson (Sydney 2000)	**Dax McCarty** (Beijing 2008)	**Allen Johnson** (Sydney 2000)	**Dax McCarty** (Beijing 2008)

Women

Coach Laurie Gregg (Atlanta 1996, Sydney 2000)	**Staci Wilson** (Atlanta 1996)	**Tobin Heath** (Beijing 2008, London 2012)
Tisha Venturini (Atlanta 1996)	**Lori Chalupny** (Beijing 2008)	**Cindy Parlow** (Atlanta 1996, Sydney 2000, Athens 2004)
Catherine Reddick (Athens 2004)	**Kristine Lilly** (Atlanta 1996, Sydney 2000, Athens 2004)	**Coach Tracy Bates-Leon** (Athens 2004)

Mia Hamm (Atlanta 1996, Sydney 2000, Athens 2004)	**Lorrie Fair** (Sydney 2000)	**Kacey White** (Beijing 2008)
Carla Werden (Atlanta 1996, Sydney 2000)	**Robyn Gale** (playing for Canada; Beijing 2008, London 2012)	**Tiffany Roberts** (Atlanta 1996)
Lindsay Tarpley (Athens 2004, Beijing 2008)	**Tracy Noonan** (Atlanta 1996)	**Heather O'Reilly** (Athens 2004, Beijing 2008, London 2012)
Coach April Heinrichs (Atlanta 1996, Sydney 2000, Athens 2004)	**Siri Mullinix** (Sydney 2000)	

As you can see both above and below, whether it be Olympics, national teams, club teams, or the various pro leagues, Tar Heels have heavily populated soccer teams in the United States. In the annals of Carolina soccer history, though, two players stand out as the greatest of the greats: Kristine Lilly and Mia Hamm. We'll look at those two players in depth before we move on to our list of other UNC soccer stars who continued playing after college.

LORI CHALUPNY. Lori Chalupny played for the U.S. National Team and for several pro soccer teams after her time as a Tar Heel.

LORRIE FAIR. A member of the 2000 U.S. soccer team, Lorrie Fair also played for the Sunnyvale Roadrunners and the Philadelphia Charge.

MIA HAMM ■ *Forward*

COLLEGE: 1989–90 1992–93 **PRO/NATIONAL TEAMS:** 1987–2004

Mariel Margaret Hamm, known more commonly as Mia, could be called the Michael Jordan of women's soccer. For one, Hamm and Jordan are both Tar Heels. Next, their accomplishments in their respective sports are simply jaw-dropping. And finally, each is probably the best-known individual in his or her respective sport. Hamm, born in Selma, Alabama, moved around quite a bit as the daughter of an Air Force pilot. Her brother, Garrett, got her interested in sports as a way to make friends and get involved when the family moved to a new community. Mia really took a liking to soccer.

MIA HAMM. Mia Hamm was the most widely known soccer player in the United States during her years active in the sport.

At age 15, she became the youngest player to ever play for the U.S. National Team. She went on to become the most prolific scorer for the United States in international competition. That record finally fell in 2013 to Abby Wambach. The Tar Heels won the NCAA Championship all four years in which she participated (she sat out the 1991 season to concentrate on the FIFA World's Cup—and yes, she was the youngest player on that championship team). In Hamm's four seasons, the Tar Heels lost just one game, and she was an All-American and All-ACC selection for three of those years. She graduated in 1994 with a degree in political science.

After her years in Chapel Hill, Hamm went on to become the first three-time U.S. Soccer athlete of the year, male or female (1994–96); in 1996, she was captain on the U.S. Olympics Soccer Team that won the gold medal and brought women's soccer to the collective American consciousness. In all, Hamm played for the U.S. women's national team for 17 years, becoming *the* face of American soccer in the process. (Speaking of faces, she was named by *People* magazine as one of the 50 Most Beautiful People in 1997.) She was named the Women's Sports Foundation Athlete of the Year for 1997, and the FIFA World Player of the Year in 2001 and 2002. Known mostly for her play in international competition, Hamm did play professionally stateside for the Washington Freedom of the WUSA from the time the league started play until it suspended operations (2001–03).

continued on next page

MIA HAMM *continued from page 173*

Known as a tenacious competitor and as the ultimate team player, Hamm is quoted as saying, "I am a member of the team, and I rely on the team, I defer to it and sacrifice for it, because the team, not the individual, is the ultimate champion." UNC teammate Julie Foudy said of Hamm, "Whenever she accepted an award, Mia would spend the first 10 minutes thanking her teammates, family, coaches, friends, doctors, trainers, past teachers, etc., for helping her achieve success. She did it honestly and never for show. Mia's unwavering commitment to the group defined who we were as a team. She set the standard for all of us to follow." ESPN named her the Greatest Female Athlete of the Past 40 Years.

She married college sweetheart Christian Corry in 1994, but the couple divorced in 2001. She married Boston Red Sox great Nomar Garciaparra in 2003, and the next year helped lead the U.S. Olympics Soccer Team to another gold medal. She then retired from the sport to concentrate on her family life. She and Garciaparra now have three children. Hamm operates the Mia Hamm Foundation, which is focused on providing support for two causes important to Hamm: raising funds and awareness for families needing marrow or cord blood transplants and continuing the growth in opportunities for young women in sports. Hamm's brother, Garrett, died in 1997 from complications related to aplastic anemia.

Also like Michael Jordan, Hamm has been a popular choice for product endorsements. Over the years, she has had endorsement deals with Nike, Gatorade, Pepsi, Nabisco, PowerBar, Mattel, Dick's Sporting Goods, and others. In essence, she has transcended her sport. "When Mia came along, our game was nothing and nowhere," her UNC coach Anson Dorrance was quoted as saying. "When she left it, it was something and significant. Mia was a part of that transition. And every little girl wanted to be Mia. She had almost a Beatles-like presence whenever she was in the stadium."

KRISTINE LILLY ■ *Midfielder*

COLLEGE: 1989–92 **PRO/NATIONAL TEAMS:** 1992–2011

"If goals are how fans remember (Mia) Hamm, then (Kristine) Lilly's consistency and durability are what set her apart," wrote ESPN's Jeff Carlisle. In that same article, Carlisle quoted former U.S. national team manager Tony DiCicco as saying, "Lilly trained with such a consistency that everyone else tried to aspire to her level." DiCicco added, "Lilly was remarkable in many ways. She had the ability to turn defense into offense so quickly that most teams weren't ready for it. She

defined the way that the U.S. wanted to compete in every game, and the work that they wanted to put in."

Lilly's 352 appearances for her national team in a 24-year career rank first in the world for male or female athletes. The Connecticut native is the only player to take the field for the United States in four different decades, and she is both the youngest and the oldest player to score a goal for the USA. Lilly scored 130 international goals, played in three Olympic Games, played in five FIFA Women's World Cups, and captained the U.S. Women's National Team from 2005 to 2007. While Mia Hamm is probably the best-known female soccer player in the world, it would be hard to argue that anyone is more accomplished in the game than Kristine Lilly. Before all the international accolades, though, Lilly led the Tar Heels to four consecutive national championships. She was a four-time All-American. The Tar Heels lost just twice and had one tie in Lilly's four-year career in Chapel Hill.

KRISTINE LILLY. Kristine Lilly appeared in 352 games for the U.S. National Team. That number ranks her as first in the world in appearances for men or women.

Like Hamm, Lilly spent most of her soccer days playing on the international circuit after college. She did, however, spend time with the Boston Breakers of the WUSA from 2001 to 2003 and then again for the Breakers of WPS in 2009–10. She was captain of the Breakers in both of its incarnations of the early and late 2000s.

Through the end of 2007, Lilly had played in 85% of the games the U.S. national team women had ever played. She retired from competitive play in January 2011. Later that year, she had her second child with husband David Heavey, a Boston-area firefighter. She couldn't stay away from the game for long, though. In 2012, she joined her old pro team, the Boston Breakers, as an assistant coach. "My professional playing career has only been with the Breakers, and now it's nice to join the team as a coach," she said. Lilly coached a season with the Breakers and now operates the Kristine Lilly Soccer Academy and is one of three founders of Team First Soccer Academy, along with fellow Tar Heels and U.S. National Women's Team players Mia Hamm and Tisha Venturini-Hoch. "Just seeing kids smile and do something you ask is pretty rewarding," Lilly was quoted as saying in regard to her coaching career. "Also, I do private lessons and seeing those kids go off and play in college is nice."

Never one to back away from a challenge, in 2004, Lilly climbed Mount Kilimanjaro in Tanzania, the tallest peak in Africa. She came up short of reaching the 19,340-foot summit by about 1,000 feet but still called her ascent "one of the most amazing experiences of [her] life."

Other Women Who Have Gone Pro in Soccer or Played on the U.S. National Team

NAME	POSITION	COLLEGE	PRO	PLAYED FOR
Yael Averbuch	*Midfielder*	2005–08	2002–13	New Jersey Lady Stallions, NY/NJ Sky Blue, Western NY Flash, WFC Rossiyanka, Kopparbergs/Göteborg FC, U.S. National Team
Meredith (Florance) Beard	*Forward*	1997–2000	1999–2003	Washington Freedom, Carolina Courage, U.S. National Team
Danielle Borgman	*Defender*	1998–2001	1997–2002	U.S. National Team, Bay Area CyberRays, Carolina Courage
Jenni Branam	*Goalkeeper*	1999–2002	2000–11	Charlotte Lady Eagles, San Diego Spirit, Arizona Heatwave, Bälinge FC, NY/NJ Sky Blue, U.S. National Team
Amber Brooks	*Midfielder*	1992–94	2013	Bayern Munich
Susan Bush	*Forward*	1999–2002	1998–2000, 2003	U.S. National Team, San Diego Spirit
Lori Chalupny	*Midfielder*	2002–2005	2001–13	Chicago Red Stars, U.S. National Team, River Cities FC, St. Louis Athletica, AIK Fotboll Dam, Atlanta Beat
Suzy Cobb	*Defender*	1981–84	1986	U.S. National Team
Robin Confer	*Forward*	1994–97	1996–98, 2001	U.S. National Team, Boston Breakers
Sarah Dacey	*Midfielder*	1993–96	2001–02	Carolina Courage, Boston Breakers
Kristin DePlatchett	*Goalkeeper*	1998–2001	2002	Atlanta Beat
Tracy Ducar	*Goalkeeper*	1991–94	1990–91, 1996–99	Boston Breakers, U.S. National Team
Joan Dunlap-Seivold	*Forward*	1983–84	1986	U.S. National Team
Crystal Dunn	*Midfielder*	2010–12	2013	U.S. National Team
Danielle Egan	*Defender*	1991–94	1993	U.S. National Team
Whitney Engen	*Defender*	2006–09	2010–13	U.S. National Team, Chicago Red Stars, Western NY Flash, Liverpool
Stacey Enos	*Defender*	1982–85	1985–86	U.S. National Team
Kristi Eveland	*Defender*	2006–09	2010	Washington Freedom
Lorrie Fair	*Defender, Center Midfielder*	1996–99	1996–2005	Sunnyvale Roadrunners , Philadelphia Charge, U.S. National Team
Nel Fettig	*Defender*	1994–97	2001–03	New York Power, Carolina Courage
Shelly Finger	*Goalkeeper*	1991–94	2002	San Diego Spirit
Kendall Fletcher	*Defender*	2002–05	2009–13	U.S. National Team, St. Louis Athletica, Philadelphia Independence, NY/NJ Sky Blue, Vittsjo GIK

NAME | POSITION | COLLEGE | PRO | PLAYED FOR
Leslie Gaston *Defender* | 1999–2002 | 2003 | Atlanta Beat
Adelaide Gay *Goalkeeper* | 2010–11 | 2013 | Portland Thorns
Robyn Gayle *Defender* | 2004–07 | 2013 | Washington Spirit, Canada National Team, Vancouver Whitecaps
Wendy Gebauer *Forward* | 1985–88 | 1987–91 | U.S. National Team
Gretchen Gegg *Goalkeeper* | 1986 | 1986–90 | U.S. National Team
Laurie Gregg *Midfielder* | 1981–82 | 1986 | U.S. National Team
Libby Guess *Forward* | 2003–06 | 2013 | Boston Breakers
Linda Hamilton *Defender* | 1990 | 1987–95 | U.S. National Team
Ariel Harris *Defender* | 2004–07 | 2009 | Boston Breakers
Ashlyn Harris *Goalkeeper* | 2006–09 | 2013 | U.S. National Team
Tobin Heath *Midfielder* | 2006–09 | 2008–13 | U.S. National Team, Paris Saint-Germain FC, Portland Thorns, New York Fury, NY/NJ Sky Blue, Atlanta Beat
April Heinrichs *Forward* | 1983–86 | 1986–91 | U.S. National Team
Lori Henry *Defender* | 1986–88 | 1985–91 | U.S. National Team
Shannon Higgins *Midfielder* | 1986–89 | 1987–91 | U.S. National Team
Courtney Jones *Forward* | 2008–11 | 2013 | Kansas City
Kalli Kamholz *Defender* | 1999–2000 | 2001 | Philadelphia Charge
Rakel Karvelsson *Forward* | 1995–98 | 2001–02 | Philadelphia Charge
Debbie Keller *Forward* | 1993–96 | 1995–98 | U.S. National Team

APRIL HEINRICHS. April Heinrichs helped to put UNC women's soccer on the map. She was an assistant coach for the U.S. National Team for the 1996 Olympic Games and head coach in 2000 and 2004.

NAME | POSITION | COLLEGE | PRO | PLAYED FOR
Meghan Klingenberg *Midfielder* | 2007–10 | 2011–13 | U.S. National Team, Boston Breakers, Tyreso FF
Jena Kluegel *Midfielder* | 1998–2001 | 2000–03 | U.S. National Team, Boston Breakers
Tracey (Bates) Leone *Midfielder* | 1985–87, 1989 | 1987–91 | U.S. National Team
Allie Long *Midfielder* | 2007–08 | 2009–13 | Washington Freedom, NY/NJ Sky Blue, Western NY Flash, Portland Thorns
Marcia McDermott *Defender* | 1983–86 | 1986–88 | U.S. National Team
Julia Marslender *Midfielder/Defender* | 1997–2000 | 2001 | Carolina Courage
Jessica McDonald *Forward* | 2008–09 | 2010, 2013 | Chicago Red Stars
Raven McDonald *Forward* | 1997–2000 | 2001 | New York Power
Rebekah McDowell *Midfielder* | 1996–99 | 2001–03 | Philadelphia Charge, Boston Breakers
Siri Mullinix *Goalkeeper* | 1995–98 | 1999–2004 | U.S. National Team, Washington Freedom
Casey Nogueira *Forward* | 2006–09 | 2007–13 | U.S. National Team, Chicago Red Stars, NY/NJ Sky Blue, Kansas City
Tracy Noonan *Goalkeeper* | 1992–95 | 1995–2003 | U.S. National Team, Boston Breakers
Heather O'Reilly *Midfielder* | 2003–06 | 2002–13 | U.S. National Team, Boston Breakers, NY/NJ Sky Blue
Carla (Werden) Overbeck *Defender* | 1986–89 | 1988–2003 | U.S. National Team, Raleigh Wings, Carolina Courage
Cindy Parlow *Forward* | 1995–98 | 1996–2006 | Atlanta Beat, U.S. National Team
Emily Pickering *Midfielder* | 1981–84 | 1985–92 | U.S. National Team
Louellen Poore *Defender* | 1988–91 | 1992 | U.S. National Team
Alyssa Ramsey *Forward* | 2000–03 | 2000–01 | U.S. National Team
Sara Randolph *Midfielder* | 2001–04 | 2001 | U.S. National Team
Catherine Reddick *Defender* | 2000–03 | 2000–10 | U.S. National Team
Amy Remy *Forward* | 1998–2001 | 2002 | Atlanta Beat
Nicole Roberts *Midfielder/Forward* | 1996 | 2001 | Carolina Courage
Vanessa Rubio *Midfielder* | 1992, 1994–96 | 2001 | U.S. National Team, Philadelphia Charge
Tiffany (Roberts) Sahaydak *Midfielder* | 1995–98 | 1994–2004 | U.S. National Team, Carolina Courage
Keri Sanchez *Defender* | 1991–94 | 1991–2003, 2009 | U.S. National Team, Boston Breakers, San Jose Cyber Rays, Los Angeles Sol

NAME | POSITION | COLLEGE | PRO | PLAYED FOR
Laurie Schwoy *Midfielder* | 1996–98, 2000 | 1997–99, 2001 | U.S. National Team, Philadelphia Charge
Beth Sheppard *Midfielder* | 1995–96, 1998–99 | 2001 | Carolina Courage
Lindsay (Tarpley) Snow *Midfielder* | 2002–05 | 2003–13 | U.S. National Team, Washington Freedom, Chicago Red Stars, St. Louis Athletica, Boston Breakers
Carolyn "Zola" Springer *Defender* | 1990–93 | 1992–93 | U.S. National Team
Amy Steadman *Midfielder* | 2003–04 | 2001 | U.S. National Team
Lindsay Stoecker *Defender* | 1997–2000 | 2001–03 | Washington Freedom
Maggie Tomecka *Midfielder* | 2000–03 | 2009–10 | Boston Breakers
Rita Tower *Forward* | 1989–90, 1992–93 | 1993–94 | U.S. National Team
Tisha Venturini *Midfielder* | 1991–94 | 1990–2003 | U.S. National Team, Delaware Genies, Bay Area CyberRays
Nikki Washington | *Midfielder* | 2006–09 | 2010–13 | Chicago Red Stars, Boston Breakers, Washington Freedom, Atlanta Beat, Portland Thorns
Kacey White | *Midfielder/Forward* | 2002–05 | 2006–12 | Atlanta Beat, NY/NJ Sky Blue, Bälinge IF, New Jersey Wildcats, U.S. National Team
Catherine "Cat" Whitehill | *Defender* | 2000–03 | 2009–13 | U.S. National Team, Washington Freedom, Atlanta Beat, Boston Breakers
Staci Wilson | *Defender* | 1994–97 | 1995–96, 2001–02 | U.S. National Team, Carolina Courage

Men Who Have Gone Pro in Soccer or Played on the U.S. National Team

NAME | POSITION | COLLEGE | PRO | PLAYED FOR
Eddie Ababio *Defender* | 2006–10 | 2011–13 | Colorado Rapids, Carolina RailHawks, Carolina Dynamo, Tampa Bay Rowdies
Jalil Anibaba *Defender* | 2010 | 2010–13 | Chicago Fire, Carolina Dynamo
Corey Ashe *Defender, Midfielder* | 2003–06 | 2007–13 | Houston Dynamo
Chad Ashton *Midfielder* | 1986–89 | 1990–98 | Colorado Foxes, Kansas City Comets, Denver Thunder, Milwaukee Wave, Wichita Wings, Dallas Burn
Gregg Berhalter *Defender* | 1991–93 | 1997–2004, 2009–11 | U.S. National Team, Los Angeles Galaxy
Michael Callahan *Midfielder* | 2005–08 | 2011–13 | Richmond Kickers, Carolina RailHawks
Scott Campbell *Midfielder* | 2005–07 | 2008 | Colorado Rapids
Chris Carrieri *Midfielder* | 1998–2000 | 2001–10 | San Jose Earthquakes, Colorado Rapids, Rochester Raging Rhinos, Chicago Fire, Richmond Kickers, Carolina RailHawks

NAME	POSITION	COLLEGE	PRO	PLAYED FOR
Donald Cogsville	*Defender, Midfielder*	1985–88	1988	U.S. National Team
Matt Crawford	*Midfielder*	1999–2000	2003–07	Colorado Rapids
Tyler Deric	*Goalkeeper*	2007	2007–09	Houston Dynamo
Alex Dixon	*Midfielder*	2008–10	2011–13	Houston Dynamo
Michael Farfan	*Midfielder*	2009–10	2011–13	Philadelphia Union
Marco Ferruzzi	*Midfielder*	1989–92	1997–2004	Tampa Bay Rowdies, Los Angeles Galaxy, Richmond Kickers, Minnesota Thunder
Danny Garcia	*Midfielder*	2012	2013	FC Dallas
Jordan Graye	*Defender*	2005, 2007–09	2010–13	D.C. United, Carolina RailHawks, Houston Dynamo
Michael Harrington	*Defender*	2003–06	2007–13	Sporting Kansas City, Portland Timbers
Matt Hedges	*Defender*	2011	2012–13	FC Dallas
Justin Hughes	*Goalkeeper*	2003–06	2007–08	Colorado Rapids
Ben Hunter	*Forward*	2005–06	2007–09	Columbus Crew, Richmond Kickers
Danny Jackson	*Defender*	1998–2001	2002–08	Colorado Rapids, Seattle Sounders
Chris Leitch	*Defender*	1998–2001	2002–11	Columbus Crew, New York Red Bulls, San Jose Earthquakes
Mikey Lopez	*Midfielder*	2011–12	2013	Sporting Kansas City
Zach Loyd	*Defender*	2006–09	2010	FC Dallas
Enzo Martinez	*Midfielder*	2009–11	2012–13	Real Salt Lake, Carolina RailHawks
Stephen McCarthy	*Defender*	2009–10	2011–13	New England Revolution
Dax McCarty	*Midfielder*	2004–05	2006–13	FC Dallas, D.C. United, New York Red Bulls
Tim Merritt	*Defender*	2001–04	2005, 2009	D.C. United, Miami FC
Caleb Norkus	*Defender, Midfielder*	1997–2000	2007–10	Carolina RailHawks
Logan Pause	*Midfielder*	2000–02	2003–13	Chicago Fire, U.S. National Team
Eddie Pope	*Defender*	1992–95	1996–2007	D.C. United, MetroStars, Real Salt Lake, U.S. National Team
Eddie Robinson	*Defender*	1996, 1998–2000	2001–11	San Jose Earthquakes, Houston Dynamo, U.S. National Team
Brian Shriver	*Forward*	2005–08	2009–13	Fort Lauderdale Strikers, Carolina RailHawks
Ben Speas	*Forward*	2011	2012–13	Columbus Crew

NAME | POSITION | COLLEGE | PRO | PLAYED FOR
David Stokes *Defender* | 2000–02 | 2003–08 | D.C. United, Carolina RailHawks
Marcus Storey *Forward* | 2001–04 | 2005–06 | Columbus Crew, Houston Dynamo
Temoc Suarez *Forward* | 1993–96 | 1997–99 | Dallas Burn
Carey Talley *Defender* | 1994–97 | 1998–2010 | D.C. United, Kansas City Wizards, FC Dallas, Real Salt Lake, Chivas USA, New York Red Bulls
Jamie Watson *Forward* | 2003–04 | 2005–08, 2011 | Real Salt Lake, FC Dallas, Orlando City
Shenon Williams *Defender* | 2008 | 2010–13 | Philadelphia Union
Kerry Zavagnin *Midfielder* | 1992–95 | 1997–98, 2000–08 | MetroStars, Kansas City Wizards, U.S. National Team

WOMEN

Head Coaching Records

(In chronological order, including record and winning percentage; a tie counts as half a win, half a loss, per NCAA practice)

YEARS	COACH	RECORD	WINNING PCT.
1979–2013	Anson Dorrance	743-49-29	.923

NCAA Winningest Coaches

(Ranked by winning percentage through 2013 season; minimum of 10 years in Division I)

COACH	SCHOOL	YEARS	WINNING PCT.	RECORD
Anson Dorrance	**North Carolina**	**34**	**.923**	**743-49-29**
Clive Charles	Portland	14	.799	226-52-13
Jillian Ellis	UCLA	14	.785	248-63-14
Randy Waldrum	Notre Dame	23	.779	387-100-28
Becky Burleigh	Florida	23	.770	401-108-33

(Ranked by victories through 2013 season; minimum of 10 years in Division I)

COACH	SCHOOL	YEARS	WINNING PCT.	RECORD
Anson Dorrance	**North Carolina**	**34**	**.923**	**743-49-29**
Len Tsantiris	Connecticut	32	.728	500-171-50
Becky Burleigh	Florida	23	.770	401-108-33
Jerry Smith	Santa Clara	26	.740	394-122-50
Randy Waldrum	Notre Dame	23	.779	387-100-28

Atlantic Coast Conference Champions

(Regular Season through 2013)

20 North Carolina	**1** Clemson	**1-1** Florida State	**0-1** Boston College
2 Duke	**1** NC State		

(Tournament through 2013)

21 North Carolina	**1** Florida State	**1** Wake Forest
2 Virginia	**1** NC State	

NCAA Championships

(Through 2013)

14 North Carolina	**1** George Mason	**1** Santa Clara	**1** Stanford
1 Florida	**1** Notre Dame	**1** Southern California	

MEN

Head Coaching Records

(In chronological order)

YEARS	COACH	RECORD	WINNING PCT.
1947–50, 1953–76	Marvin Allen	174-81-23	.667
1951–52	Alan Moore	8-9-1	.472
1978–88	Anson Dorrance	172-65-21	.708
1989–2010	Elmar Bolowich	280-144-40	.632
2011–2013	Carlos Somoano	21-2-3	.865

(Ranked by victories)

RECORD	COACH	YEARS
280-144-40	Elmar Bolowich	1989–2010
174-81-23	Marvin Allen	1947–50, 1953–76

GREGG BERHALTER. Defender Gregg Berhalter spent time on the U.S. National Team and with the Los Angeles Galaxy after leaving Chapel Hill.

EDDIE POPLE. Eddie Pople played professionally for three teams and for the U.S. National Team after his days at UNC came to a close.

RECORD	COACH	YEARS
172-65-21	Anson Dorrance	1978–88
21-2-3	Carlos Somoano	2011–13
8-9-1	Alan Moore	1951–52

(Ranked by winning percentage)

WINNING PCT.	RECORD	COACH	YEARS
.865	21-2-3	Carlos Somoano	2011–13
.708	172-65-21	Anson Dorrance	1978–88
.667	174-81-23	Marvin Allen	1947–50, 1953–76
.632	280-144-40	Elmar Bolowich	1989–2010
.472	8-9-1	Alan Moore	1951–52

Atlantic Coast Conference Teams

(Ranked by wins through 2013 season)

RECORD	TEAM	WINNING PCT.	SEASONS
691-315-98	Virginia	.670	68
657-342-70	Duke	.647	75
655-301-88	**North Carolina**	**.670**	**65**
642-310-82	Maryland	.661	65
581-222-64	Clemson	.707	45
463-395-75	NC State	536	62
390-335-86	Boston College	.534	45
382-215-74	Wake Forest	.624	32
334-308-63	Virginia Tech	.519	40
0-8-0	South Carolina	.000	1

(Ranked by winning percentage through 2013 season)

WINNING PCT.	TEAM	RECORD	SEASONS
.707	Clemson	581-222-64	45
.670	**North Carolina**	**655-301-88**	**65**
.670	Virginia	691-315-98	68
.661	Maryland	642-310-82	65

KERRY ZAVAGNIN. Kerry Zavagnin anchored the defense on the 2000 Major League Soccer Cup-winning Kansas City Wizards.

WINNING PCT.	TEAM	RECORD	SEASONS
.647	Duke	657-342-70	75
.624	Wake Forest	382-215-74	32
.536	NC State	463-395-75	62
.534	Boston College	390-335-86	45
.519	Virginia Tech	334-308-63	40
.000	South Carolina	0-8-0	1

Atlantic Coast Conference Champions

(Tournament through 2013)

10 Virginia	3 Duke	2 Clemson	1 NC State
6 Maryland	3 **North Carolina**	1 Boston College	1 Wake Forest

NCAA Championships

(Through 2013)

6 Virginia	2 Clemson	1 Wake Forest	3 Maryland
2 **North Carolina**	1 Duke		

OLYMPIC SPORTS

OLYMPIC SPORTS OLYMPIC SPORTS

You may wonder, and rightfully so, what Olympics sports are doing in a book called *Gone Pro*. Well, for most sports, a professional major league represents the pinnacle of competition. But for such pursuits as swimming, diving, and what's known as "athletics" (track and field and other walking and running events), the highest level of competition occurs every four years at the Olympic Games. So we're counting participation in the Olympics as having "gone pro."

This designation does get a bit tricky, though, because over the years more sports have been added, including some that feature pro athletes. This is true for sports such as basketball and tennis, for instance. So we've decided that we won't include the Olympics accolades here for those UNC athletes who competed in sports that have their own chapters, such as baseball/softball, basketball, and soccer. Even excluding those sports for this chapter, Carolina has a lot to show in the realm of the Olympics, beginning with Harry Williamson, who ran the men's 800 meters in 1936. (More on him later.) That's a long history of Olympics athletes.

Modern Olympics History

The ancient Olympics took place at Olympia in Greece every four years from at least 776 BC until it was banned in AD 393 by the Roman Emperor Theodosius. It consisted of a series of athletic competitions to honor the Greek god Zeus, though originally it was just one competition, a stadium-length sprint of somewhere around 200 meters. Any Greek-speaking free man could compete. Greece's city-states suspended any wars they had going at the time in order to allow passage to and from the competitions.

Other sports were added: boxing, chariot racing, horse racing, other running events, wrestling, pankration (an ancient version of mixed martial arts), and pentathlon (discus, javelin, jumping, running, and wrestling). Athletes generally competed naked except for one footrace run in some 50 pounds of armor. Winners got a wreath of laurel leaves.

To 19th-century intellectuals who idealized the glories of ancient Greece and Rome, it all seemed so noble and, well, manly. Several Olympics-style competitions took place as early as 1796 and at various places in Europe throughout the 1800s. In 1890, French Baron Pierre de Coubertin founded the International Olympic Committee. In 1896, it held its first modern Olympic Games in Athens, Greece. The Games have gone on every four years since, except for interruptions during World War I and II. In 1924, the IOC

ANN MARSHALL. Ann Marshall won Olympic Gold as part of the 4x100 relay team in 1972. *(see page 201)*

MARION JONES. Marion Jones was a dominant force for the United States in the 2000 Olympic Games, winning three gold and two bronze medals before having them stripped years later for use of performance-enhancing drugs. *(see page 208)*

Track and Field Athletes through the years

FLOYD SIMMONS. Floyd "Chunk" Simmons (left) is awarded a bronze medal in the decathalon at the 1952 Olympic Games. He won bronze in the 1948 Games too [inset]. *(see page 210)*

added a Winter Olympics for cold-weather sports in the same year as the Summer Olympics. Starting in 1994, the IOC shifted the Winter Olympics schedule so that it alternates with the Summer Games every two years.

Coubertin admired the British system of physical education at schools. He and other aristocrats of the time thought the lessons learned by the upper classes on the playing fields of Eton had contributed greatly to the worldwide expansion of British power and colonization. Not wanting to confine sports to a small coterie of professionals, he conceived of his Olympics as a competition for amateurs. Unlike many of his peers, he thought physical education—and Olympics eligibility—should be available to the working classes as well as the aristocracy.

The modern Olympics remained open only to amateurs—theoretically—for most of the 20th century. As the Games became more popular and, thanks to television and corporate sponsorship, more lucrative, ways of subsidizing athletes within the rules proliferated. Critics increasingly dismissed the IOC's attempts to preserve the ideal of the 19th-century gentleman athlete as "shamateurism." Starting in the 1970s, professional athletes gradually were granted eligibility. Today, boxing, wrestling, and soccer still exclude professionals on a limited basis; for all other events, income source is irrelevant.

Much earlier, the old boys began allowing women to compete, though grudgingly. The 1900 Paris Olympics included women's events in the genteel sports of lawn tennis and golf. Women's sports were gradually added over the years until, with the debut of women's boxing in 2012, no Olympics sports remained restricted to men.

Political controversies, boycotts, accusations of drug use to enhance performance, scandals involving bribery by cities hoping to become Olympics hosts, massive cost overruns, and other issues have dogged the modern Olympics.

Still, the Games draw avid public interest and global TV audiences estimated at close to 5 billion people. Whatever the reason—national pride, love of sport, or perhaps even the purity of athletic competition that so enthralled the Games' founders—the Olympics continue to thrive.

The IOC frequently tinkers with the Games, adding and subtracting sports between Olympiads. (Bring back tug of war!) TV networks have struggled with time-zone differences and the rise of the Internet. How do you maintain suspense for a delayed broadcast of an event that took place in the middle of the previous night local time, especially when everything that happens goes online as soon as it occurs?

Still, some marketing options remain unexplored. Imagine the boost in TV ratings if, in a bow to ancient tradition, athletes competed naked. Don't think it hasn't been considered.

Summer Olympic Games

1896	Athens, Greece	**1960**	Rome, Italy
1900	Paris, France	**1964**	Tokyo, Japan
1904	St. Louis, Missouri, USA	**1968**	Mexico City, Mexico
***1906**	Athens, Greece	**1972**	Munich, West Germany
1908	London, England	**1976**	Montreal, Quebec, Canada
1912	Stockholm, Sweden	**1980**	Moscow, Russia
1916	Berlin, Germany; canceled due to WW I	**1984**	Los Angeles, California, USA
1920	Antwerp, Belgium	**1988**	Seoul, South Korea
1924	Paris, France	**1992**	Barcelona, Spain
1928	Amsterdam, Netherlands	**1996**	Atlanta, Georgia, USA
1932	Los Angeles, California, USA	**2000**	Sydney, Australia
1936	Berlin, Germany	**2004**	Athens, Greece
1940	Tokyo, Japan; canceled due to WW II	**2008**	Beijing, China
1944	London, England; canceled due to WW II	**2012**	London, England
1948	London, England		
1952	Helsinki, Finland		
1956	Melbourne, Australia, and Stockholm, Sweden (for equestrian events)		

**No longer recognized by the International Olympic Committee as an official Olympics; now called the 1906 Intercalated Games*

Winter Olympic Games

1924	Chamonix, France	**1972**	Sapporo, Japan
1928	St. Moritz, Switzerland	**1976**	Innsbruck, Austria
1932	Lake Placid, New York, USA	**1980**	Lake Placid, New York, USA
1936	Garmisch-Partenkirchen, Germany	**1984**	Sarajevo, Yugoslavia
1940	Sapporo, Japan; canceled due to World War II	**1988**	Calgary, Alberta, Canada
1944	Cortina d'Ampezzo, Italy; canceled due to World War II	**1992**	Albertville, France

1948	St. Moritz, Switzerland	1994	Lillehammer, Norway
1952	Oslo, Norway	1998	Nagano, Japan
1956	Cortina d'Ampezzo, Italy	2002	Salt Lake City, Utah, USA
1960	Squaw Valley, California, USA	2006	Turin, Italy
1964	Innsbruck, Austria	2010	Vancouver, British Columbia, Canada
1968	Grenoble, France	2014	Sochi, Russia

In the section that follows, we offer a bit of information about the sports at the University of North Carolina that are traditionally considered Olympics sports. This allows you to get a full picture of the Tar Heels and their history of excellence in these athletic endeavors.

SWIMMING AND DIVING

YANN DE FABRIQUE. Yann de Fabrique competed for France in the 1992 and 1996 Olympic Games. *(see page 201)*

THOMPSON MANN. Thompson Mann is best known for breaking the one-minute mark in the backstroke, which he did at the 1964 Olympic Games in Tokyo. *(see page 201)*

Men's Atlantic Coast Champions

(Number of titles per school; includes co- and tri-championships; through 2013)

24 NC State	**16** Virginia	**1** Clemson
17 North Carolina	**7** Maryland	

Women's Atlantic Coast Champions

(Number of titles per school; through 2013)

16 North Carolina	**4** Clemson	**1** Florida State
11 Virginia	**2** NC State	**1** Maryland

Men's Head Coaching Records

(In chronological order; through 2012)

YEAR	COACH	RECORD	WINNING PCT.
1938–44	Dick Jamerson	39-7	.847
1944–45	Willis Casey	4-0	1.000
1945–46	Ralph Casey & Willis Casey	4-3	.571
1946–48	Dick Jamerson	15-2	.882
1948–49	Ralph Casey	6-1	.857
1949–52	Dick Jamerson	31-2	.939
1952–57	Ralph Casey	37-6	.860
1957–74	Pat Earey	145-59	.711
1974–75	Paul Doty	6-4	.600
1975–77	Jim Wood	10-6	.625
1977–2007	Frank Comfort	226-90-1	.715
2007–13	Rich DeSelm	37-9	.804

(Ranked by victories)

RECORD	COACH	YEARS
226-90-1	Frank Comfort	1977–2007
145-59	Pat Earey	1957–74
85-11	Dick Jamerson	1938–44, 46–48, 49–52

RECORD	COACH	YEARS
47-10	Ralph Casey	1945–46, 48–49, 52–57
37-9	Rich DeSelm	2007–13
10-6	Jim Wood	1975–77
8-3	Willis Casey	1944–46
6-4	Paul Doty	1974–75

(Ranked by winning percentage)

WINNING PCT.	RECORD	COACH	YEARS
.885	85-11	Dick Jamerson	1938–44, 46–48, 49–52
.824	47-10	Ralph Casey	1945–46, 48–49, 52–57
.804	37-9	Rich DeSelm	2007–13
.727	8-3	Willis Casey	1944–46
.715	226-90-1	Frank Comfort	1977–2007
.711	145-59	Pat Earey	1957–74
.625	10-6	Jim Wood	1975–77
.600	6-4	Paul Doty	1974–75

Women's Head Coaching Records

(In chronological order)

YEAR	COACH	RECORD	WINNING PCT.
1974–75	Maxine Forrest	9-2	.818
1975–77	Jim Wood	11-1	.916
1977–2007	Frank Comfort	253-49	.838
2007–13	Rich DeSelm	35-12	.744

(Ranked by victories)

RECORD	COACH	YEARS
256-52-1	Frank Comfort	1977–2007
35-12	Rich DeSelm	2007–13
11-1	Jim Wood	1975–77
9-2	Maxine Forrest	1974–75

(Ranked by winning percentage)

WINNING PCT.	RECORD	COACH	YEARS
.916	11-1	Jim Wood	1975–77
.830	256-52-1	Frank Comfort	1977–2007
.818	9-2	Maxine Forrest	1974–75
.744	35-12	Rich DeSelm	2007–13

TRACK AND FIELD

Men's Atlantic Coast Champions

(Number of titles per school, indoor; through 2012)

26 Maryland	**9** Florida State*	**2** Virginia Tech
12 Clemson	**3** **North Carolina**	**1** NC State

*Participation in 2007 championship vacated by the NCAA Committee on Infractions

ALLEN JOHNSON. Allen Johnson won a gold medal in the 110-meter hurdles in the 1996 Olympic Games. He also competed in the 2000 and 2004 Games. *(see page 208)*

NADINE FAUSTIN. Hurdler Nadine Faustin was a three-time Olympian for Haiti. *(see page 205)*

(From left) UNC track and field stars Shalane Flanagan, Vikas Gowda, and Laura Gerraughty all competed in the 2004 Olympic Games. Flanagan and Gowda also competed in the 2008 and 2012 Games. *(see pages 206 and 207)*

(Outdoor, through 2013; includes co-champions)

26 Maryland	8 NC State	1 Virginia Tech
11 Clemson	5 **North Carolina**	1 Virginia
9 Florida State*		

**Participation in 2007 championship vacated by the NCAA Committee on Infractions*

Women's Atlantic Coast Champions

(Number of titles per school, indoor; through 2013)

15 **North Carolina**	2 Virginia Tech	1 Georgia Tech
5 Clemson	1 Florida State	1 Virginia
2 Miami		

(Outdoor; through 2013)

14 **North Carolina**	5 Virginia	2 Miami
6 Clemson	2 Florida State	2 Virginia Tech

Atlantic Coast Conference Cross-Country Champions

(Men, through 2012)

16 NC State	**7** Clemson	**4** Wake Forest
11 Maryland	**7** Duke	**1** Florida State
9 **North Carolina**	**4** Virginia	**1** Virginia Tech

(Women, through 2012; includes co-champions)

21 NC State	**2** Duke	**1** Clemson
5 Florida State*	**2** Virginia	**1** Wake Forest
3 **North Carolina**		

Participation in 2007 championship vacated by the NCAA Committee on Infractions

FIELD HOCKEY

Women's Atlantic Coast Conference Championships

(Through 2013)

18 **North Carolina**	**10** Maryland	**3** Wake Forest

Head Coaching Records

(In chronological order; through 2012)

YEARS	COACH	RECORD	WINNING PCT.
1973–75	Ann Gregory	13-8-5	.596
1976–80	Dolly Hunter	54-27-3	.660
1981–13	Karen Shelton	527-138-8	.800

(Ranked by victories)

RECORD	COACH	YEARS
527-138-8	Karen Shelton	1981–13
54-27-3	Dolly Hunter	1976–80
13-8-5	Ann Gregory	1973–75

(Ranked by winning percentage)

WINNING PCT.	RECORD	COACH	YEARS
.800	527-138-8	Karen Shelton	1981–13
.660	54-27-3	Dolly Hunter	1976–80
.596	13-8-5	Ann Gregory	1973–75

Athlete Bios

We've covered all the University of North Carolina athletes below who have appeared in the Olympic Games. Those who competed in sports that don't have their own chapters have bios provided here and in the pages that follow. We then list the additional athletes who are covered in other chapters representing their respective sports, such as basketball, soccer, baseball, or soccer, for instance.

CYCLING

DANUTE BANKAITIS-DAVIS

COLLEGE: Ph.D. from UNC in 1988 **OLYMPICS:** 1988

The story of Danute Monika "Bunki" Bankaitis-Davis is a good one, though not necessarily for her Olympics prowess. Of course, she did make the U.S. Olympics Team, so there's that. She finished 14th in the Women's Road Race event as a 30-year-old UNC doctoral student after completing bachelor's and master's degrees from Cleveland State University, where she played volleyball. Today she is co-founder and serves as executive vice president of Source Precision Medicine, otherwise known as Source MDx, based out of Boulder, Colorado.

JOHN FRIEDBERG ■ COLLEGE: 1979–83 OLYMPICS: 1992

At the age of 31, several years after he received his degree in psychology from UNC, John Friedberg competed in the men's team sabre event. He finished ninth. He's now a Syfy account executive for NBC Universal Cable Entertainment.

FIELD HOCKEY

KATE BARBER ■ COLLEGE: 1994–97 OLYMPICS: 2008

Kate "Tiki" Barber was voted the ACC's Rookie of the Year in 1994 and started all 92 games of her college career. She had a long history of international play, finally retiring in 2009. She then went back to Chapel Hill and served as an undergraduate assistant on Coach Karen Shelton's staff while she finished her degree in physical education. She was captain of the 2008 field hockey team that finished in eighth place.

ILLSE DAVIDS ■ COLLEGE: 2006–10 OLYMPICS: 2012

Born in Cape Town, South Africa, Illse Davids competed at the Junior World Cup in Santiago, Chile, in 2005. She was invited to train with South Africa's National Team in 2006, the same year she became a student-athlete at the University of North Carolina. Davids was a solid performer in Chapel Hill, helping to lead the team to the 2009 National Championship. She competed for South Africa in the London Olympics in 2012, in which her team finished 10th. Davids remains an active member of the South Africa National Team.

RACHEL DAWSON ■ COLLEGE: 2003–07 OLYMPICS: 2008, 2012

Field hockey runs deep in the Dawson family, as two of Rachel Dawson's older sisters (Natalie and Sarah) played for the U.S. National Team, an organization with which Rachel is still active. Her sister Megan played for Carolina. Dawson joined the U.S. team in 2005 while still a student-athlete at UNC and is now the group's veteran member, having competed in the 2008 (finished eighth) and 2012 (finished 12th) Olympic Games.

KATELYN FALGOWSKI ■ COLLEGE: 2007–11 OLYMPICS: 2008, 2012

Katelyn Falgowski was first named to the U.S. National Team in 2005 while still in high school. Known by the nickname "Falgo," she competed in her first Olympic Games while a student-athlete at UNC and competed in her second a year after finishing her sterling career at UNC. There she was named the NCAA Division I Player of the Year and led the Tar Heels to a runner-up national finish. Sisters Kerry and Carly played field hockey at UNC and William & Mary respectively.

JESSE GEY ■ COLLEGE: 2004–08 OLYMPICS: 2008

After leading UNC to the 2007 National Championship, Jesse Gey graduated from UNC in 2008 with a communications degree and that same year competed in the Beijing Olympics. In late 2010, she spent a year away from playing and instead coached at UNC while applying for graduate schools. She returned to the U.S. National Team in 2011 and played until retirement in 2013. "I had an amazing time traveling the world and representing my country on the field with some of my best friends," Gey said. "After a lot of soul searching, I realized that I am ready to move on to the next adventure in my life." As of 2013, she was living in Philadelphia and was the field hockey manager for Longstreth, a sporting goods company.

CARRIE LINGO ■ COLLEGE: 1997–2001 OLYMPICS: 2008

After a UNC career filled with honors, including winning a National Championship in 1997, Carrie Lingo graduated in 2001 with degrees in communications and psychology. The following year, she joined the U.S. National Team, where she had a successful 11-year career that included an appearance in the 2008 Olympics. But after seven surgeries to her right knee in 12 years, Lingo said, "My leg just can't take the training anymore. It's ready to retire." As of 2013, Lingo was living in her hometown of Rehoboth Beach, Delaware.

KAREN SHELTON ■ COLLEGE: 1976–79 (at West Chester State) OLYMPICS: 1984, 1 BRONZE MEDAL

In a bit of an unusual circumstance, rather than being a UNC student-athlete, Karen Shelton was already the head coach of the Carolina field hockey team when she won a bronze medal as part of Team USA in 1984. She played on the U.S. National Team since her college days at West Chester State in Pennsylvania, where she earned a degree in health and physical education in 1979. She then spent a year as an assistant coach at Franklin & Marshall College before taking the job as head coach at UNC in 1981. In addition to her bronze medal while employed at UNC, Shelton has more than 500 wins in her career and led Carolina to six NCAA championships, the last coming in 2009. After 32 years at the helm, Shelton defines field hockey in Chapel Hill.

AMY TRAN ■ COLLEGE: 1998–2002 OLYMPICS: 2008, 2012

Born in Hershey, Pennsylvania, Amy Tran had a sweet career as a field hockey goalkeeper. She joined the U.S. National Team in 2002 and was in goal during Olympic Games in Beijing and London. She was a starting goalkeeper all four years at UNC following a redshirt year in 1998. Her sister Katy also played field hockey at Carolina.

Upon her 2013 retirement from the sport, Tran said, "The Olympic Games is the ultimate test of athletic competition and excellence, and I am so honored to have participated in two Games." Now married with the last name Swensen, she is an assistant coach at Old Dominion in Norfolk, Virginia.

HANDBALL

JOHN KELLER ■ COLLEGE: 1985–89 OLYMPICS: 1996

John Keller's father, also named John, was a pro baseball player. The younger John was a tight end for the Tar Heels, catching 16 passes in 1986 and being named to the Academic All-ACC Team in 1988. So, naturally, his athletic pursuit following his football days was team handball. Team handball? Yep! Keller qualified for the 1996 U.S. Olympic Handball Team, which finished ninth. He's now president of the Atlanta-area company Proteus On-Demand Facilities, which provides temporary structures for events, emergency response, and extended-term needs.

STEVEN PENN ■ COLLEGE: 1987–91 OLYMPICS: 1996

Steven Penn was a star athlete for Brevard High School who went on to play as a wide receiver at Carolina. Penn was a freshman when John Keller (mentioned above) was a junior tight end. Later on, Penn joined his former football teammate in team handball, with Penn being named to the 1996 Olympic team.

CHRYSS WATTS ■ COLLEGE: 1984–88 OLYMPICS: 1992, 1996

An all-around athlete, Chrysandra Watts played basketball and was a track star in high school. She carried those two sports over to Carolina, where she earned three varsity letters in track and four in basketball. She then became part of the U.S. National Team in handball 1989–1997, allowing her to compete in two Olympic Games, serving as captain for the 1996 team. She was team handball Female Athlete of the Year in 1995 and 1996 and served on the board of directors for USA Team Handball for a number of years thereafter.

SWIMMING AND DIVING

YANN DE FABRIQUE *[pictured, page 191]*

■ **COLLEGE:** 1992–95 **OLYMPICS:** 1992, 1996

Born in Florida and a star swimmer at Carolina, Yannick Jerôme de Fabrique competed for France in the 1992 and 1996 Olympics. Just 19 years old at his first Olympics, he participated in the 4x200 freestyle relay and the 400-meter freestyle. As a 23-year-old in 1996, he competed in those two events again and the 1,500-meter freestyle. His best finish was eighth in the 1996 4x200 freestyle relay. He now lives in Southern California and works as an operations executive in the health care industry.

JANIS HAPE ■ COLLEGE: 1977–80 OLYMPICS: 1976

The U.S. women's swim team was thought to be the best in the world going into the Montreal Olympics in 1976, but unexpected dominance by the East Germans led to just one medal by the Americans. Janis Hape, now Janis Hape Dowd, said years later in an interview, "To this day, I wish I'd done better." Still, she was a star swimmer in her days in Chapel Hill, and her name is part of an annual meet at UNC, the Janet Hape Dowd Nike Cup Invitational. Just a few years ago she said, "I truly feel that the person I am today is because of my swimming experiences, particularly because of the dedication and hours of training it takes to reach your goals, all while going to school." Married with three children, she now lives in Charlotte, North Carolina.

THOMPSON MANN *[pictured, page 191]*

■ **COLLEGE:** 1961–64 **OLYMPICS:** 1964, **1 GOLD MEDAL**

Harold Thompson Mann is best known as the 21-year-old who broke the one-minute mark in the 100-meter backstroke at the 1964 Olympics in Tokyo. He did so as the lead man in the 4x100 relay. In 1965, he claimed all four Amateur Athletic Union (AAU) backstroke titles. He then retired from swimming and entered the Medical College of Virginia. He completed postgraduate training in San Francisco and had a full-time practice in Virginia for many years. Dr. Thompson Mann is now a board-certified internist and the assistant chief of medicine at Anna Jaques Hospital in Massachusetts.

ANN MARSHALL *[pictured, page 188]*

■ **COLLEGE:** 1975–78 **OLYMPICS:** 1972, **1 GOLD MEDAL**

Barbara Ann Marshall, known commonly by her middle name, swam for the gold medal–winning U.S. women's 4x100 relay team in the 1972 Olympics and barely missed a bronze in the women's 200-meter freestyle. She was just 14 years old. She went on to become the first female swimming scholarship recipient at the University of North Carolina but continued to compete internationally. Among her numerous accomplishments, in 1975, Marshall scored five individual gold medals and a silver at the 1975 Pravda International Meet in Leningrad, Russia, and was named the meet's Outstanding Swimmer. She's now a senior client associate at Merrill Lynch in Fort Lauderdale, Florida.

DAVID MONASTERIO ■ COLLEGE: 1989–93 OLYMPICS: 1992

The ACC Swimmer of the Year in 1990–91, David Monasterio built upon his success in Chapel Hill by making it to the 1992 Olympics, where he competed for Puerto Rico. The 21-year-old participated in five events, with his best finishes being 12th place in both the 4x100 freestyle relay and the 4x100 medley relay. He now works for SunPower Corporation in Spain.

PHIL RIKER ■ COLLEGE: 1965–68 OLYMPICS: 1964

Joining the aforementioned Thompson Mann in the 1964 Olympics was 18-year-old Phil Riker III, who finished fourth in the 200-meter butterfly. While at Carolina, he won the NCAA Championship in the 100 fly in 1966 and was strong in the 200 fly, 400 medley relay, and 800 medley relay throughout his days in Chapel Hill.

YI-KHY SAW ■ COLLEGE: 2005–09 OLYMPICS: 2004

Yi-Khy Saw swam the 1,500-meter freestyle in the 2004 Olympic Games for his home country of Malaysia, prior to entering the University of North Carolina on a swimming scholarship. He spent four years as a top-notch Tar Heel swimmer and currently lives in British Columbia, Canada.

CHRIS STEVENSON ■ COLLEGE: 1982–86 OLYMPICS: 1984

You might think that the swimming days of Dr. Christopher L. Stevenson, who graduated from UNC in 1986, are long in the past. After all, he's now an associate professor of chemistry and environmental studies at the University of Richmond, and his foray into the Olympics was back in 1984 when he was a star swimmer for the Tar Heels. But Stevenson is still involved with U.S. Seniors Swimming, where he set a world record a few years ago. In 2013, he was elected as the organization's vice president of local operations. He still loves swimming and recalls his Olympics experience fondly.

"My mom is Greek, and I lived in Greece for three years," he said in an interview several years ago about his experience competing for the Greece team. "I could compete because of my Greek heritage." His best finish was 12th in the 100-meter butterfly. He also competed in the 100 backstroke, 200 backstroke, and 200 butterfly.

"It was an amazing experience," he said. "People dream of going to the Olympics. I was happy placing 12th."

STAN TINKHAM ■ COLLEGE: 1950–53 OLYMPICS: 1956 women's swimming coach

Shortly after his days of swimming in Chapel Hill, Stan Tinkham began coaching at Walter Reed Army Hospital. He was chosen to coach the U.S. women's swimming team in the 1956 Melbourne Olympics as a 24-year-old. Shelley Mann took home the first Olympic gold in the butterfly. After the Olympics, Tinkham returned to Walter Reed for two years before becoming manager of the Connecticut Belair pool in Silver Spring, Maryland. He then started the Northern Virginia Aquatic Club, a premier national competitive swim and water polo program, which he led until the Club closed in 1988.

SUE WALSH ■ COLLEGE: 1980–84 OLYMPICS: 1980

Sue Walsh was a top junior swimmer in 1979 when she visited Chapel Hill for the first time. Coming from the Buffalo, New York, suburb of Hamburg, Walsh said, "I just loved the place from the beginning. Still do. I can't imagine having gone anywhere else." She made the 1980 Olympic Team in the 200-meter backstroke, but politics got in the way of her Olympic experience. The United States declined to send its team to Moscow to compete. But she went on to become one of the most decorated swimmers in UNC history and then had a long career with UNC. She currently serves as Director of Endowment & Legacy Gifts for the Rams Club.

WENDY WEINBERG

■ COLLEGE: 1980–83 OLYMPICS: 1976, 1 BRONZE MEDAL

OK, Wendy Weinberg never swam for the University of North Carolina, but she does hold a master's degree in sports medicine from Chapel Hill. Weinberg swam in the Olympics as an 18-year-old, winning a bronze medal in the 800-meter freestyle. She then went on to swim for a year with the University of Virginia, but a series of injuries ended her swimming career. Those injuries, though, led her in a new direction. She transferred to Chapel Hill to study sports medicine. Now known as Wendy Weil, she is a longtime physical therapist in McLean, Virginia.

TRACK & FIELD

BILL ALBANS ■ COLLEGE: 1949–50 OLYMPICS: 1948

William Everett Albans was known back in the day as "Wild Bill." His accomplishments in Chapel Hill are pretty wild too. In 1949, a year after he finished 10th in the triple jump in London, Albans led the Tar Heels to the Southern Conference Indoor Championships with five first-place finishes. In 1950, he had more points at the NCAA Championships than any other competitor, including a first-place finish in the 220-yard low hurdles. By the end of his Carolina career, he had set more school and conference records than anyone in Tar Heel track and field history. He died in 1990 in Puerto Rico.

JIM BEATTY ■ COLLEGE: 1953–57 OLYMPICS: 1960

So you've wondered who first broke the four-minute barrier in the mile? It was none other than Jim Beatty, who achieved the feat indoors with a 3:58.9 performance in February 1962 in Los Angeles, besting the existing record by 2.5 seconds. Beatty ran for UNC, where he dominated ACC distance events. He temporarily retired from competitive running immediately after college, but then he moved to California to train with legendary Hungarian coach Mihály Iglói. From there, he made the U.S. Team and competed in the 5,000 meters. His Olympics performance wasn't particularly memorable, but Beatty continued to get better. He won the AAU mile in 1962 and was AAU indoor mile champion from 1961 to 1963, taking home the Sullivan Award in 1962 as the nation's top amateur athlete. He was the first American to hold records simultaneously in all events from 1,500 to 5,000 meters. He won a silver medal in the 1,500 at the Pan American Games in 1963. Beatty went on to serve in the North Carolina legislature and currently owns Charlotte-based Jim Beatty & Associates.

LATASHA COLANDER-RICHARDSON

■ COLLEGE: 1994–98 OLYMPICS: 2000, 2004, 1 GOLD MEDAL

LaTasha Colander-Richardson won three championships at the National Scholastic Outdoor meet and was a star sprinter and hurdler before attending the University of North Carolina. Once she arrived in Chapel Hill, she won 14 ACC titles and was a four-time All-American. She continued her track prowess after graduation and earned a spot on the 2000 Olympics team, running the 400 meters as well as the 4x400 relay, for which she won a gold medal. About that medal, though. It was stripped by the International Olympic Committee in 2008 when fellow UNC and Olympic teammate Marion Jones pleaded guilty to lying to investigators about her use of performance-enhancing drugs. Jones surrendered all of her medals won in 2000, but her teammates appealed. The Court of Arbitration for Sports announced in 2010 that it had overturned the decision by the IOC to disqualify the team.

In the meantime, LaTasha Colander-Richardson continued to compete and participated in the 2004 Olympics in the 100 meters and 4x100 relay. She remained an active competitor in track until 2006. Now married to Kris Clark and the mother of three, LaTasha Colander Clark has written both an autobiography and a children's book and is the head coach of the cross-country and track and field teams at Paine College in Augusta, Georgia.

SHARON COUCH ■ COLLEGE: 1987–91 OLYMPICS: 1992, 2000

A 1991 graduate of the University of North Carolina, where she was one of the most decorated female student-athletes (including three-time ACC Most Valuable Performer), Sharon Couch was a member of five U.S. World Championship Teams as a long jumper. In the 1992 Barcelona Olympics, she finished sixth in the long jump. At the 2000 Sydney Olympics, she advanced to the semifinals in the 100-meter hurdles. Now known as Sharon Seagrave, she joined the University of Tennessee track and field staff in 2010 as an assistant coach for women's sprints.

DOMINIC DEMERITTE ■ COLLEGE: 1995–99 OLYMPICS: 2000, 2004

Born in Nassau, Bahamas, Dominic Demeritte ran track at UNC and competed for the Bahamas in two Olympic Games. Known as a sprinter who competed in events such as the 100, 200, and 400 meters, Demeritte competed in the 200 meters and the 4x100 relay at the 2000 Olympics. By 2004, he was specializing in the 200 meters, which is the event he ran in the Olympics. He holds Bahamian records in the indoor and outdoor 200 meters as well as the 400 relay. He currently lives in Marietta, Georgia, where he is involved in several sports management and sports training projects.

ERIN DONOHUE ■ COLLEGE: 2000–04 OLYMPICS: 2008

A high school national champion in the mile, Erin Donohue attended Carolina to compete in middle-distance running events and the javelin throw. As a junior, she was a member of the 2003 NCAA Champion distance-medley relay team. Upon graduation, she established herself as a national presence in the 800 meters and 1,500 meters. In the Olympics, she competed in the 1,500 meters.

NADINE FAUSTIN *[pictured, page 194]*

■ COLLEGE: 1995–99 **OLYMPICS:** 2000, 2004, 2008

A three-time Olympian for Haiti, Nadine Faustin competed in the 100-meter hurdles each time. She also competed at the World Championships in 1999, 2001, 2003, and 2005 and the World Indoor Championships in 2001, 2003, 2004, and 2006. She's also done quite well at the Central American and Caribbean Games, including a gold medal there in 2005. But before all that, she was an All-American hurdler at UNC, where she graduated with a degree in physical education and sports sciences.

She married Anthony Daniel Parker, who became her coach in 2003. Nadine Faustin-Parker was part of the UNC track & field staff for four years and then the head women's track & field coach and an assistant for the men's team at Mansfield University in Pennsylvania. She's now an assistant coach for the University of Cincinnati.

SHALANE FLANAGAN *[pictured, page 195]*

■ **COLLEGE:** 2000–04 **OLYMPICS:** 2004, 2008, 2012, **1 BRONZE MEDAL**

Shalane Flanagan may be familiar with the lyrics from the band Cake, "She's going the distance. She's going for speed." Shalane Flanagan is one of UNC's most-decorated distance runners. She was the American-record holder in the 10,000 meters and was a two-time cross-country national champion at UNC. While she is adept at the 3,000 and 5,000 meters, she's been increasing her distance specialties over the years. In the 2004 Olympics, she competed in only the 5,000 meters. In 2008, she added the 10,000 meters, winning a bronze medal in that event. In 2012, she concentrated on running the women's marathon, finishing 10th.

Flanagan's parents are both distance runners (her mother, Cheryl Treworgy, is a former world record holder in the marathon). She's married to fellow UNC track and field star Steven Ashley Edwards. Flanagan remains active in running and has been a volunteer assistant coach for UNC's cross-country team.

NICOLE GAMBLE ■ COLLEGE: 1995–99 OLYMPICS: 2000

Specializing in the triple jump, Nicole Gamble became the first University of North Carolina woman ever to win an NCAA field event title when she reigned supreme at the 1999 NCAA Indoor Championships. Overall, she was a 13-time All-American at Carolina and won eight ACC Championships. She went on to compete in the triple jump at the 2000 Olympics.

LAURA GERRAUGHTY *[pictured, page 195]*

■ **COLLEGE:** 2002–06 **OLYMPICS:** 2004

Laura Gerraughty finished her UNC career as the most-decorated female thrower in the program's history, competing in the shot, discus, hammer, and weight throws. Just a few of her collegiate accomplishments: 2006 NCAA Outdoor champion; 2006 NCAA Indoor runner-up; 2004 Olympic Trials champion; 2004 USA Indoor shot put champion; two-time ('03 & '04) NCAA Indoor shot put champion; and 2004 NCAA Outdoor shot put champion. She threw the shot for the United States in the 2004 Olympic Games. Injuries forced her to retire from competitive throwing after college.

VIKAS GOWDA *[pictured, page 195]*

■ **COLLEGE:** 2002–06 **OLYMPICS:** 2004, 2008, 2012

The name Vikas Gowda has been floating around the world of the discus for more than a decade, and the former UNC star isn't showing signs of slowing down. A solid competitor in the discus and shot put, he competed in discus for India in the 2004, 2008, and 2012 Olympics. It was also in discus that he won a National Championship in 2006 at North Carolina. Representing India, he won gold in discus in the World Challenge Meeting at Kingston, Jamaica, in 2013.

KEN HARNDEN ■ COLLEGE: 1993–95 OLYMPICS: 1996, 2000

Born in and competing for Zimbabwe, Ken Harnden ran at the 1996 Olympics in Atlanta and the 2000 Olympics in Sydney in both the 400-meter hurdles and the 4x100 relay. A 1995 graduate of the University of North Carolina, Harndan won an NCAA Championship in the 400-meter hurdles and was a member of the 4x400 relay team that won a title in 1995. Sandwiched between his Olympics appearances, he won a bronze medal at the Commonwealth Games in the 400-meter hurdles in 1998. Harndan is currently associate head coach and director of sprints, hurdles, and relays for the Florida State University track and field team, where he was twice named NCAA National Assistant Coach of the Year. His younger brother Iain Harndan also competed for Zimbabwe in the 2000 Olympics in the 400-meter hurdles.

MONIQUE HENNAGAN

■ **COLLEGE:** 1994–98 **OLYMPICS:** 2000, 2004, **2 GOLD MEDALS**

Monique Hennagan had impressive performances at the 1993 and 1994 World Junior Championships, setting the stage for a solid career of running in Chapel Hill, where she won two NCAA titles: the indoor 400 meters and the outdoor 800 meters. She was an eight-time ACC individual champion, including winning the 400 meters four straight years. Hennagan competed in the 400 meters and 4x400 relay at the 2000 and 2004 Olympic Games, winning gold in each relay event. Her 2000 gold medal was stripped in 2008 after Carolina and Olympic relay teammate Marion Jones admitted to doping. In 2010, the Court of Arbitration for Sports overturned the decision by the International Olympic Committee to disqualify the team other than Jones. The 2004 gold also became tainted when Olympic relay teammate Crystal Cox admitted to doping in 2010. The IOC stripped Cox of her gold medal but thus far has allowed the rest of the team to keep its medals.

ALLEN JOHNSON *[pictured, page 194]*

■ **COLLEGE:** 1989–93 **OLYMPICS:** 1996, 2000, 2004, **1 GOLD MEDAL**

Allen Johnson was an all-around athlete recruited to Chapel Hill for the decathalon. The rigorous endeavor, though, kept him regularly injured, so he opted to specialize in hurdles and long jumping. He continued to improve and won the 55-meter hurdles at the NCAA indoor track meet in 1992. In 1993, Johnson finished second in the 55-meter hurdles and 11th in the long jump at the indoor meet and second in the 110-meter hurdles at the NCAA outdoor meet. But Johnson just kept getting better after college.

He began accumulating medals and increasing his world standing leading up to the 1996 Olympics in Atlanta. There Johnson won gold in the 110-meter hurdles, the same event that he competed in for the 2000 and 2004 Olympics. While Johnson didn't win another medal in the Olympics, he did finish his career as a seven-time World Champion (four gold in the 110-meter hurdles and three indoors in the 60-meter hurdles). He officially retired in 2010 and went back to Chapel Hill to finish his sociology degree in 2012, while his daughter Tristine was at UNC and part of the track and field team.

MARION JONES *[pictured, page 188]*

■ **COLLEGE:** 1993–97 **OLYMPICS:** 2000, 2004

The rise and fall of Marion Jones is complicated and typically a tremendous source of disappointment to fans of UNC athletics. The story, though, begins so well. Jones was a high school star who came to UNC on a basketball scholarship and, as a freshman, led the Tar Heels to a first women's National Championship when the 1993–94 team finished 33-2. Her prowess in track was also apparent, as she won All-American honors and then led the basketball team to a 30-5 record in 1994–95. A basketball injury, though, kept Jones out of the 1996 Olympics in track. She played one final season of basketball before giving it up to concentrate on track.

Just after graduation from UNC, she won three gold medals at the USA Outdoor Track & Field Championships, thus landing in the national spotlight. In 1998, she won 34 individual events, losing only a late-season long jump competition. In 2000, Jones announced her goal of winning gold in all five Olympics events for which she was entered. She finished with three gold and two bronze medals, but then-husband C. J. Hunter, a shot putter who met Jones while he was an assistant coach for the UNC track and field team, failed drug tests and was not allowed to compete in the 2000 Olympics. This also opened the doors to speculation about Jones's possible doping.

For years, Jones adamantly denied ever taking steroids, and she had a disappointing showing in the 2004 Olympics. By then she had divorced Hunter and married sprinter Tim Montgomery, who also tested positive for performance-enhancing drugs, thus further fueling speculation about Jones. Finally in 2007, Jones confessed that she had lied to a grand jury when she stated that she had never taken PEDs. Her

Olympic medals were promptly taken back. She was later sentenced to six months in jail for perjury. After her jail time, Jones tried for a career in the WNBA. For more about that, check out her entry in the Basketball chapter (page 74).

LYNDA LIPSON ■ COLLEGE: 1989–93 OLYMPICS: 2000

A three-time All-America selection and six-time ACC champion at UNC, Lynda Lipson won ACC outdoor titles in the shot put and the javelin and was second in the discus in 1993. She set an ACC record in the discus with a mark of 181-0 and placed sixth in the javelin at the NCAA Outdoor Championships. She won the 1997 and 1999 U.S. National Championships in the javelin prior to competing in the javelin in the 2000 Olympics. Now known as Lynda Blutreich, the former American record holder in javelin is married to former Olympian Brian Butreich, who competed in the discus throw in 1992. Brian is an assistant track and field coach at the University of Oklahoma, while Lynda works for the Norman City Schools. They have two daughters.

EDDIE NEUFVILLE ■ COLLEGE: 1995–99 OLYMPICS: 1996

While on scholarship to run track at UNC, 19-year-old Eddie Neufville had the opportunity to compete for Liberia in the 1996 Olympics where he ran the 4x100 relay. "I felt very blessed, honored, and fortunate to have competed at the Olympic Games for my country, especially at such a young age," Neufville said. "It was a feeling of accomplishment and also a feeling of giving back to Liberia. Liberia was in the midst of a civil crisis in 1996. The opportunity to represent Liberia and provide a positive picture of Liberia was very satisfying. It was out of this world!" He graduated from UNC in 1999 and went to law school at Washington & Lee. He is the founder and principal of the Law Office of Edward W. Neufville, III, LLC, in Silver Spring, Maryland.

ALICE SCHMIDT ■ COLLEGE: 2000–04 OLYMPICS: 2008, 2012

Alice Schmidt won NCAA titles in consecutive years in the 800 meters, also setting UNC and ACC records in the process. In addition, she was also a two-time NCAA runner-up in the event. Schmidt specialized in the 800 after college, becoming the 2005 USA Indoor runner-up and 2006 Indoor champion. She competed twice in the Olympics in the 800 meters.

OLA SESAY

■ **COLLEGE:** 1997–2001 (transfer from Kentucky) **OLYMPICS:** 2012

Born in Sierra Leone, Ola Sesay competed in the 2012 Olympics for her home country. In fact, the 33-year-old long jumper was the flag bearer for Sierra Leone in London. But before that, she wore the Carolina blue as a dominant long jumper in the ACC and was accomplished in the triple jump as well. She went on to receive a doctorate from Duke in physical therapy and works as a physical therapist today in Arlington, Texas.

BLAKE RUSSELL ■ COLLEGE: 1993–97 OLYMPICS: 2008

"My college career was weird because I started so far back," Blake Russell said. "Initially I was one of the worst runners on the team. I went from not making the traveling squad as a freshman to making it and running okay as a sophomore and then I kept getting better and better." She finished her collegiate career as a conference champion and school record holder in the 1,500 meters. She continued her career as a distance runner after college, running the marathon in the 2008 Olympics and falling just short of making the team for the 2012 Olympics. She and her husband, John, a former track star at Wake Forest, just had their second child in 2013. They live in Pacific Grove, California.

FLOYD "CHUNK" SIMMONS *[pictured, page 188]*

■ COLLEGE: 1946–49 OLYMPICS: 1948, 1952, 2 BRONZE MEDALS

UNC's first two-time Olympian, Floyd Macon Simmons Jr., was best known by the nickname "Chunk." He was a fantastic athlete who competed in the decathalon and won consecutive bronze medals in London and Helsinki. Simmons lived quite the life: World War II veteran, Tar Heels track star, two-time Olympian, movie and TV actor (his biggest role was in the 1958 musical *South Pacific*), and accomplished artist and photographer. Simmons played football for the Tar Heels, too, and was pretty darn good. Unfortunately, he played tailback behind one of UNC's all-time greats, Charlie "Choo Choo" Justice. Simmons still competed in senior events until his early 80s. He died in Charlotte, North Carolina—the city of his birth—in 2008 at the age of 84.

TISHA WALLER ■ COLLEGE: 1988–92 OLYMPICS: 1996, 2004

When Tisha Waller's older sister Petra was in high school, she was a sprinter until a broken leg ended her career. Not to be deterred, young Tisha was inspired by her sister's pre-injury accomplishments and began to get into track and field. She made it to Chapel Hill on a track scholarship but really began to build momentum after college. To name a few of her accomplishments, she is a five-time USA outdoor champion ('96, '98, '99, '02, '04); five-time USA indoor champion ('96, '98, '99, '00, '02); 1998 Goodwill Games champion; American indoor record holder; 2003 Visa Humanitarian Award recipient. And, oh yeah, the Olympics: Waller participated in the high jump at the 1996 Olympics and then again in the 2004 Olympics—at the age of 33. Once a schoolteacher, Waller is now a solutions architect at Houghton Mifflin Harcourt in Atlanta.

WRESTLING

PERRIN HENDERSON ■ COLLEGE: 1955–59 OLYMPICS: 1956

Born in Charlotte, North Carolina, Perrin Henderson was a solid athlete. He was a swimmer as a teen and then earned varsity letters in cross-country and wrestling while at the University of North Carolina. He was a member of the ACC Champion cross-country team in 1957 and was captain of the wrestling team. He competed in the 1956 Olympics as a wrestler and then went on to finish his degree in economics from Chapel Hill in 1959. He left his formal athletic pursuits behind upon graduation, attending the UNC Law School and then graduating from the U.S. Navy Officer Candidate School in 1961. After leaving the Navy in 1964, he entered the real estate business. He died in 2007 at the age of 69.

The List Continues . .

The following UNC athletes and coaches are covered in other chapters, but we felt we should at least mention their Olympics accomplishments here. Scan the list, and then read more about your favorites in the chapters for their respective sports.

Baseball

B. J. Surhoff (1984)	**Scott Bankhead** (1984)	**Andrew Miller** (2004)

Basketball: MEN

Larry Brown (1964, coach 2004)	**Mitch Kupchak** (1976)	**Sam Perkins** (1984)
John Lacey (1964)	**Tom LaGarde** (1976)	**J. R. Reid** (1988)
Charlie Scott (1968)	**Coach Dean Smith** (1976)	**Henrik Rodl** (competed for Germany) (1992)
Bobby Jones (1972)	**Coach Bill Guthridge** (1976)	**Vince Carter** (2000)
Walter Davis (1976)	**Michael Jordan** (1984, 1992)	**Coach Roy Williams** (2004)
Phil Ford (1976)		

Basketball: WOMEN

Coach Sylvia Hatchell (1988)

Soccer: MEN

Eddie Pope (1996)	**Ken Harnden** (2000)	**Eddie Neufville** (2000)
Dominic Demeritte (2000)	**Allen Johnson** (2000)	**Dax McCarty** (2008)

Soccer: WOMEN

Coach Laurie Gregg (1996, 2000)	**Tisha Venturini** (1996)	**Catherine Reddick** (2004)
Mia Hamm (1996, 2000, 2004)	**Carla Werden** (1996, 2000)	**Lindsay Tarpley** (2004, 2008)
Coach April Heinrichs (1996, 2000, 2004)	**Staci Wilson** (1996)	**Lori Chalupny** (2008)
Kristine Lilly (1996, 2000, 2004)	**Lorrie Fair** (2000)	**Robyn Gale** (competed for Canada) (2008, 2012)
Tracy Noonan (1996)	**Siri Mullinix** (2000)	**Tobin Heath** (2008, 2012)
Cindy Parlow (1996, 2000, 2004)	**Coach Tracy Bates-Leon** (2004)	**Kacey White** (2008)
Tiffany Roberts (1996)	**Heather O'Reilly** (2004, 2008, 2012)	

Softball

Natalie Anter (competed for Italy) (2004)

GOLF & TENNIS

In attempting to figure out the most logical organization for this book, tennis and golf seemed to make sense together as classic country club sports. By that, we mean just about every country club in America offers tennis courts and a golf course, whereas not too many offer baseball or football fields. Fortunately for the two sports, a concerted effort has been made in recent decades to attract interested young people, opening doors to new generations of enthusiasts from all walks of life.

In Chapel Hill, golf and tennis have experienced a tremendous amount of success over the years. The Tar Heel men's golf team has a history going back to 1928, while the history of the men's tennis team goes back even further. The University Tennis Club was founded in 1884, with intercollegiate competition beginning a decade later. Tennis was officially recognized as a varsity sport in 1908.

MEN'S GOLF

It's not surprising that, in the early days of collegiate golf, the Ivy League schools were dominant. From the time the initial college championship was awarded in 1897, through 1933, Harvard, Princeton, and Yale captured the title every year except for 1921, when Dartmouth was the winner. Eventually, teams such as Houston, Stanford, Oklahoma State, Texas, Florida, LSU, and North Texas State started winning multiple championships. Yale still holds the most golf championships with 21, followed by Houston with 16, Princeton with 12, and Oklahoma State with 10, as the only teams with double-digit championships. Alabama took the 2013 title in June.

North Carolina has never won a team NCAA National Championship in golf, though it has made numerous impressive showings nationally. It has had two individual champions, though, as John Inman took the title in 1984 and Harvie Ward won it in 1949. You'll see John Inman's name in this section in a couple of capacities. He was just mentioned as a player, but he was also a Carolina coach. Inman led his alma mater for 13 years and became the first person to win the ACC title as both a player and a coach.

UNC Top 25 NCAA Team Finishes

1953 2nd	**1985** tie 16th	**1996** 16th
1960 tie 4th	**1986** 12th	**1997** 10th
1962 12th	**1987** 8th	**1998** 25th
1977 12th	**1989** 13th	**1999** 10th
1978 5th	**1990** 7th	**2000** 10th
1979 tie 6th	**1991** 2nd	**2002** 17th
1981 tie 18th	**1992** 23rd	**2003** tie 9th
1982 9th	**1993** 3rd	**2006** 17th
1983 tie 8th	**1994** 11th	**2007** tie 21st
1984 4th	**1995** 19th	

Atlantic Coast Conference Team Championships

(Outright-Co-champions)

18 Wake Forest	**6** Duke	**0-1** NC State
12-2 Georgia Tech	**1** Florida State	**0-1** South Carolina
10-1 **North Carolina**	**0-1** Maryland	**0-1** Virginia Tech
8-1 Clemson		

Atlantic Coast Conference Individual Championships

22 Wake Forest	**7** Clemson	**3** Maryland
13 **North Carolina**	**6** Duke	**2** Virginia
8 Georgia Tech	**6** NC State	**1** Florida State

List of Head Coaches

(Years listed include that spring and the previous fall season)

1928 (no coach)	**1961–72** Ed Kenney	**1978–98** Devon Brouse
1929–34 John Kenfield	**1973** Clyde Walker	**1999–2011** John Inman
1935–60* Chuck Erickson	**1974–77** Mike McLeod	**2012–13** Andrew Sapp

**UNC did not field a team for three years in the early 1940s due to World War II.*

Player Bios

JIM FERREE ■ COLLEGE: 1951–53

A Tar Heel from the beginning, Jim Ferree was born in Pinebluff, North Carolina, and grew up in Winston-Salem where his father, Purvis, was a pro at Old Town Golf Club.

Ferree played on UNC's 1951–53 golf teams and was the 1953 Southern Conference Champion.

Ferree played on the PGA Tour for 11 years, 1956–66, winning one tournament: the 1958 Vancouver Centennial. He then spent several years as the Director of Golf at Long Cove Club in Hilton Head, South Carolina, before heading back to the Senior Tour in 1981. There he won two tournaments: the 1986 Greater Grand Rapids Open and the 1991 Bell Atlantic Classic. His Jim Ferree Education Endowment has assisted organizations such as the UNC Lineberger Cancer Center.

BOBBY GALLOWAY ■ COLLEGE: 1959–60

Leading the 1960 Tar Heels to an ACC Championship, Bobby Galloway was poised to make a solid run in the world of golf. That same year, he led UNC to a fourth-place finish at the NCAA Championships where he was an individual quarterfinalist. After graduating from Carolina, he won the Winston-Salem City-County Championship four times before turning pro in 1964.

Galloway, who simply went by the name Bob after college, had a solid pro career from the mid-1960s through the 1970s. His best PGA finish was in 1965, a 10th-place finish in Memphis. His regional accolades include being the Carolinas PGA champion in 1971, winning the North Carolina Open in 1972, and being named the Carolinas Professional Golfer of the Year in 1976.

Galloway was a former co-owner of Pine Tuck Golf Club in Rock Hill, North Carolina, in the 1970s, and then had his amateur status reinstated in 1980. He's back in Chapel Hill, where he assists the men's and women's golf teams from time to time and owns a golf club repair center. Galloway has won 10 tournaments as an amateur and has been a rules official on amateur and collegiate circuits.

PAT MOORE ■ COLLEGE: 1988–92

Pat Moore was a three-time All-ACC performer and an All-American in 1991. Having won five collegiate titles, it seemed he was destined to do well as a pro. The majority of his success, though, came in one year: 2002. Playing on the **buy.com** tour, Moore won three tournaments, had nine top-10 finishes, and finished first on the final earnings list with $381,965. He was that tour's player of the year, and his three victories in 2002 gave him an immediate promotion to the PGA Tour.

Unfortunately, Moore has struggled with back injuries almost ever since. He has played in only 26 PGA Tour events over the years and made the cut just four times. Moore has had a Major Medical Extension that extended into 2013, but he has hopes to get back to pro golf eventually.

TOM SCHERRER ■ COLLEGE: 1988–92

While in Chapel Hill, Tom Scherrer led UNC to two top-10 NCAA finishes, including second place in 1991 when he was also a member of the Walker Cup Team and finished fourth in the NCAA Championships. Of that Walker Cup, Scherrer says, "My Walker Cup was probably one of my fondest memories of any tournament I ever played in." The year before, he won the North and South Amateur; he finished second to Justin Leonard of the University of Texas in the 1992 U.S. Amateur.

Scherrer turned pro in 1992. He has four professional wins: one on the PGA Tour and three on the developmental tour. His best year as a pro was 2000 when he won the Kemper Insurance Open and posted four top-10 PGA finishes. He was an avid hockey player growing up but admits that golf is a little easier on the body. "I've lost teeth playing hockey and not yet in golf," he said.

E. HARVIE WARD JR. ■ COLLEGE: 1945–49

Edward Harvie Ward Jr. has a story that simply wouldn't happen today. A phenomenal golfer for UNC, Ward maintained his amateur status through his peak years, becoming one of the most accomplished amateurs in U.S. golf history.

A native of Tarboro, North Carolina, Ward won an individual NCAA Championship in 1949 and then dominated the amateur circuit thereafter. He won the British Amateur in 1952, the Canadian Amateur in 1954, and the U.S. Amateur in 1955–56. Of Ward's run in the 1950s, golf historian Herbert Warren Wind wrote, "The most talented amateur of the decade, no question about it, was Harvie Ward, the consummate stylist from North Carolina." Arnold Palmer was quoted as saying, "He was an extremely fine player and one of the fiercest amateur competitors I ever knew. He was a great guy, and one who certainly made his niche in the world of golf as one of its finest players."

Ward attended prep school and had a 30-month stint in the military before attending UNC, where he earned a degree in economics. He played the Masters several times as an amateur, finishing fourth in 1957 and tied for eighth in 1955. He was also a regular at the U.S. Open, where he finished sixth in 1955. Ward finally turned pro in 1974, returning to North Carolina to become head golf professional at Foxfire Country Club, west of Fayetteville. He won the North Carolina Open in 1977. He served at two Florida golf clubs before landing back in North Carolina at Pinehurst in 1989. He occasionally played Senior PGA events from 1980 to 1990.

JOHN INMAN ■ COLLEGE: 1981–84

JOHN INMAN. John Inman played for and coached the Carolina men's golf team. In between, he spent 12 years on the PGA Tour.

A legend in the annals of Carolina golf, John Inman won the NCAA Championship in 1984, as he broke Ben Crenshaw's NCAA record with a 17-under-par score. In that same year, he won the Western Amateur and was awarded All-ACC and All-America status (as he had the two previous years). Inman finished 1984 by winning the Fred Haskins Award as the National Player of the Year. In 1982, he won the ACC Tournament.

Inman turned pro in 1985 and played for 12 years on the PGA Tour, winning two events. He then went back to Chapel Hill to become head coach of the men's golf team starting in the 1998–99 season. He coached through the 2010–11 season and had considerable success, leading UNC to three top-10 NCAA finishes and one ACC Championship. He was the first player to win ACC Championships as a player and a coach. He ended his tenure as golf coach to return to the pro game. Upon his retirement, Inman said, "It has been a privilege and an honor to coach the UNC men's golf program for the last 13 years. I am very proud of the team's many accomplishments and the enduring relationships that we have forged, but it is time that I begin a new chapter of my life and explore other professional options. I will always be a Tar Heel."

UNC Director of Athletics Dick Baddour said, "John Inman has represented our University, the department, and its golf team with nothing but class both as a student-athlete and head coach. He is devoted to his team, loves the University, and we love him." Reaching 50 years of age in 2012, Inman was then eligible for the Champions Tour (formerly the Senior PGA Tour). One of six kids, he is the younger brother of pro golfer Joe Inman, who played collegiately for Wake Forest.

DAVIS LOVE III ■ COLLEGE: 1982–85

While UNC has produced its fair share of great golfers, none have won more accolades than Davis Love III. It was clear during his time in Chapel Hill that Love was going to be special on the golf course. In 1982, he won the Wolfpack Invitational, his first collegiate tournament. His other accomplishments include All-America and All-ACC honors 1983–85 and ACC Tournament Champion in 1984. Of course, for someone born a day after his father (Davis M. Love Jr.) competed in the 1964 Masters Tournament, golf seemed destined to be a big part of his life.

Davis Love III was the PGA Rookie of the Year in 1986. He has 20 PGA victories.

After his days in Chapel Hill, he became the PGA's Rookie of the Year in 1986. He has posted 20 PGA victories in his career, including the PGA Championship in 1997 and the Players Championship in 1992 and 2003. He has second-place finishes in the Masters (1995) and the U.S. Open (1996). He was a five-time member of the World Cup team and a six-time member of both the Ryder Cup and Presidents Cup teams. Love has had the most success at what is now known as the RBC Heritage, which has gone by a variety of names depending on the sponsor but was originally known as simply the Heritage Classic. Love has won the event, located on Hilton Head Island, South Carolina, five times, more than any other golfer. His best year in terms of wins and earnings was 2003, when he recorded four wins and tallied more than $6 million in prize money.

In 1994, Love teamed with his younger brother Mark—who is also his caddy—to create Love Golf Design, a golf course architecture company. In 1997, Love released his book *Every Shot I Take,* which includes commentary on the lessons about golf and life he learned from his late father. In 2005, he founded the Davis Love Foundation, which "contributes to the well-being and progress of society by supporting both national and community-based programs that focus on children and their families."

E. HARRIE WARD JR. *continued from page 217*

Ward coached numerous players throughout his career, the most notable being Payne Stewart. He died at his home in Pinehurst in 2004 at the age of 78. Upon Ward's death, golf great Jack Nicklaus said, "Harvie was a wonderful man and one of the great amateur players of his era. Amateur golf was so much more important in his era as the place where the top golfers of the day competed, and he was considered one of the best. He was able to beat the best, both here in the U.S. and internationally. As much as he will be remembered for his accomplishments in golf, I think he will be remembered even more for his warm and friendly nature."

MARK WILSON ■ COLLEGE: 1993–97

Born on Halloween in 1974, Mark Wilson racked up numerous treats in his three years as part of the UNC men's golf team. He was a two-time All-ACC performer who won the ACC Championship in 1996 and tied for third place in 1997. He was the 1996 Ben Hogan Award winner for his excellence in athletics and academics.

Wilson turned pro in 1997 and spent his early years on the NGA Hooters Tour. He won his PGA Tour Card in 2004 and since then has bounced back and forth between the PGA Tour and the FedEx Cup. He has won five PGA events and finished the 2011 season ranked No. 22 in the FedEx Cup. He has 26 top-10 PGA finishes. Wilson lives with his wife, Amy, near Chicago, where they have contributed heavily to charitable causes.

WOMEN'S GOLF

The women's golf team at North Carolina doesn't have as long a history as the men's, but its competitiveness has been on par. The women achieved varsity sport status in 1974 and began being sanctioned by the NCAA in the early 1980s. The Tar Heels have finished in the top 20 nationally 15 times.

Since the NCAA took over as the governing body for women's intercollegiate golf in 1982, a handful of teams have won the NCAA title multiple times, including Arizona State (7), Duke (5), San Jose State (3), Southern California (3), UCLA (3), Arizona (2), Florida (2), and Tulsa (2, although one was later vacated). Southern Cal won its third title in 2013.

In the ACC, Duke has been the dominant force in the women's game, much to the chagrin of Carolina fans. Duke has won the ACC title 18 times. That said, women's golf in the ACC has definitely been controlled by the state of North Carolina, as the only other two teams to have won conference championships are Wake Forest (5) and the Tar Heels (2).

Jan Mann, the current head coach of the Tar Heel women's golf team, is just the third coach in the program's history. Dot Gunnells served as coach for 18 years, from 1975–76 through the 1992–93 season. Sally Austin then coached for 16 years, from 1993–94 through 2008–09, when Mann was hired. Mann had previously been head coach at Virginia and her alma mater, UNC-Wilmington.

UNC Top 25 NCAA Finishes

1982 tie 16th	**1994** 16th	**2007** 21st
1984 12th	**1995** 8th	**2009** 7th
1989 8th	**1998** 15th	**2011** tie 8th
1992 8th	**2003** 13th	**2012** 10th
1993 tie 8th	**2004** tie 15th	

Atlantic Coast Conference Team Championships

18 Duke	**5** Wake Forest	**2 North Carolina**

Atlantic Coast Conference Individual Championships

15 Duke	**7** Wake Forest	**2 North Carolina**

List of Head Coaches

1975–93 Dot Gunnells	**1993–2009** Sally Austin	**2009–13** Jan Mann

Player Bios

SALLY AUSTIN ■ COLLEGE: 1973–77

A native of Raeford, North Carolina, Sally Austin was a member of the Tar Heels' first varsity team in 1973–74. Earning four varsity letters and graduating in 1977 with a degree in business administration, Austin continued playing golf as an amateur, winning the 1979 North Carolina Women's Amateur Championship. She later turned pro and got her LPGA card for the 1987 season. Other than her one season on the LPGA, Austin played on other mini-tours, the Asian Tour, and the European Tour.

She returned to her alma mater in 1993 to coach the Tar Heels' women's golf team, which she did successfully until 2009. In 2004, Austin received the LPGA Coach of the Year Award for 2004, given annually to a female golf professional who is actively engaged in teaching and/or coaching golf at the college, university, or high school level. Her highlights in 15 seasons as head coach include finishing in the top 25 at the NCAA Championships six times, along with 14 NCAA Regional appearances, including 11 in a row from 1994 to 2004.

Austin stepped down from coaching at UNC in 2009. Since then, she has continued to dabble in coaching at various golf academies and, dare we say it, as a volunteer assistant coach at North Carolina State.

CATHY JOHNSTON-FORBES ■ COLLEGE: 1981–83

Cathy Johnston, as she was known then, was born in High Point, North Carolina, but spent a lot of time in Wilmington where her father worked as golf pro for Echo Farms Golf & Country Club. She started playing golf at the age of seven, competing

DONNA ANDREWS ■ COLLEGE: 1985–89

Virginia native Donna Andrews is a five-time winner of the Virginia State Amateur Championship and a two-time winner of the North and South Amateur title (1984, 1988). She had an outstanding career at UNC, in which she earned All-American honors in 1989. Andrews joined the LPGA Tour in 1990 and was a solid force on the tour through the 1990s. Her first victory came in 1993 at the PING-Cellular One LPGA Championship. She was also named the *Golf Digest* Most Improved Player in 1993, as she finished ninth in the overall LPGA standings. Her pro career peaked in 1998 when she won one tournament, was runner-up in four others, finished the season as the top-ranked American, and ranked third on the money list. A dislocated shoulder in 1999 marked the beginning of the end for her pro career.

DONNA ANDREWS. Donna Andrews was named the LPGA Most Improved Player in 1993.

After missing the second half of the 1999 season, she came back with solid but not spectacular years in 2000 and 2001. She knew she wanted to be around golf but was less interested in the grind of the tour. So in 2001, Andrews landed a part-time gig with ESPN as an on-course commentator, greatly reducing her playing schedule. She also began teaching golf.

Andrews served as president of the LPGA players division in 2003–04 and worked full-time for ESPN in 2004–05. She was named head golf instructor at Pine Needles Resort and Lodge in Southern Pines, North Carolina, in 2006. She continues to operate the Donna Andrews Golf School there.

in—and winning—several junior tournaments before heading to Chapel Hill, where she was a star for the UNC women's golf team.

She landed on the LPGA Tour in 1986 and won her only tournament on the tour in 1990: the du Maurier Ltd. Classic. A steady player on the tour, Johnston-Forbes passed the $1 million mark in career earnings in 2000. She has moved on to play a few tournaments on the Legends Tour (formerly the LPGA Senior Tour) and offers private golf instruction. For several years, she organized the Cathy Johnston-Forbes Golf Classic in Wallace, North Carolina, with proceeds going to Easter Seals. She is married and has two children. Her brother, Clyde, is a noted golf course architect.

STEPHANIE KORNEGAY ■ COLLEGE: 1974–78

The recipient of UNC's first women's golf scholarship, Stephanie Kornegay won four individual titles in tournaments while at UNC. She played for a year on the LPGA Tour but still teaches golf in Charlotte while acting as vice president of the Kornegay Company in her hometown of Mount Olive, North Carolina. Kornegay has her pilot's license so that she can fly back and forth between Mount Olive and Charlotte.

SUZY McGUIRE ■ COLLEGE: 1986–89

Known as Suzy Whaley since her 1991 marriage to PGA golfer Bill Whaley, she is probably best known in the golf world for her appearance in a PGA tournament in 2003. In fact, Whaley was the first woman to qualify for, and participate in, a PGA Tour event in 58 years. By winning the Connecticut PGA Section Championship in 2002, she automatically qualified for the 2003 Greater Hartford Open.

Before her forays into pro golf, Suzy McGuire started playing the game at age nine under the influence of her golfing mom in Syracuse, New York. Her true passion, though, was ski racing. Making an Olympic development team at age 12, she had dreams of competing in the Olympics as a ski racer before an injury in 1983 led her back to golf. That led her to play four years on the UNC women's golf team, graduating in 1989 from Chapel Hill with a degree in economics.

The Whaleys currently live in Connecticut. Their two daughters, Jennifer and Kelly, are both golfers. Suzy has become a noted coach, gaining accolades such as two-time LPGA Northeast Teacher of the Year and being named a top-five national female teacher by *Golf Digest*. As a nearly 20-year veteran of the LPGA Teaching and Club Professionals, she was the recipient of the 2012 Nancy Lopez Golf Achievement Award, which recognizes an LPGA professional who gives back to the game in the spirit of Nancy Lopez. Whaley is currently the teaching professional at the TPC at River Highlands in Cromwell, Connecticut, and offers private instruction as well. She stays very active in the game of golf, serving on several boards and speaking at education seminars.

MINDY MOORE ■ COLLEGE: 1973–77

Part of the inaugural class of varsity women's golfers in Chapel Hill, Mindy Moore graduated from UNC in 1977 with a degree in industrial relations. She had some solid play as an amateur thereafter, winning the 1978 and 1979 Florida Four-Ball Championship, as well as the 1979 Palm Beach Amateur, before joining the LPGA tour in 1981.

Moore's career-best finish was in 1985 at the S&H Golf Classic. In 1986, she recorded her career-low score of 66. Always popular among her peers, she served as the Association's president in 1987. Moore is currently based out of Daytona Beach, Florida, where she is the Senior Vice President of Professional Development and Member Services for the LPGA.

MARCY NEWTON HART ■ COLLEGE: 1996–2000

A 2000 graduate from UNC in recreation and leisure studies administration, Marcy Newton Hart (just Marcy Newton back then) turned pro just a few months after her collegiate eligibility had expired. A native of Thomasville, North Carolina, the Tar Heel won three tournaments in her UNC days but is still trying to score her first victory on the LPGA Tour.

Married to Robert Hart since 2002, she was known for hosting the Marcy Hart LPGA Charity Classic Pro-Am, which benefitted Friends for an Earlier Breast Cancer Test in Greensboro, North Carolina. Hart's best year on the LPGA Tour was in 2006, when she had $235,243 in earnings, including a career-best finish at the Wegmans LPGA, where she tied for third. She resides in High Point, North Carolina.

MEAGHAN FRANCELLA ■ COLLEGE: 2002–04 (at UNC after transferring from the University of Memphis)

In 2003, Meaghan Francella won the ACC title, marking just the second time it had been won by a UNC player. That squad also finished 13th in the NCAA Championships. Francella had another solid performance her senior year, as the 2004 team finished tied for 15th in the NCAA Championships. Upon finishing her eligibility, she began playing on the LPGA Futures Tour, where she won the 2006 Lakeland Duramed Futures Classic. She also finished fifth in earnings on the Futures Tour that year.

Francella went on to play on the LPGA Tour beginning in 2007, earning her first win at the 2007 MasterCard Classic, holding off Annika Sörenstam in a four-hole playoff. "Words can't describe how I feel right now," she said after the win. "Annika is the best player in the world. I was a little intimidated, but I just tried to stay patient. I didn't want her to intimidate me. I just tried to stay focused. . . . I was like, 'Am I really doing this?' I felt like I was dreaming." Understandably, 2007 was also her best earnings year, as Francella won more than $500,000, which was good for 29th on the Tour that year.

In 2010, Francella won the HSBC LPGA Brasil Cup, which is an unofficial LPGA event. Overall, she has had seven top-10 finishes on the PGA Tour, but she has struggled somewhat since 2010, failing to make a top-20 finish on the Tour.

ASHLEY PRANGE ■ COLLEGE: 2000–04

On campus with the aforementioned Meaghan Francella, Ashley Prange joined Francella in leading the Tar Heels to top-20 NCAA finishes in 2003 and 2004. Prange also recorded three individual wins and 15 top-10 finishes while at Chapel Hill. She spent most of her seven years of pro golf on the Futures Tour, where she had 25 top-10 finishes, including two victories, both in 2006: the Greater Tampa Duramed Futures Classic and the Northwest Indiana Futures Golf Classic.

KATIE PETERSON ■ COLLEGE: 1985–89

KATIE PETERSON. A year after she graduated from UNC, Katie Peterson was ranked as the No. 1 amateur in the country. She joined the LPGA Tour a year later.

After her years at UNC came to a close, Katie Peterson spent a decade on the LPGA Tour, from 1991 to 2000, but she never matched the accolades she received while in Chapel Hill. At Carolina, Peterson won five individual championships in her four years, the only woman to accomplish such a feat. During her senior season of 1988–89, she was also the first first-team All-America in UNC women's golf history and led the team to an eighth-place finish in the 1989 NCAA Championships.

After graduating from UNC in 1989 with a degree in journalism, she was ranked as the No. 1 amateur in the country in 1990 and then went on to a join the LPGA Tour in 1991. Peterson, who went by Katie Peterson-Parker for much of her pro career, never won an LPGA Tour event but was involved in a classic finish in 1995, when she lost to Michelle McGann on the third hole of a sudden-death playoff in the Youngstown-Warren LPGA Classic. Now known as Katie Haley after marrying husband Steve, she offers golf instruction at Meridian Valley Country Club and is a pastry chef in Kent, Washington.

ASHLEY PRANGE *continued from page 225*

That same year, she won the Golf Channel's *The Big Break V: Hawaii,* a reality TV competition program. The win, among many other things, gave Prange an exemption into the LPGA's Safeway Classic that year and entry to all of the remaining Futures Tour events. She played mostly LPGA events in 2007 but found herself back on the Futures Tour in 2008.

She decided to give collegiate coaching a try, beginning with a stint as an assistant at Stetson University from 2009 to 2011. She was then head women's golf coach at Jacksonville University for the 2011–12 season before being named an assistant coach at the University of Central Florida in 2012.

MEN'S TENNIS

The men's tennis program at the University of North Carolina has a long and storied history that includes the tale of a candy man. The University Tennis Club was founded in 1884 and began playing intercollegiately in 1894. Tennis was not recognized as a varsity sport, though, until 1908. The team functioned (quite well in terms of wins, actually) without a coach through 1927, though organization was sometimes a problem. No teams were fielded in 1911, 1915, and 1919. Many people think of Tar Heel tennis really launching in the 1927–28 season when John Kenfield started his tenure as coach.

Kenfield was 35 years old and a vice president at Curtiss Candy Company in Chicago. Kenfield is noted for naming the Baby Ruth and Butterfinger candy bars, both brands now owned by Nestlé. But candy wasn't Kenfield's only game. An avid tennis player, he was also a tennis instructor at the Lake Shore Country Club in the Chicago suburb of Glencoe. Kenfield then saw an ad placed by the University Athletic Association in the American Lawn Tennis Journal seeking UNC's first full-time tennis coach. The warmer climes of Carolina seemed like a good change of pace, so Kenfield answered the ad.

Kenfield coached the Tar Heels from 1928 until his retirement in 1956. Ten of his 28 teams finished their dual match seasons unbeaten. His overall coaching record was 434-30-2, which equals a .933 winning percentage. His teams averaged a 16-1 record each year during his 28 seasons. Now that is a strong foundation from which to build, but also a long shadow cast upon the program. A stroke in 1956 led to his retirement. He died in January 1958. The tennis facility built in 1992 bears the name of this phenomenal character in the story of UNC tennis.

Success did not end when Kenfield retired. In fact, in 2012, UNC passed the all-time 1,500-win dual-match mark, the most dual victories for any collegiate tennis program in the history of the sport on the NCAA level. Throughout its history, the Tar Heels have had a winning percentage near 80, the highest of all the men's varsity sports. Long tenures have been a hallmark of men's tennis coaches at UNC. Don Skakle coached for more than 20 years, and current coach Sam Paul is approaching the 20-year mark.

Head Coaching Records

(In chronological order, including record and winning percentage; a tie counts as half a win, half a loss, per NCAA practice)

YEARS	COACH	RECORD	WINNING PCT.
1908–27	(no coach)	52-15-5	.757
1928–55	John Kenfield	434-30-2	.933
1956	Ham Strayhorn	18-1-1	.925
1957–58	Vladimir Cernik	19-11	.633
1959–80	Don Skakle	418-55	884
1981–93	Allen Morris	244-124	.663
1994–2013	Sam Paul	324-155	.676

(Ranked by victories)

RECORD	COACH	YEARS
434-30-2	John Kenfield	1928–55
418-55	Don Skakle	1959–80
324-155	Sam Paul	1994–2013
244-124	Allen Morris	1981–93
52-15-5	No Coach	1908–27
19-11	Vladimir Cernik	1957–58
18-1-1	Ham Strayhorn	1956

(Ranked by winning percentage; a tie counts as half a win, half a loss, per NCAA practice)

WINNING PCT.	RECORD	COACH	YEARS
.933	434-30-2	John Kenfield	1928–55
.925	18-1-1	Ham Strayhorn	1956
.884	418–55	Don Skakle	1959–80
.757	52-15-5	(no coach)	1908–27
.676	324-155	Sam Paul	1994–2013
.663	244-124	Allen Morris	1981–93
.633	19-11	Vladimir Cernik	1957–58

Player Bios

JOEY BURKHARDT ■ COLLEGE: 2010–12 (at UNC)

Ranked as high as No. 12 nationally by **tennisecruiting.net** while at Menendez High in St. Augustine, Joey Burkhardt went on to play his freshman and sophomore seasons at the University of Florida before transferring to Carolina. Having just graduated in 2012, Burkhardt is still trying to climb up in the ATP rankings in singles and doubles as a young professional.

TAYLOR FOGLEMAN ■ COLLEGE: 2005–09

A native of New Orleans, Taylor Fogleman was a four-year letterman and two-time first-team All-American in Chapel Hill, where he led the Tar Heels to 87 wins and four consecutive trips to the NCAA Tournament. He then joined the pro ranks and reached a career-high ranking of 551 in doubles in 2010. He is now an assistant tennis coach for the women's team at Tulane, alma mater of his mother, Jana, who played tennis there 1977–81. He was named 2013 Southern Region Assistant Coach of the Year by the Intercollegiate Tennis Association (ITA).

BRYAN "BITSY" GRANT JR. ■ COLLEGE: 1929–33

Though not truly a professional because he played in a day when tennis was for amateurs, a nod must be given to Bitsy Grant. Born on Christmas Day 1910 in Atlanta, Grant was a gift to Carolina tennis. In fact, when asked in 1955 to rate his best players, longtime UNC tennis coach put Grant at the top of the list. Grant led the 1931 team to an undefeated season and the Southern Conference title. At only 5'4", he became known as Itsy Bitsy the Giant Killer after wins over the likes of Don Budge and plenty of other top-notch contemporaries. Especially adept on clay, Grant won the U.S. Clay Court title three times, played on three U.S. Davis Cup teams, and won 19 national senior singles titles. He was a regular fixture in the American top 10 for the majority of the time after he left Chapel Hill until 1941. His highest world singles ranking was sixth. He was inducted into the International Tennis Hall of Fame in 1972.

In the 1950s, Atlanta built the Bitsy Grant Tennis Center, a public complex with 13 clay courts and 10 hard courts. Grant played there regularly for the rest of his life and won numerous seniors tournaments though the late 1970s. He died of cancer in Atlanta in 1986.

JOSE HERNANDEZ ■ COLLEGE: 2009–12

Ranked 37th in the world junior rankings by the International Tennis Federation while in the Dominican Republic, Jose Hernandez then took his talents on the court to Chapel Hill. After a successful four-year career in Carolina, Hernandez has been climbing his way up the rankings on the pro circuit. He has also played for the Dominican Republic's Davis Cup Team. As of the summer of 2013, Hernandez was showing great promise as a pro in both singles and doubles.

DON JOHNSON ■ COLLEGE: 1987–91

When most of us think of tennis, we typically think of singles, but Don Johnson was a star in doubles, which is why you may not know the name—at least in terms of tennis. (Not to be confused with the former *Miami Vice* actor.) After lots of success in Chapel Hill, Johnson graduated with a degree in economics in 1991—just after leading UNC to its first ACC Championship in a dozen years as the tourney's MVP. He then joined the ATP tour, where he played until 2004. Johnson was part of 23 doubles finals, including Wimbledon in 2001 with Jared Palmer and a mixed doubles title at Wimbledon the year before with Kimberly Po. Johnson and Palmer achieved the No. 1 world ranking for a while in 2002.

After retiring from tennis, Johnson was an assistant tennis coach for UNC for three seasons. He is now involved in business development, sales, and marketing for Vstrator, a video analysis company based in Raleigh, North Carolina, with a core mission to "provide simple, life-enhancing coaching tools and collaborative networks to improve performance for everyone, everyday, everywhere."

RAIAN LUCHICI ■ COLLEGE: 2003–06 (at UNC)

Romanian Raian Luchici attended the University of Georgia as a freshman before transferring to Carolina, where he had a fantastic tennis career, teaming up at times for doubles play with Nick Monroe, who is featured below. Luchici went pro and has played a number of singles and doubles tournaments. His highest rankings came in 2008, when he reached 387 in doubles and 526 in singles. He is currently a tennis pro at Universal Tennis Academy in Atlanta.

FRED McNAIR ■ COLLEGE: 1969–73

Similar to Don Johnson, featured above, Frederick V. McNair IV is another Carolina tennis star who went on to a successful career in doubles tennis. After a sterling four years on the courts (including being an NCAA doubles finalist in 1973) and in the classroom in Chapel Hill, McNair graduated with a degree in American Studies and immediately joined the ATP tour, where he played until 1982. He and partner Sherwood Stewart were ranked as the No. 1 doubles team in the world in 1976, when they won the French Open. Overall, McNair was part of 16 doubles titles and finished as a runner-up more than 20 times. He had several doubles partners over the years but had the most success with Stewart. He was a member of the 1978 U.S. Davis Cup team.

VIC SEIXAS ■ COLLEGE: 1947–49

VIC SEIXAS. Vic Seixas won the singles and mixed doubles titles at Wimbledon in 1953.

After serving as an Army pilot in World War II, Elias Victor Seixas Jr., won the Southern Conference singles title in 1948 and finished as the runner-up in 1947 and 1949. He teamed with Clark Taylor to capture the doubles championship in 1949. He then went on to an astounding career in singles, doubles, and mixed doubles. In singles, his highlights include championships at Wimbledon (1953) and the U.S. Open (1954). In doubles, his accomplishments include winning the Australian Open (1955), French Open (1954–55), and U.S. Open (1952, 54). And in mixed doubles, he won titles at Wimbledon (1953), the French Open (1953), and the U.S. Open (1953–55), which was then called the U.S. National Championship.

Seixas (pronounced SAY-shus) was also on the U.S. Davis Cup team from 1951 to 1957, with his 55 Davis Cup singles matches being the most of any American player until John McEnroe broke his record. His 75 U.S. Open singles victories were a record that stood until it was broken by Jimmy Connors. Seixas officially turned pro at age 50 to play on the Senior Tennis Tour, which he cofounded (though it's now called the Grand Masters Tour).

Having played in an era in which trophies rather than money were the prizes, in 1999 Seixas told the *Los Angeles Times*, "I started figuring a couple of years ago, with the current prize money at the time, how much money I would have won in just the seven years or so that I played Wimbledon in singles and doubles. I was up to about $5 million and I stopped counting." His biggest paycheck from tennis was $2,000 for winning a Senior event. Long a resident of Mill Valley, California, Seixas has been involved with, among other things, the Club at Harbor Point as a member and consultant. His most recent tennis accolade came in 2011, when he was inducted into the Southern Conference Hall of Fame. He was inducted into the International Tennis Hall of Fame in 1971.

After retiring from tennis, McNair succeeded his father and grandfather as president and CEO of McNair & Company, Inc., in 1987. The company, founded in 1931, is an estate-planning firm based in McLean, Virginia. He and his wife, Linda, have four children.

NICK MONROE ■ COLLEGE: 2000–04

Benjamin Nicholas "Nick" Monroe grew up in Oklahoma City and attended UNC, where he had much success on the tennis courts. He graduated with numerous accolades, including the Arthur Ashe Regional Sportsmanship Award and the National and Regional NCAA/ITF John Van Nostrand Sportsmanship Awards. He played a handful of Futures tournaments between 2001 and 2004 before becoming a full-time pro in 2005. He reached his first final in doubles in a 2013 event in Buenos Aires, Argentina. He achieved a doubles ranking of 67 in March of that year.

TRIPP PHILLIPS ■ COLLEGE: 1996–2000

As a senior at UNC, Tripp Phillips was honored with the prestigious Patterson Medal, given annually to the school's top male and female senior athletes. He was the first UNC tennis player to receive the award since Vic Seixas in 1950. After graduating from UNC in 2000, Phillips began his professional career in 2001. He achieved a career-high ATP doubles ranking of 29 in 2006 and reached a singles ranking of 343 in 2003. In 2006, Phillips teamed with Australia's Ashley Fisher to reach the semifinals of the 2006 U.S. Open and to win the ATP event in Tokyo.

That same year, Phillips joined the UNC staff as an assistant to Sam Paul but still continued to compete professionally in doubles. In 2007, he earned seeds in three of the four Grand Slam tournaments, reaching the round of 16 in the U.S. Open. The following year, he qualified for Wimbledon and won the ATP event in Indianapolis. He and his wife, Laura, live in Chapel Hill with their two sons.

ROLAND THÖRNQVIST ■ COLLEGE: 1990–93

Swedish-born Roland Thörnqvist enjoyed a sterling career on the courts at UNC and joined the professional tour in 1993. Citing a lack of money, he headed back to Chapel Hill the following year to work as an assistant on Sam Paul's staff while finishing his degree. Thörnqvist later said, "I loved it, I just loved coaching. I had wanted to play full time and be a real pro. But once I started coaching with Sam, I really enjoyed it—really, really did enjoy it. And I thought I was decent at it too."

From there, he became the coach for the University of Kansas women's team before returning to UNC as the women's head coach from 1999 to 2001. Thörnqvist became head coach of the University of Florida women's tennis team in 2002, where he has had amazing success. Winning championships in 2003, 2011, and 2012, Thörnqvist became just the fourth person to win more than two NCAA women's championships.

WOMEN'S TENNIS

Back in 1971, eight women's sports at the University of North Carolina were elevated to varsity status. Tennis was one of those. UNC became a charter member of the new Association for Intercollegiate Athletics for Women (AIAW). Women's tennis immediately became a hit in Chapel Hill, led first by legendary coach Frances Hogan, who guided the team through its initial days with the AIAW—where the Tar Heels were a constant presence. Hogan had been a force on campus previously, coaching tennis as part of the physical education department and as women's athletic director.

Hogan stepped down from coaching in 1976 and was replaced by Kitty Harrison, who would leave quite a mark on the program over the course of more than two decades. Harrison was elected to the North Carolina Tennis Hall of Fame in 2004 after retiring in 1998 as the winningest tennis coach in ACC history in terms of total dual-match victories.

As of this writing, the program is being led by Brian Kalbas, who has made his own mark in 10 years at the helm. Kalbas has led the program to the NCAA tournament each year of his tenure, highlighted by its first NCAA tennis title in 2007; the national semifinals in 2010; and the 2013 ITA National Women's Team Indoor Championship, in which sixth-seeded Carolina defeated the top seed and defending champion, UCLA.

While no women have gone on to pro careers out of Chapel Hill, Cinda (short for Lucinda) Gurney remains the most decorated player, winning the ACC's Player of the Year Award three consecutive years, 1991–93.

Head Coaching Records

(In chronological order, including record and winning percentage; a tie counts as half a win, half a loss, per NCAA practice)

YEARS	COACH	RECORD	WINNING PCT.
1974–76	Frances Hogan	26-3	.896
1976–98	Kitty Harrison	351-224	.610
1998–2001	Roland Thörnqvist	42-30	.583
2001–03	Jen Callen	44-14	.758
2003–13	Brian Kalbas	209–73	.741

CINDA GURNEY. Cinda Gurney won the ACC Player of the Year award for three consecutive years.

(Ranked by victories)

RECORD	COACH	YEARS
351-224	Kitty Harrison	1976–98
209-73	Brian Kalbas	2003–13
44-14	Jen Callen	2001–03
42-30	Roland Thörnqvist	1998–2001
26-3	Frances Hogan	1974–76

(Ranked by winning percentage; a tie counts as half a win, half a loss, per NCAA practice)

WINNING PCT.	RECORD	COACH	YEARS
.896	26-3	Frances Hogan	1974–76
.758	44-14	Jen Callen	2001–03
.741	209-73	Brian Kalbas	2003–13
.610	351-224	Kitty Harrison	1976–98
.583	42-30	Roland Thörnqvist	1998–2001

Index

C

D

E

F

S

T

About the Author

Meherdil Irani

By high school it had become clear to Tim W. Jackson that he was not going to be a pro athlete or a rock star, but he thought he might write about sports and music. His first journalism job began in the summer after his junior year of high school when he was hired by his hometown newspaper to write about local sports. He received a journalism degree from the University of Alabama, where he worked as a sports editor for the school paper and later as editor of its arts & entertainment weekly. While still in college he found himself writing about antiques and art for a national publication, and upon graduation, served on the copy desks of *Southern Living* and *Cooking Light* magazines before becoming editor of *Canoe & Kayak* magazine.

In 2006, Jackson received an MFA in Creative Nonfiction from Goucher College. He taught journalism classes at the University of Alabama and Radford University, and directed student media organizations at the latter. He founded a nonprofit news site and was a Knight Digital Media Center Fellow. Through it all he has been a freelance writer and editor for some 20 years.

Not a Tar Heel by birth, Jackson moved to the mountains of Western North Carolina a few years ago. He now works for Keen Communications as its senior acquisitions editor from his home office near Asheville. He lives with his wife, Taryn, dogs Holly and Timber, and rabbit Kiwi, while his teenaged daughter, Anna, lives up the road in Bristol, Virginia. Jackson loves North Carolina, and now that this book is finished he might have some spare time to hike, pick up his guitar again, watch a bit of sports on TV, and ride the Carolina backroads on his motorcycle.